THE COVENTRYS
OF
CROOME

The Coventry coat-of-arms.

THE COVENTRYS

OF

CROOME

Catherine Gordon

PHILLIMORE

IN ASSOCIATION WITH

THE NATIONAL TRUST

2000

Published by
PHILLIMORE & CO. LTD.,
Shopwyke Manor Barn, Chichester, West Sussex
in association with the National Trust

ISBN 1 86077 139 4

Printed and bound in Great Britain by
BUTLER AND TANNER LTD.
Frome, Somerset

Contents

List of Illustrations

Frontispiece: The Coventry coat-of-arms

Colour Plates

Illustration Acknowledgements

I would like to thank the following for supplying the illustrations: Joan Atherley, 1; reproduced by courtesy of the Mercers' Company Archives, 2; reproduced by courtesy of the Trustees of the Croome Estate (CET), I-V, VIII-XIX, XXI-XXV, 3-5, 7, 10, 12, 14, 24, 25, 37-42, 47, 48, 50, 51, 54, 57, 63, 67, 68, 70, 71-3, 75, 76, 79-81, 85, 87, 88, 91-3, 95-107, 111; photography by Robert Anderson, II-V, VII-XVI, XVIII, XX-XXV, 4, 5, 8, 13, 14-16, 24, 37-40, 47, 65, 67, 68, 72-4, 79, 80, 81, 91, 99, 110; V&A Picture Library, Victoria and Albert Museum, 6; Catherine Gordon, 9, 55, 56, 61, 82, 83, 90; Newey, 11, 18, 21, 49, 60; Warwickshire Record Office, 19; by permission of the Trustees of the Carew Pole family, VI, VII, 27-33, 35; Tom Oliver, XXVI; reproduced by kind permission of the Duke of Beaufort, 20, 22, 23, 26, 100; Photographic Survey: Courtauld Institute of Art, 22, 30-3; National Trust, 34, 110; reproduced by courtesy of the Society of Antiquaries, London, 36; by courtesy of the Trustees at Sir John Soane's Museum, 46, 52, 53, 58, 59, 62, 77; Worcestershire Record Office, 11, 69, 78, 84, 94; The Museum of Worcester Porcelain, 86; by courtesy of the National Portrait Gallery, London, 89; Angela Chapman, 108, 109; *Coventry Memoirs* by William Dean, 66; *Life in Worcestershire at the end of the Seventeenth Century* by Charles S. Tomes, 17.

Acknowledgements

First of all, I would like to thank the Earl and Countess of Coventry, Peter Scott and the other Croome Estate Trustees, Julian Hoare and Peter Beresford, for providing me with the opportunity to study in detail the documents and artefacts in their trust. Their support and encouragement has been much appreciated and it has been a great pleasure and privilege to undertake this project on their behalf.

I am most grateful to His Grace the Duke of Beaufort for his permission to study the Coventry papers within the Badminton archive and for allowing me to reproduce selected items within the text. Margaret Richards, archivist at Badminton, has been a great help in this respect. I am also most grateful to Sir Richard Carew Pole for his permission to study at length the archive at Antony, to reproduce illustrations from his collection within the text, and also for his advice, hospitality and photographic skills. Kate Harris, Librarian and Archivist to the Marquis of Bath, has also provided me with the benefit of her knowledge of the Coventry papers at Longleat. The staff of numerous museums, libraries and public record offices have assisted with my research, notably at the V&A Museum, Sir John Soane's Museum, the Courtauld Institute, at the county record offices in Cornwall, Gloucestershire, Warwickshire and Worcestershire, and at Birmingham Central Library and Archives Division and the British Library. Christine North, Chief Archivist of Cornwall Record Office and Stephen Astley, Assistant Curator (Drawings), at Sir John Soane's Museum, have proved especially helpful.

Numerous other individuals have provided invaluable assistance. I would like to express my special thanks to Lady Maria Coventry, John Henderson, Bob Cross, Pip Webster, Joan Atherley, Angela Chapman, John Rudge, Nicholas Kingsley, David King, Mr. and Mrs. Gerrard, Malcolm Wolford, Mr. and Mrs. Newey, Ronald Halcon, and Jackie Wright. I am also most grateful to David Tweedie, who has provided essential support and guidance, and Robert Anderson for his outstanding photographs.

I have been most fortunate to benefit from the help, support and expertise of the National Trust throughout the course of my research, and I would like to thank Tom Oliver, Project Manager at Croome Park, in particular, for his valued contribution to the text. Finally, I am most grateful to Jill Tovey, Estate Archivist at Croome, for her advice and assistance, her patience and her tolerance, in dealing so thoroughly with my endless requests, and for sharing her extensive knowledge of the archive.

Foreword

Catherine Gordon has written this book about my family history and the history of Croome after taking some three years to research the facts nationwide. She has written the text in a way that is highly readable and informative and, in many places, has included anecdotes which are extremely amusing. In her endeavours she has been greatly assisted by Jill Tovey, the Archivist at Croome.

I myself was born at Croome Court, though sadly because of World War Two had to leave at the age of six, returning for just over a year in 1946. My earliest memories of Croome are merely restricted to an episode when the family doctor had been called to Croome and, when leaving, my father, the 10th Earl, placed a thunderflash under his car. This caused great consternation and subsequent amusement.

More recently, my wife and I had the pleasure of getting together with my Godfather, the celebrated wildlife artist Raoul Millais, and greatly enjoyed several of his stories about his exploits with my father, who was his best friend. Not least, he related that when my father inherited the title and Croome Court, Raoul received a telephone call to 'come over immediately because there is the most fabulous wine cellar'. On arrival, my father took him down to the cellar where the floor was about 18in. deep with champagne corks. He related that they had 'a very merry afternoon'!

It is nice to think that the humour which pervades the reports of my antecedents still exists in my family.

I know, without any doubt, that I speak on behalf of all my family, past, present and future, in expressing our gratitude to Catherine for the mammoth task she has taken on and executed with such excellent results.

This excellent historical and anecdotal book has been written up to, and including, the death of my father, killed in battle, at Givenchy, France, in 1940. This effectively brought to a conclusion the association of the Coventry family with Croome Court. We have visited his grave on several occasions and would like to take this opportunity of paying tribute to the kindness of the villagers of Givenchy who tend his gravestone, and those of others who were killed there, with such care. Although it was not possible to bring my father home to be buried, Croome Court was always his home—as it was to so many of the Earls of Coventry.

Coventry.

I

Introduction

The Coventry family came to Croome, in south Worcestershire, four hundred years ago. According to tradition, the place was then 'a deep, dead, fetid morass', a shallow bowl of marshland marooned among the lowland plains of the Severn and Avon valleys.[1] The 6th Earl described it as 'as hopeless a spot as any on this island'. The image was irresistible, especially as it highlighted the miraculous transformation that was effected at Croome during the 18th century under his ownership; but it was not strictly true. Admittedly, when his ancestor Thomas Coventry, a successful lawyer, purchased Croome in the late 16th century, enclosure and drainage had yet to transform the large areas of waterlogged and barren soil into lush pastureland, but the place had undoubted promise. Part of the estate was under cultivation, and included orchards, two mills and abundant timber. The countryside immediately to the north of the estate was owned by his wife's family, and to the west there was good access to the River Severn, which was fast becoming the nation's main artery of trade. The thriving city of Worcester and the market towns of Pershore and Upton upon Severn lay within a day's journey, and fine views extended westwards to the undulating Malvern ridge, and south-east towards the smooth mound of Bredon Hill and the receding Cotswold escarpment. It was a practical and affordable investment for a gentleman-lawyer, and a prudent and timely purchase for it presaged a rapid increase in the wealth and influence of his family. During the 17th century, there were several distinguished lawyers and statesmen among his descendants, most memorable of whom was his son Thomas, 1st Baron Coventry (1578-1640), who became Recorder of London, Solicitor-General to the King, and Lord Keeper of the Great Seal of England. Two of Lord Keeper Coventry's sons from his second marriage emulated his success. Henry Coventry (1618-86) became a Groom of the Bedchamber, Ambassador to Sweden and a Secretary of State, and his younger brother Sir William Coventry (1620?-86) was a Secretary to the Admiralty, a Commissioner to the Treasury and was knighted in 1665. The Coventry Act of 1671 was brought into effect as a direct result of a confrontation between the 1st Baron's grandson, Sir John Coventry (d.1682), and the king. It did little more than declare 'nose-slitting' a felony, but it gave nominal emphasis to the family's influence on affairs of state during this period.

Success bred opportunity, and all five of the Lord Keeper's daughters married well, notably Margaret, the wife of Anthony Ashley Cooper, 1st Earl of Shaftesbury, Anne, who married Sir William Savile, and Mary, who married Sir Henry Frederick Thynne.

Desirable new connections such as these were accompanied by a steady expansion of the estate into Gloucestershire, Warwickshire, Oxfordshire, Somerset, Middlesex and elsewhere. By the end of the 17th century, the family's increasing prominence and loyalty to the crown were duly recognised when Thomas, 5th Baron (1629-99), was created Earl of Coventry and Viscount Deerhurst by William III. This enabled the family to maintain its high profile at a time when its political influence was fading, and it stimulated new ambition in keeping with the Hanoverian age.

Early in the 18th century, constitutional change and the growing cult of enlightenment and tolerance nurtured an increasing fascination for classical art and literature. There was a drift away from the court and the capital towards the country seats of the nobility, which became centres of political intrigue, culture and patronage. Although Croome Court had been rebuilt twice in the mid-17th century and altered since, to George William, 6th Earl of Coventry (1722-1809), it appeared unfashionable and provincial. A programme of major improvements to the house, gardens and adjacent land was required before Croome could hope to rival new Palladian palaces, such as Wanstead in Essex, of 1715-20, or Houghton Hall, begun in 1722 on the Walpole estate in Norfolk. This task became the 6th Earl's lifelong obsession. Blessed with undoubted taste of which he was proud, and vast wealth which he wished to flaunt, he commissioned 'Capability' Brown and Robert Adam to fulfil his ambition on a scale that attracted the amazement and admiration of his contemporaries. Brown moulded a magnificent landscape from the marshland and medieval deer parks at Croome, and rebuilt the house, church and village to enhance his design. It was Brown's first major architectural and landscape project, a seminal work to which Robert Adam contributed some of his finest and more unusual designs. The 6th Earl proceeded to fill his new park with a plant collection second only to that at Kew in its variety and rarity, yet still he was not satisfied. While Croome was in progress, work began on the Coventry family's lavish new home in London, Coventry House, Piccadilly, and again Adam was invited to provide it with an interior of enviable elegance and beauty. Arguably, the 6th Earl's admirable judgement deserted him only once, and that was in the choice of his first wife, Maria Gunning (1732-60), the celebrated Irish beauty. A man of such aesthetic discernment could not fail to be seduced by her charms. She perfected the scenery at Croome, and initially her spontaneity was refreshing. But soon her lack of refinement began to pall. Manipulative, and with a renowned lack of tact, only her premature death spared the 6th Earl's reputation from further ridicule.

The history of the family during the early 19th century was marred by a series of tragic accidents and bitter quarrels among the immediate descendants of the 6th Earl. These threatened to dislodge the family from its lofty perch more successfully than could the repercussions of reform and revolution. The management of the estate grew slack, and the numerous legal entanglements absorbed useful resources. Difficulties persisted until the mid-19th century, when another dominant and inspiring personality emerged in George William, 9th Earl (1838-1930). He was the archetypal Victorian aristocrat and patron, a country gentleman and keen sportsman, who mingled as comfortably among his tenants as among London society. He inherited the title in 1843, aged only five, and led the family through the changes of the Victorian and Edwardian eras into the inter-war years to become the longest-serving peer in the House of Lords. As industrialisation took its toll on the countryside, he campaigned to secure a future for British agriculture and rural life. It was a thankless cause and, when he died in 1930, the ideals and inheritance for which he had fought for so long were disintegrating around him.

The three most successful eras of the family history, spanned by the lifetimes of the Lord Keeper and his children, and of the 6th and 9th Earls, are the best documented. Consequently, the many less prominent but equally interesting individuals, who give breadth and perspective to the story, have become obscured; these include Thomas, 2nd Baron Coventry (1606-61), who rebuilt Croome House in the mid-17th century, and Gilbert, 4th Earl (1664-1719), who spent several years in the Netherlands and created an elaborate formal garden at Croome. When the latter failed to produce an heir, William (1678-1751), a distant relative and descendant of the Lord Keeper's brother, already a middle-aged man with a well-established parliamentary career, inherited the title and estates. The 7th Earl (1758-1831) was dogged by ill fortune. Disowned by his father, he spent almost his entire adult life blind following a hunting accident. His grandson, George William, Viscount Deerhurst (1808-38), was similarly afflicted when he lost the sight in one eye in a grim repetition of his grandfather's predicament.

There were also numerous accomplished females among the Coventrys, many of whom played a more active part in the management of the estate than is often supposed. Some were talented writers, others were ardent collectors and kept the customary notebooks crammed with culinary and medicinal recipes. Notable among them was the Lord Keeper's daughter, Dorothy (d.1679), the pious wife of Sir John Packington, and the alleged author of *The Whole Duty of Man*, and also Lady Anne Somerset (1673-1763), wife of the 2nd Earl, who steered the family through a period of financial crisis. For much of her long life, she lived at the Coventry's house in Snitterfield, Warwickshire, where she became a tireless philanthropist and cultivated a circle of influential friends. There was Harriet Cockerell (1812-1842) of Sezincote, the wife of Viscount Deerhurst, son of the 8th Earl, who was a talented young diarist in the tradition of her distant relative, Samuel Pepys, and Blanche Craven (1843-1930), the wife of the 9th Earl. She was as popular as her husband, a devoted and tolerant wife, the mother of nine children, a beautiful and gracious society hostess, and totally committed to her public duties. She compiled vast albums of newspaper cuttings of the family's achievements and rode a tricycle around the park well into her 80s. Even her death seemed an expression of her moral virtue, for she expired just three days after her husband, their partnership complete.

The Coventry family played an integral part in almost every aspect of county life. Like other local aristocratic families, such as the Beauchamps of Madresfield, the Foleys and Dudleys of Witley Court, the Lytteltons of Hagley, the Sandys of Ombersley, and the Plymouths of Hewell Grange, they were closely involved with local politics, the militia and the law, and patrons of numerous local charities and public institutions. They also made a significant contribution to the development of agriculture, industry and transport within the county. They belonged to the locality as much as it belonged to them, and

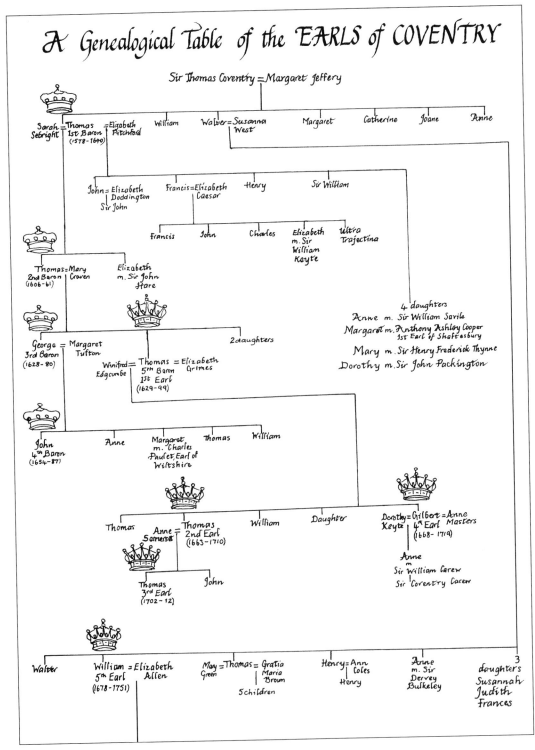

1   A genealogical table of the Earls of Coventry.

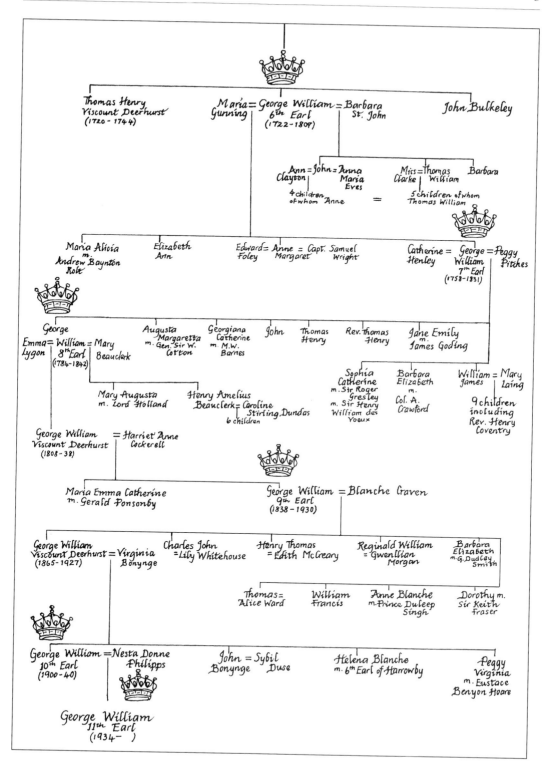

when a new Coventry heir was born it seemed quite natural for their tenants to celebrate the event as if the infant was their own. This was a formidable responsibility and the price of privilege, but during the lifetime of the 9th Earl it became clear that even his commitment could not withstand the forces of social and economic change. After the tragic and heroic death of the 10th Earl in 1940, Croome Court and its contents were sold, and the sense of loss within the local community was immense. The most devastating aftershock occurred when the M5 motorway carved a cruel path through the heart of the Croome estate. It was a ghastly incision, which could have proved terminal. The scar is permanent, but the parkland straddles the thundering torrent of traffic with an astonishing resilience and detachment. Elsewhere in the locality, evidence of the Coventry family's former influence and patronage is everywhere. It continues to give form and context to this patch of south Worcestershire, so integral a part did the family play in such a widespread community for several centuries.

* * * * * *

This history of the Coventry family and the Croome estate was instigated to commemorate the tercentenary of the earldom in 1997. It is by no means the first. In the early 18th century, an invaluable summary of the Coventry ancestry was included within a report on the family's financial affairs of c.1714, following the death of Thomas, the 2nd Earl in 1710.[2] A short but memorable history is also included by William Dean in his *An Historical and Descriptive Account of Croome* of 1824. Voluble in its praise, if a trifle vague in detail, this is more than compensated by the quite astonishing and meticulous plant list included in the book, the *Hortus Croomensis*. More recently, there has been much valuable research published on Croome Court by scholars of Capability Brown and Robert Adam and of the 6th Earl's outstanding collection of furniture and tapestries. These form a vital reference source to the history of the family and, of course, to any study of architectural and furniture design of this period. The scope of this book is much broader and inevitably less detailed. It aims to provide the background story, the foundation within which the seeds of individual achievement could take root and accumulate with each generation.

    I have been most fortunate to be permitted to explore the remarkable family archive at Croome as extensively as time could permit. During the 1950s, Colonel Osbert S. Smith, grandson of the 9th Earl, began to collate and catalogue this material, and in recent years his work has been extended and developed by Jill Tovey, the estate archivist. In 1997 the Royal Commission on Historical Manuscripts acclaimed the archive as 'most important and interesting'. It includes a wide range of material, accounts, bills, inventories, deeds, sale particulars, parish records, maps, surveys, architectural drawings, official papers, diaries, journals, albums and a wealth of correspondence. The personal correspondence is particularly abundant during the early 19th century, and many of these letters have a startling directness that seems to defy time and convention. Most of these documents survive in excellent state of preservation as they have been handled so rarely, and examining them has been a daunting but absorbing task, a source of endless speculation, frustration, and great pleasure.

However, the Croome archive does not represent the total story. During the 17th century, many documents and artefacts passed into the possession of other important family archives, largely owing to inter-marriage, for example those at Longleat in Wiltshire, Badminton in South Gloucestershire, and at Antony in Cornwall. Other documents are located within public archives at museums, libraries and county record offices. Inevitably, the earlier chapters of this book rely more on official documents and published material, while in later chapters much can be gleaned from newspaper cuttings and photographs that date from the late 19th and early 20th centuries. During the 17th and 18th centuries, the remorseless observations of Samuel Pepys and Horace Walpole vivify the details whenever possible.

This history of the Coventry family mirrors that of many of the English aristocracy in its general outline, but it is the distinctive personalities, the response to contemporary events, the personal and public relationships and the detail with which these are recorded that builds its special identity. Within the text, only one convention demands explanation. After the time of the 6th Earl, it became the custom to christen the son and heir George William. To avoid confusion, the various Earls of Coventry are referred to by their chronological number rather than by name.

This history can only hope to serve as a general introduction to the Coventry family archive at Croome and promote further and more specialised study of the Coventry family history. Although intended to commemorate the tercentenary of the earldom, by fortunate coincidence my research began not long after the National Trust started work on the restoration of the landscape park at Croome. This allowed a new optimism to pervade the depressing story of disintegration during the 20th century. The work of the National Trust at Croome, and the re-emergence of this important early design by Capability Brown, have proved an exciting stimulus to my own studies. The research into the design of this historic landscape undertaken for the National Trust in 1996 by Camilla Beresford and other experts on the Trust's behalf has contributed enormously to our current understanding of its design and has proved an additional and invaluable reference source. Tom Oliver, the Trust's Project Manager at Croome Park, has also supplied much useful advice on the history of the landscape. I was delighted when he agreed to contribute a chapter to this book, which outlines the recent history of the park, gives context to its acquisition by the National Trust, and provides a fascinating insight into the scale and detail of the restoration work in progress.

Croome played a central role in the history of the Earls of Coventry, and its role in the history of landscape design was no less significant. Now that it is to be protected and maintained for the nation to enjoy, there could be no more fitting tribute to the achievements of this important Worcestershire family.

II

Origins

The medieval history of the Coventry family is largely obscure and fragmentary. It is also rife with red herrings, as the regional associations of the name provide ample opportunity for confusion and coincidence to conceal the absence of solid fact. Early historians cite John Coventry, the 14th-century London mayor and executor of the will of the legendary Dick Whittington, as the most illustrious ancestor of the Earls of Coventry. The eminent Warwickshire antiquarian, Sir William Dugdale (1605-86), had little doubt about the connection and, even if the genealogical link remains unproven, the power of repetition has lent conviction to this assumption. Tradition, after all, is often founded on truth.

2 'Richard Whittington on his Deathbed'. John Coventry is shown at the far left of the picture.

John Coventry (d.1429) was a successful and respected London mercer and alderman, but he is remembered chiefly for his association with Richard Whittington (1393-1423), three times Lord Mayor of London, and famous for his fabled feline companion.[1] In *The Aldermen of the City of London,* Beaven cites his father as William Coventry, a mercer, and descendant of Henry de Coventre (d.1282), a vintner, sheriff and alderman of London. This is confirmed by earlier sources, including a 17th-century pedigree in the Croome archive, which is more specific about his father's place of birth, referring to him as 'William Coventrie of ye Citty of Coventrie'.[2] John Coventry was born during the late 14th century, and, by 1410, he was earning a successful living in London as a dealer in fine textiles. Presumably his reputation as a fair and honest tradesman led to his appointment in 1416 as Sheriff of London, the chief law-officer of the city.

From 1420 until his death in 1429, he served as alderman of the Aldgate ward, and he was elected Mayor from 1425-6.[3] During this period of civic leadership, John Coventry lived with his wife, Alice, and their sons, Thomas and Richard, in a house in King Street, Cheapside, with the curious name of 'Le Cage'. The house appears to have been a property of some importance and had formerly been owned by his father, and before him by two earlier mayors, William de Walleworth and Adam Franceys.[4] Its name may derive from its previous function as either a prison, an inn, or even a shop, as 'West Chepe' was a principal London shopping street in medieval times and home to numerous goldsmiths and mercers. As the Coventres were members of the Mercers' Company this seems the most likely explanation. John Coventre would have met Richard Whittington early in his career as both men shared a common trade and similar civic interests. Whittington supplied fine cloth to the Crown and later lent vast sums of money to the king, which gained him considerable influence at court and in the city. Evidently, he held Coventry in high regard, for, in 1420, he appointed him an executor of his will. This was no small responsibility, as Whittington had amassed great wealth and owned much property in the city. As a widower without issue, his fortune was to be spent on a major building programme for the benefit of the citizens of London. The proceeds from the sale of his house and other property in the city funded the collegiation of his parish church, St Michael de Paternoster, where masses for his soul and the souls of his wife and parents were to be held. Almshouses and a hospital were constructed nearby, and the remainder of the money funded various other important projects, including the rebuilding of Newgate prison, the repair of St Bartholomew's Hospital, and the repair and enlargement of the Guildhall. It is a little ironic that, despite Whittington's outstanding beneficence, he is remembered chiefly for heeding the advice of a peal of bells and the talents of his cat.

When he became mayor, John Coventry played an important part in the bitter struggle for power between Humphrey, Duke of Gloucester (1391-1447), younger brother of Henry V, and his uncle, Henry Beaufort, Bishop of Winchester (d.1447). This quarrel began after the death of Henry V in 1422, and was due primarily to Gloucester's ambition at home and abroad. During Gloucester's absence abroad, Beaufort had been appointed chancellor. This had angered the merchants of London because of his favourable attitude towards their counterparts in Flanders and because the city council had placed certain trading restrictions upon them. On Gloucester's return, Beaufort decided to exploit the situation and, on 30 October 1425, he persuaded the mayor, John Coventry, to hold London Bridge against Gloucester to prevent him from entering the city. Shops were closed, and crowds gathered on the bridge in support of their mayor, but opposition was strong and soon the situation developed into a riot. The dispute continued for the following six months and was not settled finally until 12 March 1426, when Beaufort resigned as chancellor. John Coventry gained in popularity from the incident, but current political instability may have prevented his re-election as mayor. He died on 29 March 1429, and was buried in St Mary-le-Bow churchyard, Cheapside, although his monument with its long inscription has since disappeared.

Documentary evidence now skims conspicuously over the ensuing gap of around a hundred years to Vincent Coventry, who came from Cassington, a village to the north-west of Oxford. His son and heir, Richard, had two sons, John and Thomas, and it was the younger brother who is believed to have established the Coventry family in Croome. This raises certain questions of a chronological nature. There is little doubt that a Coventry family held land in Oxfordshire from around the 13th century or even earlier.[5] It is a coincidence, but not necessarily significant, that a Thomas Coventry was pursuing a prominent civic career in Oxford at the same time as John Coventry became Mayor of London. He was appointed city bailiff in 1403, and became one of the three city coroners in 1418, an alderman and also Mayor of Oxford in 1419 and 1427-8.[6] It would be satisfying to establish a link between the two men, but no personal details of Thomas Coventry's life survive among the Oxfordshire archives. By the 16th century, references to people with the name of Coventry in Oxfordshire occur quite frequently. For example, in 1535, Wroxton mill was let to a Thomas Coventry;[7] and in 1563, Thomas Biggs, a yeoman of Horton, was left property at Woodstock and Handborough by the widow of John Coventre, a gentleman in the service of Sir John Croke.[8] The earliest references to a Vincent Coventry relate to a series of property transactions that occurred during the late 16th century. He purchased the manor of Cassington from his landlord, Thomas Norwood, in 1574.[9] At the same time, he sold three and a half yardlands in Cassington to Richard Cherry, one of the executors of his will,[10] and he and a John Hebborne bought a large parcel of land in the parish of Piddington, which included 36 messuages with orchards and gardens and 1,850 acres of land and wood.[11] He was obviously a wealthy man, and this is confirmed by his will and also by an inventory of his house in Cassington.[12] This house, formerly known as Moat Farm, included a hall, parlour, a best chamber, five additional chambers, a kitchen, dairy and buttery. The rooms were comfortably furnished and filled with a fine collection of carpets, silver, pewter, damask and linen. There were a dozen horses in his stables and 22 cattle in his byre. In his will, he left large bequests to his numerous children, and over £40 per annum towards 'ye mending of ye comon hihways'.[13] He would fulfil his presumed role as the affluent ancestor of the Coventry family perfectly, but as he died in 1610 he was the contemporary rather than the grandfather of Thomas Coventry of Croome (1547-1606). It is possible that the two men shared the same grandfather or great-uncle with the family name of Vincent. However, this does not explain why Vincent is said to have come from Cassington, if the family did not purchase the manor until 1574. Vincent Coventry sold part of the manor before he died in 1610, and his son and heir, John, mortgaged and eventually disposed of the remainder in 1633 to Edward Reynolds of Oxford.[14] If the Earls of Coventry had ancestors from Oxfordshire, the precise details of this connection cannot be easily explained.

Further complications arise concerning the family's estates in Lincolnshire. In 1870, a London genealogist wrote to the 9th Earl claiming to have traced the Coventry ancestry back to the 12th century. He referred to a Liulph de Coventre, who is recorded to have owed money to the Crown in 1158, and a Walter de Coventre, who held half a knight's fee in Lincoln in 1260, among others. The details are deliberately scant to tempt Lord Coventry to subscribe to his forthcoming book on the Norman baronage. It seems unlikely that Lord Coventry was tempted as no trace of the book survives in the library catalogue at Croome, but the letter provides some explanation for a mysterious bundle of 17th- and 18th-century papers among the Croome archive.[15] These relate to land and property in the county apparently owned by Thomas, 1st Baron Coventry, including the manors of Stixwold and Twigmore, and a house and associated grounds at Canbury, also referred to in his will.[16] There is even a specific reference to drainage works in Cambridge, Lincolnshire, dated 20 October 1619.[17] This date is significant as the 1st Baron did not start to extend his estate till after 1620. It is reasonable to assume that his holdings in Lincolnshire were inherited or purchased some time after his father's death in 1606, but neither the family archive at Croome nor the county archive at Lincoln can shed little light on the problem. There were several prominent figures called Coventry who lived in the county during the medieval period, notably a Richard Coventry, who served as Commissioner of Sewers responsible for the major programme of fen drainage between 1582-6. But the only document that makes specific reference to the Coventrys of Croome concerns the 1st Baron's second wife, Elizabeth, who inherited an interest in his Lincolnshire estates after his death.[18] Much of the Lincolnshire estate belonged to the 1st Baron's younger brother Walter, through whom it passed back to the Coventrys of Croome after the title reverted to William Coventry in the 18th century.

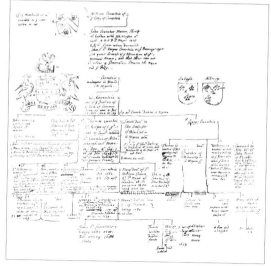

A 17th-century pedigree within the Croome archive puts forward the most plausible alternative to Sir Thomas Coventry's ancestry. Although illegible in part, this implies that the descendants of John Coventry were established in Bewdley, Worcestershire, at least a generation prior to Sir Thomas Coventry's acquisition of Croome D'Abitot. Only inaccuracies elsewhere in this pedigree fail to inspire confidence in this claim.[19]

3   17th-century pedigree of the Coventry family.

Sir Thomas Coventry (1547-1606)

Sir Thomas Coventry is thus the earliest direct and indisputable ancestor of the Coventrys of Croome. Although his achievements pale beside those of his talented descendants, he laid the foundation of his family's reputation as lawyers and statesmen during the 17th century. More importantly, he established the family estate at Croome, which provided the focus of his descendants' wealth, influence and ambition.

Thomas was born in 1547, probably in Worcestershire. As the family estates were inherited by his elder brother, John, Thomas decided to pursue a career in law. He went to Balliol College, Oxford, where he was awarded his degree in June 1565. The following year, at the age of 19, he was made a fellow of Balliol, and he moved to the Inner Temple. By 1589, he had made his debut as an advocate, and four years later he was elected Autumn Reader. That year London was stricken with plague and his reading had to be postponed. When the city was able to resume its normal business, a new Sergeant-at-Law, John Heale, was chosen to take his place and Coventry had to wait until the following year for his opportunity. Unfortunately, this important and long-awaited stage in his career was again temporarily blighted when he became involved in a controversy concerning the canvass for the appointment of solicitor-general. He is said to have incited the wrath of Francis Bacon (1561-1626), the lawyer, philosopher, and brilliant but devious politician, who was equally impatient for high office at this time. In a frank letter to Sir Robert Cecil, Secretary of State and later Lord Treasurer, Bacon accused Coventry of buying Sir Robert Cecil's interest for two thousand angels.[20] Such indiscretions and intrigues were, quite literally, the common currency of court life, but the incident may have influenced Bacon's judgement some twenty years later when he used Coventry's eminent son as a pawn in his power struggle with Sir Edward Coke. Thomas Coventry was fortunate to emerge from the charge relatively unscathed, but the last years of Elizabeth I's reign marked a period of frustrated professional ambition.

On 10 October 1602, the arms of the Coventry family were confirmed by William Camden, Clarenceux King of Arms, a confirmation based on the principle that the family had established a right to them due to their long usage, rather than a creation and assignment of new arms. This has a *sable a fesse ermine* between three gold crescents with eagle supporters, and a scarlet cockerell on a wheatsheaf perched upon the helmet. The motto *Candide et Constanter* is most appropriate to their legal background.[21]

The confirmation proved a good omen. In 1603, James I was crowned king and at last Thomas Coventry received the recognition he had sought all his life. Almost at once, he was made Sergeant-at-Law, and from 1605-6 he served as King's Sergeant. Within months of this appointment, in early 1606, he became one of the Justices of the Court of Common Pleas and he was knighted. He had waited a long time for this rush of recognition, but he had only a few months to reflect on his success. He died on 12 December 1606 and he was buried in the church on his new country estate at Croome.

Like many successful and affluent professional men of his day, he had been eager to purchase a country estate. Land ownership was the basis of power. It was necessary to assert his status, increase his income and establish the connections to promote his further advancement. Vast tracts of land had become available after the Reformation, which had swelled the ranks of the squirearchy in Worcestershire as elsewhere, among them the Packingtons of Westwood and Harvington, the Talbots of Grafton, and the Lechmeres of Hanley Castle. Around 1576-7 (the exact date remains elusive) he married Margaret Jeffery, the eldest daughter of William Jeffery, or Jefferies, and his wife Alice, of Earls Croome in Worcestershire.[22] According to Nash, the county historian, William Jeffery had been Cofferer of the Household to Henry VIII and had been granted Earls Croome by Edward VI. Later sources state that Henry VIII granted the manor to Thomas Wymbish. He sold it to Edward, Lord Clinton, Earl of Lincoln, who sold it to Thomas

Jeffery, William's father.[23] Whatever the case, William Jeffery was a man of wealth and property. He died before Thomas Coventry married his eldest daughter, Margaret, and Earls Croome manor was then under the ownership of his son, Leonard. When the opportunity arose in 1592 to purchase the adjoining manor of Croome D'Abitot from the Clare family of Kidderminster, Thomas Coventry seized it with alacrity.[24] It was a sensible investment, a secure and welcome retreat from the hustle and pestilence of London, and its convenient location adjacent to his wife's family home presented opportunities for expansion. The Jeffery family remained in Earls Croome till around 1700, and after this date the manor became absorbed within the Croome estate.

At the time, Croome manor lay within Oswaldeslawe's hundred. Thomas Habington (1560-1647) described this as an area 'conteyning the thyrd parte of the county of Worcester … graunted by kynge Aedgar, An.Do.964, to Oswald, then Bishop of Worcester'.[25] Croome, also written as Crumbe and Croomb until the 18th century, had formed part of the manor of Ripple before the Conquest and was held by Oderic, a Saxon lord. According to Domesday Book, it consisted of around one hundred acres of meadow and woodland with an estimated value of 40 shillings.[26] After the Conquest, the manor was held by the Norman D'Abitot family, who controlled a vast tract of land in the region. Urso d'Abitot was county Sheriff, and his brother Robert was Steward of the Household to William I. The manor had thereby acquired the second half of its title to distinguish it from the adjacent manors of Earls Croome, a former possession of the Earls of Warwick, and Hill Croome, which is situated on high ground to the south. The D'Abitot family and their descendants continued to hold land in Croome till 1530, when the manor passed by will to Gilbert Clare. It was Gilbert's grandson, Francis, who sold it to Thomas Coventry in 1592.[27]

Croome was then a combination of large open fields, meadows and marshland, with substantial patches of woodland and smaller area of heath and downland. The fields were grouped primarily to the north and west of the parish and were divided into strips for the cultivation of wheat, barley and leguminous crops, with the meadows providing animal pasture, although the livestock would also graze the fields after harvest. The precise extent of the woodland remains uncertain, but much of it was located on the areas of common land that skirted the parish, notably the shallow ridge of heathland that stretched along the western boundary, known as Cubsmoor Heath. Much of the land was marshy and poorly drained, but the wettest and most unwholesome patch was largely confined to an area known as Seggey Meer Common, to the south-west of the parish, the site of the present artificial lake and river. Two mills are recorded within the parish in 1584. These lay to the north-east, one upon the land now occupied by Church Hill. Of the 21 families recorded to be living in Croome at the end of Elizabeth I's reign, nearly all were accommodated in small timber-framed cottages within the small and sprawling village that stood to the north-east of the present mansion. The original parish church lay to the west of this settlement. Although it was demolished in the mid-18th century, drawings made prior to its demolition within the archive show that it had a relatively tall nave with a south aisle and gabled dormer windows. At its western end rose a short, square tower with an embattled parapet, later enhanced by a small ogee dome and finial (see no. 7, p.24). Little is known about its interior detail, but the south arcade would have been its most dominant architectural feature and, according to Habington, a figure of a knight was painted on one of the north windows. He was dressed as a Crusader, in a coat of mail and a white habit marked with a red cross, and he held a shield Argent, with a 'Crosse Gules' and 'a Launce, or rather a horseman's staffe'. The manor house itself was located between the church and the main part of the village, on the site of the present mansion house. It is just possible that this early house was built of brick as were several major domestic buildings in the county that date from the 16th century, including Grafton Manor, near Bromsgrove, Madresfield Court, near Malvern, and The Nash, nearby in Kempsey. It is more probable that Croome Court was originally a timber-framed building of modest pretensions of the hall and cross-wing type, two or three storeys high, and with massive external chimneys, common throughout the county during this period. Both Pirton Court and Earls Croome Court (as rebuilt by the Jeffery family) nearby were timber-framed buildings of a similar type, scale and date.

Sir Thomas and his family would have spent as much time at Croome as his commitments allowed between 1592 and 1603. He and his wife Margaret had seven children, three sons and four daughters.[28] Thomas, his son and heir, was born in 1578 and went to Oxford in the year his father purchased Croome so he would have had little benefit from the place in his youth. Their second son, William, settled at Redmarley D'Abitot, now in north Gloucestershire, and had four children, Thomas, Susanna, William and Mary.[29] As its name suggests, this manor descended from the same Norman family as Croome, and had been acquired by the Coventry family on the marriage of Sir Thomas's eldest son to his first wife, Sarah Sebright. Walter (d.1640), the third and youngest son, married Susanna West in London in 1628. She appears to have been a widow, and the daughter of a man by the name of Harvey from Chigwell in Essex. They had three children, Thomas, Walter and John, and the earldom reverted to the descendants of his second son, Walter, in the 18th century. Less is known about Sir Thomas's four daughters, Margaret, Catherine, Joane and Anne. Margaret may never have married or reached maturity; Catherine married a local man, William Childe of Northwick, near Worcester, in 1602; Joane married Edward Rogers from Surrey in 1612; and Anne married George Frampton, from Buckland in Dorset, around 1597 and they had six children, Grace, Mary Martha, Robert, Ursula and Walter.[30]

Towards the end of his life, Sir Thomas Coventry began to extend his estate. He purchased Hardewick in the parish of Eldersfield on the southern perimeter of the county, which he acquired from John Delamere.[31] However, he died before he could develop these plans further, and it was his son and grandson, who made most of the major additions to the estate before the outbreak of the Civil War.

Sir Thomas had achieved much: professional distinction, the approval of the king, a knighthood and a modest country estate, but these provided mere footholds for his son's ascent.

III

A Judicious Ascent

Thomas Coventry, 1st Baron Coventry (1578-1640)

In his *History of the Great Rebellion*, Clarendon described Lord Keeper Coventry as '… rather exceedingly Liked, than passionately Loved'.[1] This did not damn with faint praise, for Clarendon was a great enthusiast for Coventry's particular style of leadership. Indeed it underlined Coventry's greatest strength. For much as he inspired lasting admiration for his intellect and integrity, it was his careful detachment from the mounting constitutional crisis that made him so indispensable. His impartiality and sound judgement, necessary but not necessarily innate to his profession, earned him the respect of both the monarch and his parliament and helped to secure his sure and swift promotion to Lord Keeper. Apparently immune to the bitter power struggles that marred the careers of brilliant but more volatile personalities, such as Bacon, Coke and Buckingham, some regarded with envy and suspicion his ability to rise above the corruption at court. As Clarendon observed, his was 'a rare ascent' indeed.

Among the numerous contemporary accounts of Lord Keeper Coventry's achievements, one is outstanding in its frankness and perception. The author chose to remain anonymous, but he claims to have known Coventry as a former supplicant.[2] He provides a vivid description of Coventry's appearance:

> The Character of his Outward Man was this. He was of Middle Stature. Somewhat Broad, and round fac'd of Hair black & upright in his compartment and gesture, of complexion sanguine, and of comely aspect and presence …

4   The Lord Keeper Coventry by Cornelius Jonson, *c*.1638.

This description conforms to the portraits of Coventry painted in his early and late middle age by Cornelius Jonson.[3] The earlier portrait reveals a stocky figure of medium height, with short dark hair, a ruddy complexion and a neatly-clipped moustache and beard which gives definition to his firm, protruding jaw, a characteristic common to many members of the family (colour plate II). In the later portrait, he seems to have aged considerably, burdened by the weight of his responsibilities. Interestingly, this anonymous author notes that Coventry had a lisp, unusual for a man of his profession:

> He was of a fine and grave Elocution in a kind of graceful Lisping, Soe, that where nature might seem to cast something of imperfection on his Speech, on due Examination, she added a grace to the perfection of his delivery, for his words rather flowed from him in a kind of native pleasingness, than by any artificial help or Assistance …

Clarendon considered that he spoke 'without much ornament of Elocution', but concedes that 'his plain way of speaking and delivery' gave him 'a strange power of making himself believed'.[4] An undoubted asset in his profession, and he appears to have been '… seldom in any distempered Mood or Motion of Choller', and gifted with 'a kind of naturall and unaffected insinuation to creep into the good Opinion of all Men, rather than any affected greatnesse'.[5] Even such a paragon of virtue could not hope to bring order to a nation on the brink of rebellion.

Thomas Coventry, 1st Baron Coventry (1578-1640), is said to have been born at Croome, probably Earls Croome as his father did not acquire the manor of Croome D'Abitot until 1692.[6] It is likely that his mother would have retreated from London to the Jeffery family home for her confinement. He was privately educated, and his father sent him at the age of 14 to Balliol, his former Oxford college, to pursue a career in the law. By 1595 he had moved on to the Inner Temple, and in 1603 he was called to the bar. This was the year his father achieved high office, and Coventry's first employment as junior counsel to the Skinners' Company in May 1604 is likely to have resulted from his father's influence.[7] While working for the Skinners' Company, Coventry became involved in a dispute with the churchwardens of St Michael's Paternoster over Whittington College. Built under the direction of Coventry's ancestor, the college had recently been acquired by the Skinners' from the Mercers' Company. In early 1605, Coventry's competence and diligence were rewarded when he obtained reversions to succeed to the town clerkship of London, and in 1606 he became a judge of the Sheriff's court. That summer he married Sarah Sebright, the daughter of John Sebright of Blakeshall, near Wolverley in Worcestershire, and the sister of Sir Edward Sebright of Besford, a few miles east of Croome. They may have met through this local connection, or through Sarah's uncle, William Sebright, who was also a member of the Inner Temple and Town Clerk of London. The marriage settlement included much of Hill Croome parish, land in the parishes of Upton on Severn and Earls Croome, half of Ryalls Court manor, and property on the southern boundary of the county, including Redmarley D'Abitot.[8] A son and heir, Thomas, was born in 1606, the year when the elder Thomas Coventry received his knighthood, but there was little time to celebrate. Sir Thomas Coventry died the following winter, and a few years later Sarah was also dead. Within a year or so of her death, Thomas remarried on 20 April 1610. His second wife, Elizabeth

Pitchford, was the daughter of John Aldersey, a haberdasher from Spurstow in Cheshire, and her mother, Ann, was the sister of Sir Thomas Lowe, a London alderman. Elizabeth's Cheshire origins are of interest in that they are the only possible explanation for a mysterious chest tomb in the churchyard of St Oswald's Church, Backford, Cheshire, that dates from around the early 17th century. Believed to be the tomb of a Richard Coventry, this might be dismissed as coincidence were it not embellished with the Coventry coat-of-arms.[9]

Elizabeth was a widow, and had formerly been married to a London grocer and apothecary, William Pitchford. According to Coventry's anonymous supplicant, Elizabeth was '... Lovely, Young, Rich, and of good Fame' and she proved to be:

> ... a wife as loveing, as (Thomas) was uxorious, and of that sort which are not unaptly styled Housewives
> ... for they that know the discipline of his house averr that he waved that Care as a contiguous
> distraction to his vocation and left her only (as an Helper) to manage that Charge which best suited
> to her Conversation.

Elizabeth gave birth to four sons and four daughters, all of whom survived childhood and contributed to the rapid increase in the wealth and influence of the Coventry family.[10]

The profession of Elizabeth's former husband, William Pitchford, provided Coventry with an opportunity to serve as counsel for the Company of Apothecaries from around 1614. In 1627 he was admitted as a brother of the Company, the first lawyer to receive this honour, and he presided at the Company's Commemoration and Election dinners.[11] He also represented the Drapers' Company and the Merchants of the Staple during this important early stage of his career.

Shortly after his second marriage, Coventry had joined the Oxford circuit with his colleagues Henry Yelverton, John Walter and James Whitelocke, but it was not until 1616 that his career began to make significant progress. That year he was selected as Autumn Reader, and between 1617-23 he served as Treasurer at the Inner Temple but, most importantly, he was chosen as a candidate for the Recordership of London. His candidacy was well-deserved, but it invited the un-welcome attention of the formidable Francis Bacon.

5   Elizabeth Pitchford, wife of The Lord Keeper Coventry, by Cornelius Jonson, c.1626.

One of the chief threats to Bacon's ambition and policies was Edward, Lord Coke (1552-1634). Coke had been Treasurer at the Inner Temple during Coventry's second year of study there. He had recognised Coventry's potential and had befriended him; possibly he was aware that Bacon harboured a long-standing grudge against Coventry's father. The conflict between Coke and Bacon was reaching its height in the autumn of 1616 over the Peacham case, when Bacon was Attorney-General and Coke was Lord Chief Justice. Peacham, a Somersetshire clergyman, had been charged with treason and this had given Bacon a chance to assert his support of the royal prerogative, which he believed preferable to referring matters to the judges who he regarded merely as 'lions under the throne'. Coke, on the other hand, was in favour of furnishing the judiciary with powers even greater than parliament, so that the High Court judges could mediate between the king and the people. When he refused to submit to the king's request to give his advice independent of his fellow judges with regard to Peacham, he was dismissed on 15 November. Coventry's candidacy for the Recordership occurred right in the middle of the Peacham case and it served as an invitation to Bacon to vent his resentment of Coke's policies. On 13 November he wrote to the King:

> … The man upon whom the choice is like to fall, which is Coventry, I hold doubtful for your service; not that he is but well learned and an honest man, but he hath been, as it were, bred by Lord Coke and seasoned in his ways'.[12]

This could have been a serious blow to Coventry's ambition, but he was elected Recorder on 18 November owing to a fortunate delay caused by Yelverton's refusal to accept his election for the post.[13] Four months later, still in his late 30s, Coventry became Solicitor-General and, on 16 March 1617, he was knighted at Theobalds, just as his father had been over a decade previously. Quite why his career was unaffected by his association with Coke is uncertain. Perhaps his sheer ability granted him some immunity, but many contemporaries believed his promotion was secured through the influence of George Villiers, Earl of Buckingham, the king's handsome companion and close adviser.[14] Even so, it did not take long for him to assert his independent authority.

Yelverton had managed to secure the appointment of Attorney-General, but his incompetence merely served as a foil to Coventry's abilities. For example, in 1619, Thomas Howard, 1st Earl of Suffolk and Lord Treasurer, was charged with embezzling £140 to improve his estate. During his prosecution in the Star Chamber, Coventry launched a fierce attack upon his dishonesty to a most receptive audience: 'Thus', he proclaimed, 'the great foundation of the Exchequer must be subverted for the building up of my Lordship's stables.'[15] It was a memorable performance, and shortly afterwards, on 11 January 1621, Yelverton was dismissed and Coventry took his place. His elevation to Lord Keeper was now virtually guaranteed.

As Attorney-General, Coventry was able to play a small part in containing Bacon's ambition. Bacon was now Lord Keeper and under pressure from Buckingham to grant favours to secure support for the king on demand. Eventually, he fell victim to charges of corruption, and it was Coventry's responsibility to make him provide specific answers

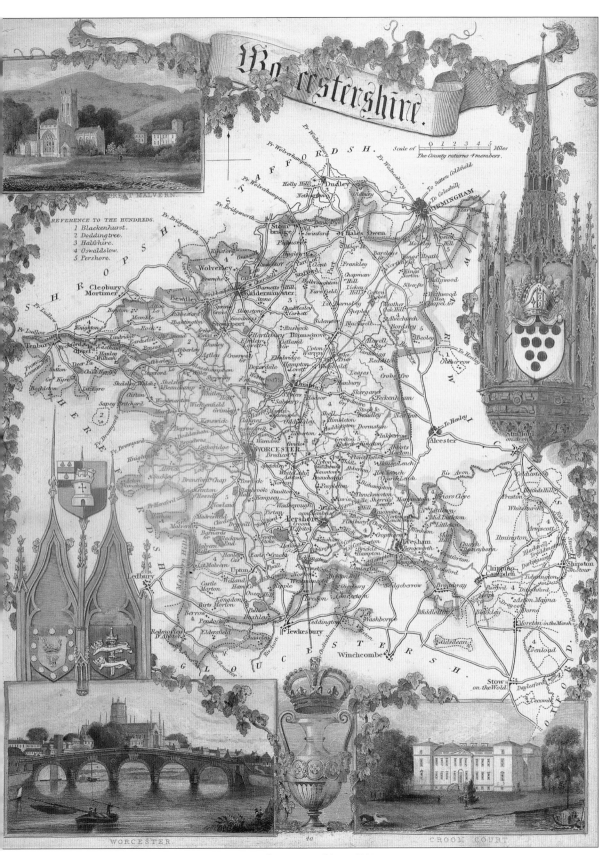

I Map of Worcestershire, *c*.1800.

II *Top left*. The Lord Keeper Coventry by Cornelius Jonson c.1626.

III *Top right*. Henry Coventry by Sir Peter Lely.

IV *Left*. Sir William Coventry by Sir Peter Lely.

V   'The Outrage upon Sir John Coventry' by T.H. Maguire.

VI *Top left*. Winifred Edgcumbe, wife of Thomas, 5th Baron and 1st Earl of Coventry.

VII *Top right*. Thomas, Viscount Deerhurst, later 2nd Earl of Coventry.

VIII *Left*. Thomas Henry, Viscount Deerhurst, *c.*1740.

to the charges brought against him in parliament. Bacon's subsequent brief imprisonment may have appealed to Coventry's sense of justice. More importantly, Bacon was obliged to step down from the political stage, which cleared a path for Coventry's advancement. By November 1625, with the new king on the throne, Buckingham recommended Coventry to succeed as Lord Keeper to replace John Williams, Bishop of Lincoln, an eminent scholar but a man he deeply distrusted.

The speed of Coventry's ascent may have owed much to Buckingham's patronage, but few could fault his integrity, impartiality and sheer professional expertise. Clarendon said of him that he

> ... was of wonderful gravity and wisdom, and understood not only the whole Science, and Mystery of the Law, at least equally with any man who had ever sate in that place; but had a clear conception of the whole Policy of the Government both of Church and of State ... He knew the temper, disposition, and genius of the kingdom most exactly ...[16]

Above all, at a time when distrust was endemic, his 'strange power of making himself believed' was a gift that neither the king nor parliament could ignore.

The Lord Keeper took into official keeping the Great Seal used to authenticate important documents issued in the name of the king. In England, the Great Seal has always been two-sided with a different device on each side. The earliest Great Seal may have belonged to Edward the Confessor, but it was the seal of William I which provided the model for later designs. This had an engraving of the monarch seated in state on the reverse and an equestrian portrait of the monarch on the obverse; the designs were reversed on later seals.[17] Since 1757, the office of Lord Keeper has been merged in that of Lord Chancellor, but during the 17th century the offices had close parallels, and Coventry was obliged to act as mediator between the king and his increasingly intractable parliament.[18] When he opened Charles I's second parliament in 1626, the Commons reverberated with a wealthy and vociferous gentry, hungry for political power and influence on religious and foreign policy. As a Royalist and officer of the crown, Coventry's official acceptance speech was unlikely to cast doubt on the royal prerogative, but soon he began to tread a delicate path between the king and his restless subjects.

His loyal conduct and tact during the following years reaped high rewards. On 10 April 1628 he was made Baron Coventry of Allesborough, or Aylesborough as it was then known, part of the manor of Pershore which he had purchased in 1622. This seemed to give him the confidence to assert his personal views more forcefully. For example, he refused Buckingham's application for the office of Lord High Constable. This infuriated Buckingham, who believed that Coventry should return the favour that he had bestowed upon him when he was made Lord Keeper. Then he annoyed James, 3rd Marquess of Hamilton by refusing to affix the Great Seal to an illegal patent he had invented. The Earl of Manchester, also a lawyer, was employed to check up on his more wilful decisions, particularly when he used his knowledge of the law to confound the king's advisers.[19] In 1628, when Coke's Petition of Right, demanding that billeting, unjust imprisonment and forced payments without parliamentary consent should stop, Coventry opposed this direct threat to the king's authority. However, he did state his support for the resolution that no man should be imprisoned without cause. Fearful of the consequences of Charles I's objection to the petition, he tried to persuade him to assent to it rather than dissolve parliament to end the debate. On 7 June, Charles I did give his assent, albeit grudgingly, but three weeks later he dismissed parliament, this time in an effort to save Buckingham from impeachment. Shortly afterwards, Buckingham died at the hands of an assassin. Parliament met again the following January, only to be dissolved by a desperate Charles I. It did not reconvene for 11 years, the last 11 years of Coventry's life.

During the 1630s, Coventry's advisory role to the king became increasingly fraught. He was much opposed to the scheme devised by Richard Weston, Lord Portland, the Lord Treasurer, to form a Spanish alliance, and in May 1634, he joined William Laud, Archbishop of Canterbury, in bringing a charge of corruption against him. He was equally wary of Laud and his influence on King Charles, although it was argued that he sometimes only pretended to disapprove of Laud's excesses when he deemed this prudent. One of the most important issues about which he spoke out was the controversial matter of Ship Money. It was traditionally the right of the monarch to levy a direct tax on property in coastal towns and cities for defence purposes in time of war without the need to consult parliament. In 1634, Charles I had levied the tax to raise funds on the excuse that there was a possibility of war. As the tax was confined to London it raised little objection at first, but after it was extended to cover the entire kingdom, in August 1635, there was a definite shift in opinion. Admittedly, much of the money raised was spent on the navy. That year, English fleets had begun to patrol the North Sea, primarily to intimidate the Dutch fishermen; but this was posturing rather than war. Coventry was in favour of the tax, and he spoke out against the dangers of a maritime war to justify its extension. 'The dominion of the sea,' he believed, 'as it is an ancient and undoubted right of the crown of England, so it is the best security of the land.' Such stirring speeches did little to mollify the mounting resentment in the shires. A policy of non-payment was adopted, led by the Buckinghamshire squire, John Hampden (1594-1645), a Puritan and a prominent voice among the parliamentary opposition to the irregular procedures of the king during the 1630s. The case was decided in favour of the Crown, but only just, and the king decided to take it no further for fear of inciting similar public protest to his inept policies. It was no surprise when one of the first acts of the Long Parliament of 1640 was to declare Ship Money illegal. Although Coventry never criticised the king's right to levy the tax, he did resist other attempts by the king to raise funds, notably his determination to enforce the payment of a loan by the city of London in June 1639. The Lord Keeper is reported to have himself lent the king £10,000 later that year. This may have been less an indication of his support of the monarchy than of his valiant efforts to dissuade the king from more ruthless measures, which would trigger the impending crisis.

In the Star Chamber, Lord Keeper Coventry sought to mitigate the severity of the sentences imposed, and he tried to stop such illegal practices as the hanging of men for resisting press gangs. Most of his official papers as Lord Keeper are among the Birmingham Archives, although a few remain within the Croome collection.[20] They represent a vast volume of paperwork which includes absolutions, licences of alienation, commissions of appeal, bankruptcy cases, grants of patents, leases, offices and appointments, licences to eat flesh, sell tobacco and wine, special pardons' etc.[21] Among them is a docket concerned with the knighthood of Peter Paul Rubens (1577-1640), who visited London as a diplomat between 1629-30 to negotiate a peace between England and Spain. He was treated with every possible honour and knighted on his return to Spain, having presented the king with a large painting of *Peace and War*. There are also commissions of the peace, that demonstrate Charles I's attempts to purge the bench of his political opponents, and numerous petitions of considerable variety and interest, from popish recusants, impoverished clergyman, or dissatisfied tenants. One was submitted by the captain and crew of the ship the *Little St George* from Bristol, who had captured a French ship, the *Gabriell*. Under English law, they were entitled to claim one third of the booty, but the Bristol merchants who owned their ship had denied them this privilege and they were seeking justice.

According to tradition, on the accession of Charles in 1625, Lord Keeper Coventry was entitled to keep the obsolete seal that had belonged to James I to convert into a piece of commemorative silver. He commissioned a pair of silver-gilt chased and embossed cups with domed covers each made from a different seal, one hallmarked 1626/7 and the other hallmarked 1627.[22] In his will of 1638 he left 'my first greate Silver Cuppe' to his son and heir, Thomas, and the other he left to his wife and thereafter to his male issue.[23] The earlier cup is now among the collection of the Victoria & Albert Museum; the later one found its way to Longleat through Sir Henry Frederick Thynne, the third son of the Lord Keeper's daughter, Mary, and her husband, Sir Henry Frederick Thynne, and it now forms part of the collection of the Marquesses of Bath. Both cups represent a very rare example of royal silversmithing, although the goldsmith responsible is unknown, and identified only by his mark which has the initials 'RB' and a mullet, a mark common to several outstanding designs of this period. Of a highly ornate and impressive design based

6 The Lord Keeper Coventry's First Seal Cup.

on heraldic devices, each has a circular base enriched with a with a narrow band of foliage, a bell-shaped plinth, a banded stem with a lion and unicorn, and a detachable vase-shaped bowl decorated with the badges of England, France and Scotland. These badges run diagonally in the opposite direction on the Longleat cup. Around the rim is engraved the words 'NUNCA PRIUATA DONY CLAUDIT AMORE CALIX: PUBLICA QUOD NUPER FIRMABAT IURA SIGILLUM'. (THIS CUP NOW ENCOMPASSES PRIVATE LOVE WHERE ONCE IT BORE THE SEAL OF PUBLIC JUSTICE.) The domed covers have a finial surmounted by the royal coat-of-arms and, as their hallmarks do not now correspond with their respective cups, it may be assumed that they were exchanged accidentally shortly after they were made.[24]

These cups alone suggest that the 1st Baron Coventry was a man of great wealth. His anonymous biographer claims that he possessed '... a Bulke of Treasure of noe Comon Sume', much of which was invested in his estate. As early as 1609 he had acquired the advowson of Ombersley church with Thomas Sandys, and later acted as its legal adviser. But it was not until his appointment as Solicitor-General in 1617 that Thomas Coventry began to invest seriously in land and property. From around 1620 he is recorded to have owned salt bulleries or phates in Droitwich.[25] A bullery or plate was a measurement by which the salt water from the salt wells was fairly distributed, and it consisted of 216 large vessels of salt water of varying quality. The possession of a phate was a privilege and could, as in Coventry's case, carry with it a burgess-ship, which became hereditary. There followed a sequence of important acquisitions, the first of which was a substantial parcel of land in Broadway, which he acquired from the Savage family in 1619.[26] By the time of his death in 1640, the Coventry family possessed land in Allesborough, Besford, Birlingham, Broughton Hackett, Buckbury, Defford, Hill and Earls Croome, Feckenham, Grafton Flyford, Hanbury, Kerswell, the Littletons, Longdon, Mitton, Newland, Offenham, Pirton, Powick, Ripple, Severn Stoke, Wadborough and Upton Snodsbury in Worcestershire. Pirton and Severn Stoke on the borders of Croome parish were particularly useful additions. Pirton included Pirton Pool, a huge medieval fishpond of around fifty acres (see colour plate IX), while Severn Stoke provided direct access to the small quay on the Severn as well as High House, a substantial manor house with numerous outbuildings and gardens perched on the steep bank south of the church overlooking the hams.[27] As it is referred to in a contemporary map as 'Lord Coventre's house', Jill Tovey has suggested that the 2nd Baron may have lived there when Croome was being rebuilt after the fire of c.1640.

As the estate continued to expand across the south-eastern half of Worcestershire, there were additional purchases of land at Cockbury, Corse, Deerhurst, Eldersfield, Hardwick, Haw, Mickleton, Postlip, Oxendon, Tirley and Woolstone, which established a firm foothold in north Gloucestershire. Elsewhere, the 1st Baron held the prebends of Bisley in South Gloucestershire, Woolvey in Warwickshire, Great Milton in Oxfordshire, Wiveliscombe in Somerset, and the manors of Clifton Camvyle and Hampton in Staffordshire, which he bought from Sir William Heveningham of Aston, Staffordshire. There were also large estates in Lincolnshire, notably a house and grounds in Canbury, and land in Stixwold and Twigmore, although 600 acres in Helyngham were sold off in 1639.[28] These investments formed an extensive power base, further reinforced by the marriages and acquisitions of his children and descendants.

Outside the capital, and even beyond the confines of his estate, the 1st Baron was able to extend his influence by other means. He had worked as a JP in Surrey and Middlesex in 1616, and in Westminster in 1619, and he was elected an MP for Droitwich in Worcestershire in 1621. He was unseated on 8 February 1621, just days before he took his place in the Commons, due to his appointment as Attorney-General, but his growing reputation provided ample compensation for this disappointment. In 1624 he became Custos Rotulorum for Worcestershire, and from 1626-40 he served as High Steward of Cambridge and, from 1633, he was High Steward of Coventry, St Albans, Kingston-upon-Hull and Bath too. He was elected Recorder of Boston in 1633, and Recorder of Coventry in 1634. It is an impressive list.

The 1st Baron was inevitably an absentee landlord. His commitments in London and elsewhere rarely permitted visits to his Worcestershire estates and it seemed sensible to build his investments in the south-eastern part of the country to include land and property in Edgware and Bois in Middlesex, and in Rotherhithe in Kent. He built himself a new house in London in 1620, Durham House in the Strand and, some years later, he began to rent Canonbury House in Islington, possibly as an informal but convenient retreat. Funds were also presented to the Inner Temple for the construction of new chambers, Fig Tree Court, in 1623.[29]

Such were his commitments that, in 1627, the 1st Baron decided to settle his Worcestershire estates on his eldest son, Thomas (1606-61), when he came of age that year and married Mary Craven. The report on the financial affairs of the family of c.1714, among the Carew Pole family archive at Antony, states that the house at Croome was burnt down during the 'time' of both the Lord Keeper and also that of his son Thomas.[30] This may refer to either their lifetimes or their actual ownership of the house. Bills and accounts within the Beaufort archive at Badminton reveal that major rebuilding works were begun by the 1st Baron's son, Thomas, c.1640. As no record survives of any other major alterations to the house between this time and Brown's remodelling of the house during the 1750s, it may be assumed that the earlier fire occurred during the second or third decade of the 17th century and the later fire just before 1640. The Croome Accounts for the half-year ended Lady Day 1624 refer to glazing and new ironwork 'about ye house', which may be the result of minor fire damage, but not until the estate was settled upon the 1st Baron's son in 1627 did the improvements begin in earnest. The entry for the half-year ended Lady Day 1627 refers to the building of a gatehouse at a cost of £192 18s. 2d., and the building of a chapel at a cost of £109 18s. 2d.[31] The gatehouse in question is illustrated in a drawing of c.1750, which shows a rectangular brick structure with three shaped gables, mullioned windows and a central archway. Could this have been constructed to complement a new brick façade on the house of a similar design? The cost of the chapel implies that it was also a substantial structure, possibly a gabled wing added onto the south elevation of the old church.

7 Croome old church from a bird's eye view of Croome House, *c*.1750.

It must have been demolished only a few years later as, in 1635, the Bishop of Worcester granted Lord Coventry's son, Thomas, a licence to restore the nave of the church and enlarge and repair the family chapel. The Antony report states that Thomas, the 2nd Baron, built 'one half' of the church at Croome, so it is probable that it was decided to relocate the chapel once more within a large new south aisle, as shown in the 18th-century drawing referred to above. There were other alterations too. A letter of 1632 from William Trap, the steward at Croome, to Hugh Dashfield, Lord Coventry's agent in London, concerns the building of a garden wall, a Backhouse (bakehouse?) and a Barnhouse, which had been delayed by hard frosts that winter.[32] The accounts imply that the gardens at Croome were already a valuable source of fresh produce by 1617, when a small sum was paid to 'the gardener of Mr Folliot of Severn Stoke' for pruning the vine and apricots. He must have been skilled at his job, for it is also evident from the accounts that baskets of apricots were regularly transported to London to grace the dining table at Durham House. The 1st Baron's son was responsible not only for the rebuilding and improvement works at Croome after 1627, but also for the purchase of some of the most important additions to the estate during the 1630s, notably Pirton, Powick, Mitton and Severn Stoke.

Most estate business throughout this period was conducted by Lord Coventry's agent, Hugh Dashfield, who refers to himself as 'Recevor of My Lord Keepers' Rents' and as 'Purse Bearer' in his correspondence.[33] From his London house, Dashfield dealt with elaborate and implausible excuses about unpaid rent and devised solutions to the problems of strayed and stolen livestock. A letter of 3 December 163[?] from John Bridges, the bailiff of the Littleton and Offernham manors, informed him that:

> ... Som of your Tenants are slacke in bringeing in their Rents which Drove me of thus longe. You Commandid me to take up any Strayes in my Lord's Right within Littleton and Offenam; ther is now a stray Sheep and the baylyese [bailiffs] of the hundred would have it but first I would know you will what shal be donn with it. Ther was also a stray Geldinge taken up by Mr Will Langston's Sheepherd proclaimed and kept 4 or 5 wickes ...

The stewards at Croome, Thomas Turbervile and William Trap, were on hand to execute Dashfield's instructions. They lived in fear of the demands of Sir Edward Sebright, Lord Coventry's brother-in-law, who felled timber from the Croome estate and was found to be 'verie unsertane of his woord'. Some indication of Coventry's income from his estates can be gleaned from the Croome accounts of this period; for example, the rents amounted to £316 8s. 8d. in 1617, and had risen to £404 0s. 6d. by 1623 and by similar amounts over subsequent years.

Such was Lord Coventry's wealth, influence and popularity by the 1630s, that it was a brave man who dared cast aspersions upon his character. When a certain Mr. J. Norton and his colleagues accused Lord Coventry of accepting bribes in 1630, the case caused public outrage. Extortionate fines, a spell in Fleet prison, and a public apology were deemed appropriate punishments, but not before two of the unfortunate villains were nailed to the pillory by their ears. In April 1635, a James Maxwell stated in a petition to the king that Coventry was too severe in his sentences and disloyal to the crown. As Coventry was renowned for his clemency and loyalty, the accusation was absurd, and Maxwell was fined a massive £3,000. Interestingly, Coventry offered to pay part of the fine. Was this an act of genuine generosity and evidence of his readiness to forgive, or was it simply a means to guarantee his continued popularity? Coventry's anonymous biographer implied the latter might be the case: '... it may well fall into the Question, whether he was more beholding to the Citty, or the Citty to him, or thus whether more may be attributed to his fortune than Meritt.' Henry Moore, a lawyer and advisor to Lord Sandwich at the Admiralty, was equally uncomplimentary. He described Lord Keeper Coventry to Samuel Pepys as '... a cunning, crafty man, [that] did make as many bad Decrees in Chancery as any man'.[34] Pepys is notably reticent about Coventry's conduct, possibly owing to his friendship with his youngest son, William. Another more surprising critic was William Dean, the head gardener at Croome, who wrote that Lord Keeper Coventry appeared neither an enlightened politician, nor a virtuous patriot.[35] But he excused the Lord Keeper from any inconsistencies because, as an officer of the crown and the mouthpiece of the king, he was often obliged to act against his better judgement. As a moderate man by nature, Coventry's concern about the more extreme measures of Charles I must have weighed as heavily upon his conscience, just as he viewed with alarm and distaste the more violent and revolutionary tendencies within parliament.

8 Monument of Thomas, 1st Baron Coventry and Lord Keeper, in Croome church.

Thomas, 1st Baron Coventry, died after a short illness at his house in the Strand on 14 January 1640. The precise cause of his death is unknown, but he had been incapacitated by 'the stone' for several weeks. His body was conveyed in great state to Croome on 17 February and he was interred in Croome church on 1 March. There his wife erected a splendid monument to his memory, carved from black and white marble, and of a quality and detail that suggests it was created in the workshop of Nicholas Stone. The semi-reclining effigy of the Lord Keeper is flanked by the figures of Justice and Virtue; Justice clasps the Great Seal of England and beneath the effigy is placed the mace and the woolsack, both intricately carved. Above rises a semi-circular canopy on four columns, surmounted by a vast coat of arms set between two allegorical figures.

The Lord Keeper's death occurred just as the constitutional unrest was reaching crisis point. In Clarendon's view, this was 'to the King's great detriment, rather than to his [Coventry's] Own'.[36] The writs that summoned the Short Parliament had been issued and, in a dying message, Coventry expressed his wish that 'his majesty would take all dictates from the parliament summoned ... with patience and suffer it without an unkind dissolution'. Shortly after his death, his worst fears were realised. The Short Parliament met on 13 April and was dissolved within three weeks. Clarendon believed that if Coventry

> ... had liv'd to the Sitting of that Parliament, when, whatever lurk'd in the Hearts of any, there was not the least Outward appearance of any irreverence to the crown, that he might have had great authority in the forming those Counsels, which might have preserv'd it from so unhappy a Dissolution.

It seems unlikely that Lord Keeper Coventry's conciliatory influence would have restrained the revolutionary tide. As disorder spread throughout the kingdom, it took little more to trigger full-scale rebellion, and by the summer of 1642 it was civil war. The simple fact that Coventry had remained unopposed as Lord Keeper during 14 years of constitutional turmoil is perhaps the most reliable gauge of his achievement.

The Children of the Lord Keeper

Thomas, 1st Baron Coventry, had ten children altogether, five sons and five daughters. His first marriage to Sarah Sebright had produced a son and heir, Thomas, and a daughter, Elizabeth, and his second marriage to Elizabeth Pitchford provided him with a further four sons, John, Francis, Henry and William, and four daughters, Anne, Margaret, Mary and Dorothy. He had one heir, at least four in reserve, and a fortune with which to attract a stream of desirable suitors for his daughters. Despite the impending civil crisis, there was every chance that the wealth and influence of the family would be sustained during the latter half of the century. It proved a reasonable and accurate assumption.

Elizabeth outlived her husband by 13 years. In his will, the Lord Keeper left her a principal residence in London, and six other houses in Worcestershire, Lincolnshire and Gloucestershire. She may have leased some of these, but she sold Durham House and moved with the family into the 2nd Baron's new home, Dorchester House in Covent Garden. She died in early May 1653 and was buried at St Gregory's, London.

After the death of his father, Thomas, 2nd Baron Coventry, began his major improvements to the family seat at Croome. An elegant and enterprising man, he was deeply attached to his Worcestershire home, and it was largely through his efforts that by the close of the century Croome assumed its pivotal role within the life and achievements of the Coventry family. Before the story of the family shifts almost entirely to Croome, it is necessary to acknowledge the achievements of his half brothers and sisters, especially Henry and William, who contributed much to the family's increasing prominence and status during the second half of the 17th century.

John Coventry (b.1611) and Sir John Coventry (d.1682), son and grandson of the 1st Baron

The two elder sons, John and Francis, are the most elusive figures, eclipsed by the success of their younger brothers. John Coventry was the eldest son of the 1st Baron's second marriage to Elizabeth Pitchford. Family histories spare him little more than a line or so, and occasionally he is confused with his only son, John, who gave his name to the Coventry Act. He probably spent much of his early life at Durham House and married Elizabeth (b.1608), daughter and co-heir of John Coles of Barton, Somerset. It was his wife's second marriage. Like his mother, she was a wealthy widow, formerly married to Herbert Doddington, heir to Sir William Doddington of Southampton. Lord Coventry gave John and his new wife the manor of Wiveliscombe in Somerset, not far from her place of birth, where they lived for several months each year. John also inherited the manors of Clifton Camvyle and Hampton in Staffordshire, which his father had purchased from Sir Walter Heveningham of Aston in Staffordshire. John was on good terms with his brother-in-law, Anthony Ashley Cooper, later 1st Earl of Shaftesbury, who admired his keen intellect and described him as 'every way an extraordinary person'. This may have been intended as a compliment, but hinted at a certain weakness of character which ultimately destroyed him. For despite, or possibly because of, the ample wealth and opportunity thrust upon him, John lacked the discipline and drive of his father. The pressure to succeed ultimately overwhelmed him and he turned to drink for consolation. With his health undermined, he retreated to Somerset leaving his son, Sir John Coventry of Pitminster, to fulfil his failed potential.

Sir John was born around 1632. The details of his early life remain obscure, but he fought valiantly for the Royalist cause and was rewarded for his loyalty when he was made a Knight of the Bath at Charles II's coronation. In 1667, his uncle, Henry, appointed him as his assistant in the negotiations at Breda, which terminated the second Dutch War. In that same year, John was elected MP for Weymouth, which he represented till his death in 1682, and from 1675 he also served as Deputy Lieutenant for Wiltshire.

Several of his contemporaries refer to his unusually loud and penetrating voice, which he employed most effectively to express his outspoken views in parliamentary debates. Like so many of his family, he displayed a strong independent streak, and despite his earlier support of the crown and the influence of his uncles, Henry and William, at court, he chose to fight for the popular cause. In 1670, when the opponents of the government proposed that a tax should be levied on playhouses, one of the Court party members argued that this was impossible 'as the players were the king's servants and part of his pleasure'. Pointedly, Sir John enquired 'whether the king's pleasure lay with the men or the women?'. This blatant allusion to Nell Gwyn and Moll Davies infuriated the king and his supporters, who vowed to take their revenge. On 21 December, when Sir John was returning home to his house in Suffolk Street, he was pulled from his carriage by a gang of hired thugs, beaten brutally and his nose was slit to the bone. His assailants are believed to have been hired by the Duke of Monmouth and included among their number such seemingly respectable figures as Sir Thomas Sandys. Sir John defended himself admirably and after the attack his nose was 'so well needled up, that the scar was scarce to be discerned'.[1] Not only did the incident increase his popularity, but a bill was rushed through parliament, known as the Coventry Act, to banish his assailants and declare acts of mutilation of a person a felony. Unhappily for the king, his plan had completely misfired (colour plate V).

Sir John's later career was shaped by his conversion to Roman Catholicism. He never married, and he left a substantial part of his estate to the college of the Jesuits at St Omer. He had inherited the manor of Wiveliscombe in Somerset from his father, and towards the end of his life he renewed the lease of the manor from the Bishop of Bath and Wells, and left money in his will to found a hospital there. The manor descended within the Coventry family till 1813, when John Coventry, son of the 6th Earl, sold his remaining interest in it for a mere £10,000.

Francis Coventry (1612-80)

Francis, the second son of the Lord Keeper's second marriage, also lived in relative obscurity. He trained as a lawyer and his father may have nurtured hopes that he would succeed him in high office, for he left all his legal books and papers to him in his will. Francis failed to fulfil these expectations and he abandoned his profession prior to the Restoration to devote his time to his various wives and children. He married three times. His first wife, Elizabeth, was the daughter of John Manning of Warbleton, Essex and the widow of Robert Caesar, a legal clerk. They had three sons and two daughters. The eldest son, also called Francis, lived at Crawley in Sussex and died unmarried in 1681, and the two younger sons, John and Charles, died in infancy. The eldest daughter, Elizabeth, married Sir William Keyte of Ebrington, near Chipping Campden. This established an important family connection, as their youngest daughter, Dorothy, became the first wife of her cousin Gilbert, later 4th Earl of Coventry. The youngest daughter gloried in the name of Ultra Trajectina (*aka* Utricia), which defies sensible explanation. She married Sir Lacon William Childe, a Master in Chancery, from West Coppice, near Kinlet in north Worcestershire, to whom she was already related through the marriage of her great-aunt Catherine.

Francis's second wife was the widow of Sir Edward Hoskins, and his third wife, Margaret Waters of Surrey, outlived him and later married Sir John Thorold. There was no issue from either of these marriages. Francis died in 1699 and he was buried at Mortlake in Surrey. He left his Staffordshire estate of Clifton Camvyle and Hampton, which he had inherited from his brother John, to his two sons-in-law, Sir Lacon William Childe and Sir William Keyte, and Keyte's brother Thomas. The Staffordshire estates were sold to Sir Charles Pye in September 1701.[2]

Henry Coventry (1619-1686)

Henry Coventry was blessed with all his father's finer qualities. He was very able and intelligent, a fine speaker, and respected by both king and parliament. Bishop Burnet described him as 'a man of wit and heat, of spirit and candour', although Pepys appears less impressed and regarded him as a 'mighty quick, ready man, but not so weighty as he should be'.[3] Pepys' views were undoubtedly tempered by his friendship with Henry's younger brother, William. Clarendon, on the other hand, considered him a much wiser man than his brother, but Henry had supported him during his impeachment, whereas Sir William's opposition to Clarendon's policies had contributed to his downfall. This episode typified the awkward relationship that existed between the two brothers once they attained high office. Although alike in some respects, not least in their appearance and ambition, they clashed on several important issues, as is evident from their correspondence among the archive at Longleat.[4] Their portraits were painted by Sir Peter Lely when they were at the peak of their careers, and these convey with great subtlety and perception their similarities and differences (colour plates III and IV). Although they share the long noses, heavy eyebrows and firm jaws, common to many members of the family, Henry's stern and steady glance contrasts with the expression of wry amusement that flickers across William's face. Both inspired respect, but Henry could inspire trust like his father, while William's frankness and independent spirit was greeted with a certain wariness and hostility among his colleagues. It was an extraordinary double act, which prompted Marvell to write in 1667:

> All the two Coventries their generals choose;
> For one had much, the other nought to lose.
> Not better choice all accidents could hit,
> While Hector Harry steers by Will the wit.

Henry studied both arts and law at Oxford. He obtained an MA and was made a Fellow of All Souls College in 1636, and two years later was awarded his law degree, apparently the only successful law student in his year.[5] At the Restoration he was made a Groom of the Bedchamber, and he became elected MP for Droitwich, which he continued to represent for the next twenty years. His first diplomatic assignment occurred in 1664, when he was appointed Envoy Extraordinary to Sweden. There he remained for the next two years and, according to Burnet, he adjusted to life in Sweden well, 'accustomizing himself to the northern ways of entertainment, and this grew upon him with age'.[6] His enthusiasm for the forest landscapes of Scandinavia nurtured his interest in trees, and he is believed to have acquired some cedar of Lebanon seeds to be sown at Croome.[7]

He returned to London in June 1666, a time of chaos and confusion. The Second Dutch War had begun in February 1665, for which his brother William at the Admiralty was held partly responsible, and shortly afterwards, London was struck by a devastating outbreak of bubonic plague. It was not a good homecoming and there was little reprieve, as the Great Fire swept through the narrow streets of the capital that September to demoralise the population still further. For Henry, the war provided fresh opportunity, as he was chosen to accompany Lord Holles to Breda to negotiate the peace settlement with the Dutch, taking with him his nephew John to act as his assistant.[8] It was not an easy task, and the successful outcome was a credit to his diplomatic skills. Rivalry with the Dutch over commerce, fisheries and the colonies was a persistent problem, and only since the Dutch had been virtually deserted by their French allies did there appear room for negotiation. To complicate matters, while Henry wrestled with clauses at Breda, the Dutch decided to embark on a daring operation to humiliate the English. In June 1667, they sailed up the Medway and launched a bold attack on Chatham docks. Fire ships were let loose, and the English flagship, the *Royal Charles*, the very vessel that had brought Charles II home from exile, was captured. Even more embarrassing for Henry, it was his brother William, recently appointed as Treasury Commissioner, who had ordered that the main body of the fleet be laid up at Chatham as an economy measure.[9] On 6 July, Henry was obliged to return to England for consultations. Certain clauses in the proposed treaty displeased the king as they infringed the English Navigation Acts, and objections were raised to the Dutch insistence on postponing consideration of the question of contraband. Eventually, the Privy Council gave in to Dutch demands, and it was John Coventry, Henry's nephew and assistant, who brought the official news of the peace to England.[10]

Henry Coventry had little time to dwell on his success, as that autumn he became involved in the controversy that surrounded the impeachment of Edward Hyde, Earl of Clarendon. Clarendon had served as Lord Chancellor since 1660, but recently he had become a scapegoat for the growing unrest caused by the treatment of nonconformists and failures in foreign policy. After the Chatham disaster, angry crowds had broken windows and uprooted trees outside his new house in Piccadilly. Clarendon and Henry Coventry respected and liked each other, and when the king finally bowed to public opinion and went ahead with the impeachment, Henry raised a strong objection in parliament and demanded that his case should be put to a committee for careful consideration.[11] He continued his appeal throughout the autumn of 1667, putting his own position at risk, and it is probable that his arguments were only tolerated as he was held in such high esteem due to his part in the Breda treaty. Some even argued that his support of Clarendon added to his reputation. Pepys records a contemporary remark by Lord Vaughan that Henry Coventry '… hath got more fame and common esteem then [sic] any gentleman in England hath at this day, and is an excellent and able person'.[12] After Clarendon's dismissal, the king decided to direct foreign policy himself with the help of his advisers, among them Sir William Coventry, who only just escaped impeachment himself for his conduct over the Dutch war. This did little to improve relations between the two Coventry brothers.

It was probably with some relief that Henry was dispatched to Sweden once more as Envoy Extraordinaire in September 1671, where he played a valuable role in the breaking of the Triple League. He returned on 3 July of the following year, and he received official recognition of his achievements when he was appointed a Secretary of State and a member of the Privy Council.

He remained in high office for eight years, but was forced to resign in 1679 owing to frequent and debilitating attacks of gout. On 11 February 1679, it was announced in the *London Gazette* that:

> His Majesty was, this afternoon, pleased to declare in council, that Mr Secretary Coventry has long solicited him, on account of his infirmity of body, for his leave to resign his place of one of his principal Secretaries of State: that his Majesty had at last been prevailed upon to grant it, though with some unwillingness, because of the great satisfaction his Majesty had always had in his services: and that his intention was that he should ever continue in his Privy Council.

Henry never married and it is possible that he was wary of such commitment. On 12 September 1676, he wrote to Sir Robert Carr, in connection with his inability to fulfil a promise he had made to him, that:

> Promises are like marriages: what we tie with our tongues we cannot untie with our teeth. I have been discreet enough as to the last, but frequently a fool as to the first.[13]

He had a house in Panton Street, near the Haymarket in Westminster, but spent much of his retirement at his estate in Enfield. He died on 7 December 1686, after being taken ill on one of his rare visits to London and he was buried at St Martin-in-the-Fields,

Westminster. The 9th Earl of Coventry removed his monument to Croome in the late 19th century, and he installed two stained-glass windows by Heaton, Butler & Bayne in the new St Martin-in-the-Fields, rebuilt by Gibbs the previous century, in commemoration of his famous ancestor. This is not the only memorial to Henry's achievements.

As he had no wife or children, he left much of his estate to various charitable causes.[14] Apart from his plate and jewellery, which were left to various friends, and presents of money, horses and packs of hounds that he gave to his servants, the poor of his Middlesex estates all received substantial legacies. Two hundred pounds was allocated to the rebuilding of St Paul's Cathedral after the Fire, a similar sum was put aside for the redemption of captives from Algiers, and his constituency of Droitwich also benefited from his generosity.

His attachment to his constituency had been confirmed when he purchased a small estate in Hampton Lovett on the outskirts of the town, which he mortgaged from his brother-in-law, Sir John Packington, in 1677. In his will, he left £100 to the burgesses of Droitwich to build and maintain a workhouse, together with funds to supply clothing and provide instruction for 40 boys and 40 girls. His two farms in Hampton Lovett, were to provide the revenue to maintain the workhouse. The original trustees were Sir Harry Coningsby of Areley, John Somers of Worcester (Lord Somers), Sir Thomas Street of Cotheridge, Richard Nash of Worcester and Richard and John Nash of Droitwich. The original idea to set up 'a manufacture' or workhouse had to be abandoned as most of the poor of the parish were employed in the thriving salt trade or in husbandry, and it was agreed to build a hospital and school instead. This still survives, much in its original state, and forms a long brick range of 18 two-storey almshouses with attractive latticed casements and tiled roofs and a large tablet to commemorate their founder. According to tradition, the Coventry Hospital, as it became known, was founded not by his will but as the result of a horse race. Henry is said to have matched his horse against one belonging to Sir John Packington, and the loser was to build and endow a hospital in the name of the winner. It is an appealing story and one that may have been perpetuated to mask an uncomfortable truth. For Henry had probably acquired Wheelers Farm and Park Farm off Sir John in 1677 to help him dispose of massive debts which he had accumulated during the Commonwealth. Originally, Henry had acquired a 99-year lease on the two farms, but when he decided to use the revenue to fund a workhouse it is probable that he purchased the reversion. In 1776, Sir Herbert Packington laid claim to the farms, as he believed that the reversion had never been purchased. When the Trustees failed to produce the title deeds, a bitter and protracted suit in Chancery took place which persisted till 1823, when a charity was established to place the hospital on a sounder financial basis.[15] Repairs were carried out, and the school was reopened with one important change in routine, the annual May dinner of roast beef and plum pudding was to be given to the children and elderly occupants rather than the trustees.[16]

Perhaps the most familiar tribute to Henry Coventry's talent and generosity is the one most easily overlooked. Coventry Street in Piccadilly, built around 1681and not far from Henry's home in Panton Street, was named after him. Set among one of the most impressive areas of development of the post-Fire rebuilding, the gesture was suitably diplomatic.

9 The Coventry Hospital, now almshouses, in Droitwich, Worcestershire.

RULES and ORDERS
To be OBSERVED and KEPT in

The Coventry Work-Houſe,
IN DROITWICH.

I. THAT the Maſter and Miſtreſs be ſober and orderly Perſons, and ſee that all the People mind their Work and obey their Orders. Whoſoever is ſtubborn, idle, or refractory, he, ſhe, or they that deny, or will not do as they are ordered, ſhall, for ſuch Offence, be ſtopped their next Meal of Proviſion; and for the ſecond Offence, be kept one Day on Half a Pound of Bread and Water; and for the third Offence, to be taken before a Juſtice, and puniſhed as the Law directs for idle and diſorderly Perſons.

II. THAT all the healthy Perſons, Boys and Girls, get up at Six o'Clock in the Morning, and the old People at Seven, in the Summer Half Year; the healthy People at Seven, and the old People at Eight, in the Winter: The Men and Boys to waſh and comb themſelves: The Women and Girls to waſh and comb and dreſs their Heads, and go to their Labour till Eight o'Clock in the Summer, and Nine in the Winter Half-Year, and then to appear clean at Breakfaſt.

III. THAT the Houſe be ſwept from Top to Bottom by the Women, each that is able to take it in Turn to clean the Rooms. The whole Houſe to be mopped every Saturday. The Miſtreſs and a Perſon appointed ſhall inſpect the Women and Beds; and the Maſter the Men, that the People may be kept clean and decent.

IV. THAT no Perſon go from Home without leave of the Maſter or Miſtreſs. That they are careful of their Work; not to embezzle, purloin, or waſte any Thing that is put into their Hands. Any Perſon ſo detected ſhall be kept on Bread and Water 'till taken before a Juſtice, and puniſhed as the Law directs.

V. THAT whoſoever goes out to work, let it be Men, Women, or Children, ſhall bring Home their Wages and give it to the ſaid Maſter of the Workhouſe, deducting Threepence out of each Shilling for their own Uſe.

VI. THAT if any Perſon ſteals any Thing, or curſe or ſwear, for the firſt Time to have their Crime pinned on their Backs one whole Day, and forfeit their Dinner: For the ſecond, to live on Bread and Water one Day: For the third to be taken before a Juſtice, and puniſhed as the Law directs.

VII. THAT the Maſter or Miſtreſs cauſe the Breakfaſt to be ready at Eight o'Clock in the Summer; the Dinner at One; and the Supper at Seven o'Clock.——In the Winter Half-Year the Breakfaſt at Nine.

VIII. THAT the Family are all in Bed at Nine o'Clock in the Summer, and Eight in the Winter Seaſon. That no Perſon ſmoke Tobacco Up-Stairs, under Penalty of living next Day on Bread and Water. That in the Winter Seaſon the Maſter or Miſtreſs ſee that all the Lights be put out.

IX. THAT no diſtilled Liquors nor Tea be allowed to be drank in this Houſe.

X. THAT the Truſtees, or any One of them, inſpect over the ſaid Houſe to ſee that the above Rules are punctually executed without reſpect of Perſons.

XI. THAT no Perſons be received into the Houſe without a Line from two of the Truſtees of the Charity.

XII. THAT Perſons able ſhall be obliged to attend Divine Service every Sunday.

The BILL of FARE for the Week's Proviſion.

	BREAKFAST.	DINNER.	SUPPER.
SUNDAY	Milk Broth	Meat and Broth	Bread and Cheeſe
MONDAY	Meat Broth	Milk or Broth, with one Ounce of Cheeſe	Ditto
TUESDAY	Milk Broth	The ſame	Ditto
WEDNESDAY	Milk Broth	Meat and Broth	Ditto
THURSDAY	Meat Broth	Milk or Broth, with one Ounce of Cheeſe	Ditto
FRIDAY	Milk Broth	Meat and Broth	Ditto
SATURDAY	Meat Broth	Milk, or Peaſe Broth, according to the Seaſon	Ditto

QUANTITY, } BREAD, one Pound every Day for each grown Perſon. CHEESE, for Supper, one Ounce. BEER, for every grown Perſon for Dinner, one Pint, and Supper one Pint, or more, at the Diſcretion of the Governor. To Children, at the Diſcretion of the Maſter and Miſtreſs, according to Age and Health.

WORCESTER: Printed by JOHN GRUNDY, FRIARS-STREET.

10 Rules and Orders of the Coventry Workhouse.

Sir William Coventry (1620?-1686)

William was easily as talented as his elder brother. He was much admired for his wit, his scholarship, and his administrative skills, and Bishop Burnet went so far as to describe him as: 'A man of great notions and eminent virtues; one of the best speakers in the House of Commons; capable of bearing the chief ministry'.[17] Unfortunately, he found little fulfilment in his career. Frustrated by the short-term policies and corrupt practices that rendered his reforms futile, he sought refuge in the company of his friends and his books.

William entered Queen's College, Oxford, in 1642, but left without taking his degree to join the army where he was given command of a foot company. During the Commonwealth, he followed the court into exile and lived in France for several years, where he developed his literary interests. When a restoration of the monarchy appeared imminent, William took active steps to seek public office. Confident of his personal abilities and the persuasive power of the family name, he left for The Hague in 1660 to visit James, Duke of York, with whom he had become personally acquainted in the army. The strategy was a success, and the Duke appointed William as his private secretary. The following year he was elected MP for Great Yarmouth, which he represented from 1661-79, and when the Duke of York became General-at-Sea, he was offered the post of naval commissioner, which he held from 1662-7.[18]

At the Admiralty, William quickly earned the respect and friendship of Samuel Pepys, who had been appointed Clerk of the Acts to the Navy Board at the Restoration. In July 1662, Pepys described William as 'a most ingenuous man and good company'.[19] By September of that year, their friendship had blossomed, and Pepys noted that his new friend was 'to admiration good and industrious, and I think my most true friend in all things that are fair'.[20] Both men shared a deep sense of commitment to their work, similar political and literary interests, and both enjoyed good company and lively conversation. Also they both kept journals, although William's has not been traced. Pepys admitted that William was the only person he had told about his journal, but this was not entirely true, for he had told a naval lieutenant about it some years previously.[21] William's determination to enquire into the malpractices and inefficiencies within the navy in an effort to reduce expenditure evidently impressed Pepys. However, neither man could claim to have an impeccable record. Pepys was concerned in case William checked his expense account, which included a recent trip to Hampton Court, allegedly undertaken on behalf of the navy. William was guilty of making money from the sale of offices, but this was such a notoriously common practice among his colleagues that it made little impact on the course of his career.[22]

In October 1662, William became a commissioner for the government of Tangier, and in September of the following year he was created a Doctor of Law at Oxford. From there it took a mere two years before he became a Privy Councillor, and he was knighted on 26 June 1665. It was at this point that his judgement came under question, and his confidence in the system, which had embraced him so readily, began to flounder. He had been in favour of declaring war upon the Dutch, but by 1666 had become weary of the whole affair. The fleet was in dire need of funds and, on 29 June 1666, he confided to Pepys that he felt he had lost his authority at the naval office. Prince Rupert, Charles I's dashing and courageous nephew, shared Sir William's concern about the mismanagement of the fleet. In a letter of 19 September 1666, he confided to him that, 'I find every day fresh reason to complayne that there is a very strong remissnesse in ye fleet as to the strict obeying of orders which if it not be [?] corrected will prove of [?] consequence'.[23] That October, Sir William informed the Duke of York that he intended to resign, although he did not tender his resignation till the following January. Meanwhile, he felt that the threat from the Dutch had abated sufficiently to allow some of the larger ships in the fleet to be laid up at Chatham. It proved a fatal error. When the Dutch crept up the Medway and towed away the *Royal Charles* as their trophy, Sir William took much of the blame for the disaster.

Fortunately, he did not have to forfeit the new post he had been offered in June as Treasury Commissioner, and his interest in naval affairs did not cease with this new appointment. Using his experience at the Admiralty, he devoted much of his time to devising means of reducing naval expenditure without detriment to its efficiency. It was a daunting task and he was obliged to resign from the Duke of York's service, although he remained in close contact with the Duke. It seems to have been a genuine friendship, founded in part on their enthusiasm for horses, and Sir William would often accompany the Duke on his rides across Putney Heath.

During autumn 1667, Sir William moved into his new house at 79, Pall Mall. Previously during the winter months he had lodgings in Old Palace Yard at Whitehall Palace and stayed in St James's Palace during the summer. After the Great Fire, Pepys observed that Sir William's rooms at the Palace were without curtains and that he had kept most of his belongings in storage. Presumably, he planned to move to alternative accommodation as soon as possible. Sir William remained in his new house for three years and spent a considerable sum on new hangings and furniture. Pepys makes specific reference to a curious circular table located within Sir William's closet. This had a large hole in the middle of it so that he could sit at its centre and be surrounded by his papers.[24] Whether he had to crawl on his hands and knees to reach his chair is unclear. He sold the house on his retirement and later it became the home of the infamous Nell Gwyn, a descendant of whom, coincidentally, became the wife of the 8th Earl of Coventry.

On 7 December 1668, Sir William confessed to Pepys that he was as weary of the Treasury as the Navy. He resented the short-sighted policies of his colleagues, who he believed 'reckoned their one good meal, without considering that there was nothing left in the cupboard till tomorrow'.[25] His general frustration with his work led to the accusation that he was a melancholy man, and in March 1669 he was satirised in a play as Sir Cautious Trouble-All by George Villiers, 2nd Duke of Buckingham, and Sir Robert Howard. This so outraged him that he challenged Buckingham to a duel, but when the King found out, he excluded Sir William from the Treasury and the Privy Council and sent him to the Tower. There he was visited by a vast number of his supporters, including his friend Pepys, who claimed that no less than sixty coaches had called at the Tower to visit Sir

William on 6 March. He was released on 20 March but, despite repeated conciliatory offers of posts at court, he decided he had had quite enough of high office. In 1670, he moved to Minster Lovell, near Witney in Oxfordshire, to grow peaches on his garden walls and enjoy his extensive library, but he did not retire entirely from public life, as he continued to serve as MP for Great Yarmouth in Norfolk for the next 16 years.

During his retirement, his name became associated with an influential tract entitled *The Character of a Trimmer*. A 'Trimmer' was a nautical expression more usually applied to the steadying of a boat by the application of ballast, but in this case was used to describe the moderate political views expounded in the tract. However, it is not entirely clear whether he or his nephew, George Savile, Marquess of Halifax, was the author. The manuscript was first circulated in 1685, possibly to coincide with the Duke of Monmouth's secret trip to England that Halifax had arranged, and it was not printed till 1688, two years after Sir William's death. Two further editions printed in the same year confirmed Coventry's authorship and a new revised edition by Halifax referred in glowing terms to him as 'universally reputed as an acute Statesman, an accomplisht Gentleman, a great Schollar, and a true Englishman'. However, in a letter to another of his nephews, Sir Thomas Thynne, 1st Viscount Weymouth, Sir William denied his authorship.[26] Sir William and Halifax were among many who feared that the growing sense of distrust that surrounded the Roman Catholic resurgence and the persecution of the nonconformists, would combine with fears of French intervention and the succession issue to provoke another civil war. In many ways, it was ahead of its time, as its discussion of the virtues of libertarianism anticipated 18th-century politics and culture, notably those associated with the writings of Edmund Burke.

Sir William died at Somerhill, near Tunbridge Wells, on 23 June 1686 and he was buried at Penshurst. He had travelled there to take the waters for a persistent ailment, quite probably gout to which his family appears to have been particularly susceptible. Like his brother Henry, he never married, and much of his estate was left to charitable causes, notably £2,000 to the Huguenots expelled from France and £3,000 for the captives in Algiers. It was typical of his tolerant and moderate views that he saw nothing inconsistent in befriending the Duke of York, a devout Catholic, and bequeathing money to help the French Huguenots.

The Lord Keeper's Daughters

The daughters of the 1st Baron Coventry, Elizabeth, Anne, Margaret, Mary and Dorothy, may not have allowed their aspirations to stray much further than an advantageous marriage, fecundity, and the felicity and ambition of their offspring and in this respect they fulfilled their duty admirably. Anne and Dorothy, at least, were capable of more, and Dorothy well-exceeded these expectations.

Little is known about the eldest daughter, Elizabeth. She married Sir John Hare of Stow Bardolph in Norfolk, a descendant of the eminent judge, Sir Nicholas Hare. The Lord Keeper was appointed guardian to a member of the Hare family, but it is uncertain whether this occurred before or after his daughter married into the family.

Anne (b.1600), the eldest daughter of the second marriage, married twice. Her first husband was Sir William Savile, 3rd Baronet of Thornhill, Yorkshire, related by marriage to the Earls of Shrewsbury and Strafford, whom she married on 29 December 1629. Sir William was a staunch Royalist. He fought against the Scots in 1639, and was elected a member of the Short Parliament. Later he became Governor of Sheffield and of York, and he died in Sheffield in January 1644. During the months following his death, Anne exhibited exceptional courage and resilience. Although Sheffield Castle was under siege, she refused to leave with her children despite the castle's ruinous condition, the depleted supply of ammunition, and fears for the safety of her unborn child. She yielded finally the following August, but only because the garrison mutinied, and she gave birth on the day after the capitulation. It seemed only reasonable to allow her to return with her children to Yorkshire, and soon she was remarried to Thomas Chichele of Wimpole, Cambridge.

Two of her sons achieved prominence and her eldest son, in particular, played a dominant role in late 17th-century politics. George, Marquess of Halifax (1633-95), was a man of outstanding intellect and ability and a leading statesman, popularly known as 'Halifax the Trimmer' or 'The Great Trimmer' owing to his association with the afore-mentioned influential tract *The Character of a Trimmer*. At the age of 32, he was created Baron Savile of Eland and Viscount Halifax, and became a commissioner of trade. His elevation to the Privy Council followed in 1672; and he was created Earl of Halifax in 1679 and Marquess of Halifax in 1682. Opposed to James II's policies, he used his influence to help secure the accession of William and Mary and he was rewarded with the appointment of Lord Privy Seal, although he resigned this office a year later to concentrate his efforts on his political pamphlets. Halifax was a close friend of his brother-in-law, Shaftesbury, but their friendship failed to withstand the complexities of political life. Henry Savile (1642-87), the youngest child of Anne Coventry and Sir William Savile, spent much of his early life abroad and on his return was appointed a Gentleman of the Bedchamber to the Duke of York, possibly thanks to the influence of his uncle, Sir William Coventry. Condemned by Clarendon for his arrogance and impudence, he became a favourite of the Duchess of York. He fought in the Dutch wars on the flagship, the *Royal Charles*, and he was imprisoned briefly for carrying his Uncle William's challenge to the Duke of Buckingham. Later he became MP for Newark, and in 1679 he served as an envoy to Paris to assist the Protestant cause, prior to the revocation of the Edict of Nantes. On his return, he became a Commissioner of the Admiralty and in March 1687 was appointed Vice-Chamberlain, but died in Paris the following October.

The Lord Keeper's second daughter of his second marriage, Margaret (1616-49), was the first wife of Anthony Ashley Cooper, 1st Earl of Shaftesbury (1621-83), whom she married on 25 February 1639. Shaftesbury, a leading political tactician under Charles II, was famous for his diminutive size and political courage. A friend of the philosopher John Locke, he is remembered above all as the founder of the Whig party. Shaftesbury was a lawyer by profession, and as a young man was welcomed into the Coventry household. After his marriage to Margaret Coventry, he moved into Durham House at the Lord Keeper's invitation. He and Margaret had no children, and after Margaret's death on 11 July 1649, Shaftesbury remarried twice. He remained a close friend of the Coventry family, which was to their mutual benefit, and he rose to become Lord Chancellor in 1672. After the impeachment of Clarendon, he and the king's other chief ministers, Sir Thomas Clifford, Lord Arlington, and the Dukes of Buckingham and Lauderdale, became known as the Cabal, a popular name for any secret clique and one that accorded with their initials most aptly.

Mary Coventry (b.1617), the third daughter of the Lord Keeper's second marriage, married Sir Henry Frederick Thynne (1615-81), the son of Sir Thomas Thynne of Longleat and his second wife, Katharine Howard. In 1682, their eldest son, Thomas, inherited Longleat on the murder of his cousin and, later that year, was created Baron Thynne and 1st Viscount Weymouth. Like his cousin, Halifax, he was in opposition to the extreme measures of James II, and was among the party that conveyed the invitation to the Prince of Orange to come to England. Throughout the reign of William and Mary he opposed government policy and, on the accession of Queen Anne in 1702, he was made a privy councillor. He took a considerable interest in Longleat, where he completed the new chapel and laid out the Dutch gardens, and his horticultural interests were acknowledged when the new English larch, introduced into England in 1705, was named the Weymouth pine in his honour. Sir Henry Frederick Thynne, the third son of Sir Henry Frederick Thynne and Mary Coventry, was secretary to his uncle, Sir William Coventry, and the executor of his will. It was through his connection with the Coventry family that the Coventry papers, and possibly the seal cup, came to Longleat.

11 Lady Dorothy Coventry, wife of Sir John Packington, by E.F. and T.F. Burney.

The Lord Keeper's youngest daughter, Dorothy (1623-79), became the wife of Sir John Packington, 2nd Baronet of Westwood (1621-80). The Packingtons held substantial estates in Buckinghamshire and Suffolk as well as Worcestershire. Packington had been made a ward of Lord Coventry in 1624 after the death of his father, and Coventry had arranged the marriage and helped nurture Sir John's political career. He became MP for Worcestershire and for the borough of Aylesbury and he served as Deputy Lieutenant for Worcestershire between 1662-3. The Packingtons' principal home in Worcestershire was in Hampton Lovett, near Droitwich, but, after this was damaged during the Civil War, Packington decided to enlarge his hunting lodge at Westwood as his main residence. He added corner wings and pavilions with pyramidal roofs to the tall compact brick block, and a fine gatehouse, all embellished with openwork flourishes and studded with the Packingtons' armorial mullets and wheatsheaves. The interior was fitted with flamboyant plasterwork and rich carving and, within these sumptuous surroundings, Dorothy embarked upon her divine contemplations. She was an immensely pious and scholarly woman and, during the Civil War, Westwood became the asylum of Dr. Henry Hammond and others who shared Dorothy's strong religious convictions, such as the Bishops Fell, Henchman and Morley and Dr. Richard Allestree. During this time, Dorothy is said to have written a powerful religious text entitled *The Whole Duty of Man*, which was published anonymously in 1658. Hammond claimed that he had read the work thoroughly prior to its publication when he was living at Westwood, and this gave rise to the belief that Dorothy was the author. After her death in 1679, several of her friends, including Fell and Allestree, confirmed that this was true but that she did not wish this to be known during her lifetime. There is little doubt that Dorothy was capable of such erudition, although the author appears to have personal experience of travel abroad as well as a working knowledge of Hebraic, Syriac and Arabic. As Dorothy is not known to have left the country, it seems most probable that the book was a collaborative effort between Dorothy and her guests.

Sir John Packington and Dorothy Coventry had three children, Elizabeth, Margaret and John, but the close ties between the Coventry and the Packington families diminished during the 18th century following the dispute over Henry Coventry's Droitwich estate. Dorothy died on 10 May 1679 and she was buried at Hampton Lovett church on 13 May, her body wrapped in linen at her special request.

V

The Estate and the Earldom

Thomas, 2nd Baron Coventry (1606-61)

Thomas, 2nd Baron Coventry had little interest in law and politics. Neither did he seek public acclaim. A striking figure, tall and elegant with a mane of dark curls, his ambition lay elsewhere. From an early age, he concentrated his efforts on the development of the family estates. As the eldest son and heir, choice may not have entered the equation, but once the estate at Croome was settled upon him in 1627, he applied himself to its improvement with enterprise and enthusiasm. This contrasted starkly with his dithering and devious behaviour during the Civil War, when he risked the honour and reputation of his family to spare his magnificent new home. Whether he was motivated more by courage than cowardice remains open to question.

Thomas, 2nd Baron Coventry, was brought up in London, but was the first member of the Coventry family to spend a substantial part of his life in Worcestershire. At the age of 19, he became MP for Droitwich. Three years later he served as MP for Worcestershire, and in 1633 he became Councillor for Wales. These offices came with the territory, and he showed no active interest in them. On 2 April 1627, he married Mary Craven at St Andrew Undershaft, London. She was the third and youngest daughter of Sir William Craven, Mayor of London from 1610-11 and the sister of the first Earl of Craven. Four children were born in quick succession, but their fifth child died at birth on 18 October 1634, and within a few hours

12 Thomas, 2nd Baron Coventry, painted by Cornelius Jonson.

Mary was dead too; she was 29. Of their four surviving children, the two daughters died young, and only the two older children, George and Thomas, reached adulthood. Thomas erected a touching monument to his wife's memory, which conveys his deep sense of loss. Her semi-reclining effigy clasps the dead infant in her arms, and at her feet kneel the two small figures of her young sons, George and Thomas, their heads bowed in mourning. Her epitaph is particularly poignant and rich in hyperbole:

> Of the most illustrious Lady Mary the pious wife of Thomas Coventrye Eldest Son of Thomas Baron Coventrye of Allesborough Lord Keeper Of the Great Seal of England. A woman indeed most admirable To whome God was liberal of beauty (and what is more rarely found in ye sex) Vertue. Of a beautifull Aspect surpassing women, of a masculine generosity. An unspotted Reputation, an upright life, a ready wit, a strong Judgement, Of a smooth Education, of a well govern'd Tongue, who not only prudently, But also soberly moderated her passions and all her Endowments, She was the fruitful mother of four children. At last Child-bed Prov'd fatal to her, a son indeed was born, but soon depriv'd of life. So whome strong to impart life, destroy'd it. This infant She herself follow'd at a small distance, accompany'd with A general lamentation.[1]

Thomas never remarried, and probably his attachment to Croome owed much to its associations with his wife. His plans for the estate must have provided a welcome distraction at this time.

Once Croome had been settled upon him, he began a sequence of improvements to the house which suggest that it was in a state of some disrepair, probably following the first fire mentioned in the Antony report. These included the new gatehouse and chapel, a new front and rear court, and various outbuildings, notably the barn and bakehouse referred to in William Trap's letter of 1632. There must have been a well-established kitchen garden too, where the vines, apricots and other produce was grown that is listed in the accounts around this date.[2] The acquisition of Feckenham, Mitton, Powick, Pirton and Severn Stoke cost a staggering £80,000, which gives some idea of the vast wealth accrued by the Lord Keeper, as well as the almost unlimited budget that Thomas had at his disposal. These added significantly to the family's local influence and income. There was still abundant timber to be had from the ancient forest

13 Monument of Lady Mary Coventry, wife of the 2nd Baron, in Croome church.

of Feckenham. The purchase of Pirton extended the northern boundary of the estate and included the great medieval fishpond now known as Pirton Pool, while Severn Stoke provided necessary access to the River Severn, one of the busiest rivers in Europe by the end of the 17th century.

When Croome house burnt down for the second time, it is likely that the 2nd Baron welcomed the opportunity to reconstruct it according to current architectural taste. Under the surveyorship of Inigo Jones (1573-1652), a new formal classicism was grafted onto the rambling and irregular streets of London, and the 2nd Baron had shown a keen interest in this new cultural phenomenon.[3] During the early 1630s he purchased Dorchester House in Covent Garden, and just a few years later he decided to build himself another town house in Lincoln's Inn Fields, known as Pine Apple House after the exotic finials upon the gate piers. Both these houses were located within the most fashionable and influential new residential developments in London.

The Covent Garden development was begun in 1630 on an area of land to the north of the Strand belonging to the 4th Earl of Bedford. Inigo Jones was responsible for the overall scheme and for the new church of St Paul's, which formed its focal point. Jones had already stunned the capital with such seminal designs as the Queen's House, Greenwich, of 1616-35 and the Banqueting House, Whitehall, of 1619-22, inspired by his travels in Italy accompanied by a copy of Palladio's *Quattro libri dell'architettura*, which he filled with scribbled notes for future reference. An Italian-style piazza, Covent Garden was London's first formal space centred around a Tuscan church, but only the rows of houses to the north and east were completed. These were built of stuccoed brick to an elegant and restrained classical design with two main storeys set above ground-floor loggias. The symmetry and spacious formality of the arrangement evidently made a deep impression upon Coventry, whose new gatehouse at Croome of 1627, with its shaped brick gables, must have appeared distinctly old-fashioned by comparison.

He seized the chance to build himself another town house when a suitable site became available in Portugal Row, Lincoln's Inn Fields. Between 1636-8, a Bedfordshire developer, William Newton, had obtained licences to build 46 new houses in the area. Some of these he built himself, but many plots were sold to private individuals, one of whom was almost certainly Thomas Coventry. Most of the houses were completed by 1640, and all were finished to a very high standard with a regular layout and classical facade, following the success of the Covent Garden piazza. Coventry is said to have spent 'divers Thousand Pounds' on the project.[4] It is uncertain who designed the houses. Inigo Jones and John Webb (1611-72) are obvious candidates, but no conclusive link has been established. Peter Mills (1598-1670), a prominent City bricklayer, and Nicholas Stone (1586-1647), the King's Master Mason, who had worked with Jones at the Banqueting House and in whose workshops the Lord Keeper's monument was taking shape, have also been associated with the scheme.[5] What is certain is that the houses included features, such as giant pilasters, prominent eaves and cornices, moulded architraves, cartouches, hipped roofs and dormers, which became part of the architectural vocabulary of many country houses of the late Stuart period. Pine Apple House would have made a gracious

14 Bird's-eye view of the north front of Croome House, *c.*1750.

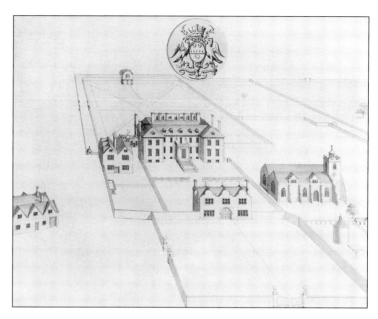

addition to this influential new housing scheme. Many of the houses at Lincoln's Inn Fields had spacious forecourts with brick piers surmounted by ornate finials, the best surviving example being at Lindsey House; so the pair of fat pineapple finials outside Lord Coventry's house would have been in good company.[6]

Work began on rebuilding Croome House in 1640, according to the contracts among the Beaufort archive.[7] These articles and accounts provide an invaluable clue to the scale and character of the new house.[8] They also imply that this second fire caused serious damage, for the articles of agreement with Richard Wells, the plumber, note that 'the said Lord Coventrye hath some store of leade of his owne that was left in ye ruines of the old house …'. The house was rebuilt on the old site, and some of the old masonry was incorporated into the new structure. Walls of over a metre in depth within the basement of the present mansion date back either to this major rebuilding or possibly even earlier. A bird's-eye view of Croome, made just prior to Brown's remodelling of the house in the 1750s, suggests that the new gatehouse was incorporated into the scheme, and probably much of the earlier garden walling and outbuildings.

What did the new house look like? It appears from the evidence available that it adopted many new features in its design and planning that reflected the aesthetic and functional changes in domestic architecture introduced during the Carolean period. It may be significant that the builder and surveyor in charge of the work was Matthew Browne, a bricklayer from St Martin-in-the-Fields, London. He would have been familiar with contemporary architectural developments in the capital; possibly he even worked on the Lincoln's Inn scheme. Other specialist craftsmen drew up separate contracts with Lord Coventry, notably Thomas Usher, a Gloucestershire stonemason, William West the carpenter and Richard Wells, the plumber. In some ways the house typified the transitional period between the flamboyance of the Jacobean style and the fully-fledged and disciplined classicism of Jones, often no more than a classical veneer on a traditional plan. However, the carpenter's contract and bill confirm that the house conformed to a more progressive, symmetrical, double-pile plan with stumpy wings flanking the main entrance on the north front. The hall formed a formal space at the centre of the north elevation, and across a central axial corridor were located three other rooms on the south side of the house. A great staircase appears to have been incorporated within the hall. Its precise location is unclear but it must have provided access to a great chamber on the first floor. The central corridor still divides the present house in two, and, as this was an old-fashioned layout by 1750, it was almost certainly retained from the 2nd Baron's time. As no major rebuilding occurred after the 1640s, Croome House seems to have been an early example of this axial plan type, which broke with medieval tradition and adopted a staircase hall as a splendid formal entrance space.

The house was built of brick and faced with ashlar, 'Hansome and Smoot' with 'as close and thinn Jointes as may be donne', with a roof of clay or stone tiles. It was of two storeys raised high upon a basement and had an attic storey with dormer windows incorporated within the steeply-pitched roof. The articles refer to the 'Mantle Trees' of the chimneys, and it is quite possible that the phalanx of massive interlinked stacks that march across the central ridge of Croome today were remodelled from these earlier chimneys. They appear in the *c.*1750 bird's-eye views of Croome House, and possibly acquired their interlinking arches and panelled detail as part of the alteration work undertaken by the 1st Earl and his two sons at the turn of the century. Certainly they had acquired their present form by 1714, when Henry Beighton made his bird's-eye view of Croome for Gilbert, 4th Earl of Coventry.[9]

The restrained and disciplined façades of Croome House revealed almost none of the mannerist influences introduced by emigrant craftsmen from the Low Countries and also adapted from Flemish pattern books around this time, such as pedimented windows and gables or broken pediments containing busts or shields. Both the drawings of the house and the mason's bill suggest that detail was confined to the dentilled cornices, window architraves and moulded cornices, rusticated quoins and moulded doorcases, although the accounts do include an entry for 'Cuttinge and settinge every Cartose, two shillings'. Presumably these cartouches were used to embellish the façades, but no evidence of them appears in the drawings.

The interior was fitted to an equally high standard, with moulded cornices, fine panelling and carved doorcases. Here the craftsmen were allowed freer rein to display their skills, and the carpenter's bills amounted to an extravagant £641 13s. 10d. in total. A high proportion of this was spent on the staircase and the doorcase in the hall and at the head of the staircase, which would confirm that these fulfilled a primary role in the layout. The main balustrade of the staircase ran for 39 feet, and included some subsidiary sections of balustrading and two balconies (possibly galleried landings). The main rooms were fitted with elaborate chimneypieces, some of which were painted to simulate white marble. Elsewhere, the wainscot was grained to resemble walnut, and white, blue and purple paint was used to enhance the architectural detail.

The 2nd Baron did not ignore the setting of his new house. A great pair of gates was made, probably for the front court, and an Evidence House was built to punctuate the southern wall of the new south court. The kitchen garden was laid out to the south-west of the house next to the parish church, as shown on Beighton's drawing of 1714, and the stables and other outbuildings lay to the north and east. Although designed to impress, practical matters were not ignored entirely. A brick drain, a metre or so wide and almost as deep, ran straight across the courtyard from the kitchen, but quite where it ran to is not clear.

Croome House may have lacked the pleasing proportions and details of the later Stuart houses inspired by the work of Roger Pratt (1620-84) and Hugh May (1622-84), but the available evidence suggests that its planning and design were quite advanced for its date and location.[10] It is interesting to speculate whether John Webb became involved with the architecture during its early stages. Certainly its success owed much to the 2nd Baron's special interest in the project and his choice of Matthew Browne to supervise the work, clearly among the more talented artisan builders working in England at this time. By coincidence, just over a century later, another man by the name of Brown, would be responsible for the third and final rebuilding of the Coventry family's country seat.

The structural work was due for completion on Midsummer's Day 1641, although the roof was not finished till April of the following year; only then could work start on the internal fittings and time was running out. By the summer of 1642, the surrounding countryside was swarming with soldiers as plans were laid for some of the most ferocious and decisive encounters of the Civil War.

The strategic role that Worcestershire played during the Civil War is well documented. It arose primarily from its location, set between the Parliamentarian support in the south-east of the country and Royalist Wales, but also because it included several important crossing points along the natural boundary of the River Severn. Worcester was predominantly Royalist, and most noble families in the region stood firmly behind the monarchy, with the notable exception of the Lechmeres of Hanley Castle and the Lygons of Madresfield. Although the Coventrys were ardent supporters of the Crown, they were not blind to the weaknesses within the English constitution. Lord Keeper Coventry had attempted in vain to restrain Charles I from stretching his royal prerogative beyond the limits of the nation's endurance. His family was obliged to suffer the consequences, and most rallied dutifully to defend the Royalist cause. Only the 2nd Baron remained decidedly reluctant to reveal his hand.

At the outbreak of the war, he served as Joint Commissioner of Array in Worcestershire, a role appropriate to his position and one that enabled him to view with increasing alarm the escalation of events in the southern half of the county. Clustered along the banks of the Severn from Powick right down to Tewkesbury, the Croome estate lay sandwiched between the Royalist garrison at Worcester and the Parliamentary stronghold in Gloucester. His fears were quite justified when the first battle of the war, the Battle of Powick Bridge, took place on 23 September 1642. The following year, Prince Maurice, nephew of the king and brother of Prince Rupert, took up the Royalist command in Worcester, which remained a Royalist stronghold till 1646. Lord Coventry had reason to feel confident of the protection of the nearby garrison, but as the conflict in the Severn valley persisted, the Royalist position grew steadily weaker. The bridge at Upton upon Severn was secured by Prince Maurice only to be regained by the Parliamentarians, who ventured as far as the outskirts of Worcester in May 1643. By 1645, the Parliamentarians under Colonel Massey had captured Evesham, and the remaining Royalist garrisons in Worcestershire were forced to surrender. After the execution of the King in Whitehall on 30 January 1649, the 2nd Baron reconsidered his position. It seemed sensible to move to Croome permanently rather than leave it vulnerable to plunder or to play host to an unwelcome tenant. He would rather risk his life than see the place burnt down for the third time.

There was another reason too. It appears that by the time of the King's execution, the 2nd Baron's sympathies had begun to shift towards the Parliamentarians. Possibly he was inspired by Cromwell's leadership, but, more probably, he felt it prudent to back the winning side. By August 1651, the county seethed with troops once more. The new King, Charles II, and his Scots army marched into Worcester to join forces with the Welsh, but there they met with a less than rapturous reception from its long-suffering citizens. Lord Coventry's movements during the next few months are recorded in some detail in the various depositions of selected witnesses brought before the Commissioners of Sequestration.[11] As such they are not totally reliable; sometimes they present conflicting evidence, and it is likely that some of Lord Coventry's more loyal servants overstated his Parliamentary sympathies to protect themselves and their master. For example, one witness claimed that Lord Coventry had planned to abandon Croome and seek refuge in the Parliamentary headquarters in either Gloucester or Warwick prior to the King's arrival in Worcester. This seems unlikely, but cannot be ruled out. He was aware that Charles II would demand his full support in terms of men, money or arms and that failure to comply with these demands would put himself and his property at risk. Yet if he did support the King, Cromwell would surely seize and destroy his property too. His position seemed hopeless. He dithered and dallied, and short of an inspired solution to his dilemma, he bolted the gates and retired to his bedchamber with an unspecified ailment.

The King grew increasingly impatient and is said to have ordered his supporters to pull Coventry 'out of his house by the ears'. The bed-ridden baron decided it would be prudent to send the King a formal apology for his indisposition, together with a promise of £1,000 and the support of his two sons. It is doubtful whether this money reached the King, or whether Coventry intended to donate the money at all. It had been deposited in a chest in the house of his steward, William Bromall, in Worcester, ready for collection by the King's men. Some witnesses claim that this money was not intended for the King at all but that it had been transferred to Worcester for safekeeping while Croome lay under threat of plunder. Also that it included £500 set aside for the poor of Worcester, and £200 allocated to the Parliamentarians should they apply to Lord Coventry for support. Lord Coventry's two sons were reported to have appeared in arms at the King's side, but whether they wielded their swords on their monarch's behalf is unknown. The King was deeply insulted by this belated and half-hearted response, so he sent soldiers to Croome to steal horses from Lord Coventry's stables, apparently a dapple-grey, a grey roan and a bay gelding. Their task was made easier by the treachery of the head groom, William Smith, who was seen to ride away with them.

As Lord Coventry paced his bedchamber to plan his next move, news reached him of Cromwell's imminent advance from Evesham. Cromwell's plan was to seize Upton bridge and thereby reach the west bank of the Severn to cut off the advancing Welsh army. No sooner had he received this news, than Lord Coventry staged a miraculous recovery and was reported to have been seen strolling through his garden giving 'civill and cheerfull entertainment to ye Parliament forces whensoever they came'. If this is true, it seems surprising that he felt safe to exhibit his loyalties quite so openly.

Fortunately, Lord Coventry's confidence in a forthcoming Parliamentary victory was justified. Perhaps Lord Coventry's knowledge of the surrounding countryside contributed to the outcome of the Battle of Worcester on 3 September 1651. Again the action centred on the bridge at Powick, part of the Croome estate. The Royalist forces were routed, and Cromwell and his army were able to march triumphantly into the city leaving the King with little alternative but to flee in disguise, conceal himself in the famous Boscobel oak and eventually seek refuge abroad.

Lord Coventry emerged from this debacle shaken but unscathed, his property intact, and with the loss of only three horses and a head groom. Only his loyalty seems questionable. Family influence and a brief spell of imprisonment in 1655 purged him of guilt, but it ruined his health, and proved a high price to pay for the survival of his country seat and the grant of a Royal Pardon at the Restoration.[12] As a conciliatory gesture to the King, on Oak Apple Day on 29 May, the date of the King's birthday, oak boughs were brought from the Croome estate to decorate the Guildhall in Worcester in celebration of his return from exile. The gesture was well meant, but remarkably tactless. It is unlikely that Charles II wished to be reminded of his undignified flight from Worcester and he never returned to the city.[13]

Thomas, 2nd Baron Coventry, died at his home in Lincoln's Inn Fields on 27 October 1661, and he was buried at Croome. A monument was commissioned by his sons of a similar design to that of their mother, with twisted columns flanking the effigy and the whole set beneath a segmental pediment. During the following century, both monuments were moved to the new church and they now face each other at the eastern end of the chancel. Although the relocation of the monuments may have been dictated by practical considerations, it seems more probable that their position was intended to honour the 2nd Baron's construction of the new family chapel at Croome.

When he died, the 2nd Baron was still a very wealthy man. Although he lavished tens of thousands of pounds on the improvement of his estate, he is recorded to have 'kept a noble house and great retinue' throughout his life and to have paid for his two sons, George and Thomas, to travel abroad 'in Foreign Parts at great Expence'.[14] He gave generously to the poor of Worcester, Evesham and Tewkesbury, and he gave money towards the repair of Worcester Cathedral after it had been damaged by Parliamentary

15   Monument of 2nd Baron Coventry, Croome church.

16   Carved oak marriage chest of 1653 to commemo-rate the marriage of George, 3rd Baron Coventry to Lady Margaret Tufton.

forces. His wealth, generosity and down-right deviousness played a key part in sustaining the family's influence within the county. At the Restoration, when many noble families were facing devastating debts, the Coventry family owed much to the 2nd Baron's idionsycracies.

George, 3rd Baron Coventry (1628-80)

When the 3rd Baron came into his inheritance, it might be assumed that he would wish to capitalise upon his good fortune. His family enjoyed increasing social and political prominence and, after the drab years of the Commonwealth, this was time of opportunity and growth. In truth, very little happened at all to the estate under his ownership. While his various uncles commanded the political arena, he was content to live in consid-erable comfort and obscurity in his father's new homes and merely observe.

George had travelled widely through-out Europe with his brother Thomas, a sensible precaution on his father's part to educate his sons and remove them from the earlier stages of the civil conflict.[15] He was back in England by 1651, as reference is made to him and his servants in the Sequestration documents, and on 18 July 1653 he married Lady Margaret Tufton (b.1636), the daughter of John Tufton, Earl of Thanet. They had five children, John, Anne, Margaret, Thomas and William. John, later 4th Baron Coventry, born on 2 September 1654, was the only surviving son. Thomas, born on 27 August 1659, died five months later, on 17 January 1660, and William, born on 6 July 1661 died aged three on 14 July 1664. The eldest daughter Anne, born in July 1656 also died young but her sister, Margaret, born on 14 September 1657, survived, and she married Charles Paulet (1661-1722), Earl of Wiltshire and later 2nd Duke of Bolton, in July 1679. They had no children, and Margaret died in 1683 in the fourth year of her marriage, aged only twenty-four.

On inheriting the title and the estate, the 3rd Baron was appointed Lord Lieutenant and Custos Rotulorum of Worcestershire and High Steward of Tewkesbury. The former two appointments, which often, but not always, went hand in hand, established a precedent among many of his descendants. The title of Lord Lieutenant of the county carried social and other implications beyond its official military obligations as, effectively, the holder of the title became the principal local vehicle of crown patronage.

There is nothing within the family archive at Croome to suggest that the 3rd Baron exploited his position or even fulfilled his obligations. Indeed, according to the Antony report, he appeared content to enjoy his good fortune and '... kept a great Retinue, & a noble & plentiful Table ...', although he never ran into debt.[16] The only work known to have been undertaken on the estate during his ownership were the minor repairs to the carriage road at Croome in 1674. Buildings fell into disrepair and there was a serious decrease in rents. But it appears that towards the end of his life he took steps to remedy the situation and made the most significant decision of his ownership when he took on a new agent, Francis Taylor (d.1722), who worked for the estate for several decades and became a close family friend.[17]

Taylor's family held a considerable amount of land and property in the Littletons, near Evesham. Francis was the local squire, and his brother, Ralph, was an eminent scholar,

17 South Littleton Manor, Worcestershire, c.1872, the home of Francis Taylor. Detail from a drawing by R.F. Tomes.

a Doctor of Divinity and Sanctae Theologiae Professor, who had been awarded the Craven exhibition at Oxford. Not long after Francis became agent to the Croome estate, Lord Coventry offered Ralph the living of Severn Stoke. He remained there until 1690, when he followed James II into exile, and on his return he was appointed Rural Dean and a prebendary of Worcester.

Francis Taylor may have been responsible for the new Red Deer Park at Croome. The Fallow Deer Park had been laid out earlier in the century, but it seems likely that the Red Deer Park was created towards the end of the 3rd Baron's ownership and may have been Taylor's first project. Roughly square in shape, it covered 175 acres of ground, with a lodge in its north-west corner and entrances on its north and west sides. The eastern part of the park included a coursing ground flanked by trees and this can still be traced along its former south-eastern boundary today.[18]

However, before Taylor could embark upon more essential improvements, the 3rd Baron Coventry died on 15 December 1680, aged 52, at the house his father had built in Lincoln's Inn Fields. He was buried in the south aisle of the old church at Croome, but no monument has survived. Within a few years both his surviving children had also died, and his widow, Lady Margaret, 'languishing and disconsolate', moved to Canterbury.[19] There she continued to correspond frequently with Taylor on estate and other matters, notably the charities she had established at Severn Stoke and elsewhere, expressing her views with some force and referring to certain people she disliked as 'that surlie clown' and 'that shirking phantastical fellow'. She was clearly a lady of some character, and she signed her letters 'your lovinge friend'. In her will, she left Taylor a portrait of herself in the style of Lely, which he hung in his manor house in South Littleton, and she gave his daughter, Judith, a gift of 25 yards of fine silk.

John, 4th Baron Coventry (1654-87)

George, 3rd Baron Coventry, was succeeded by his eldest and only surviving son, John. John was 26, and is described in his epitaph as 'comely, & tall of stature, & gracefull in mien & deportment' with an 'incomparable candour & sweetness of temper'. He never married and his mother was deeply attached to him. Like his father, he spent much of his time at Croome, where he '… kept a noble & plentiful house, great Hospitality, suitable Retinue, Hounds, Hawks, running Horses …', and under Francis Taylor's instruction, he began to develop an informed interest in the estate.[20]

Shortly after he came into his inheritance, Taylor provided him with a useful report on the Estate, in which he referred to the

> two large Parks well stored with Deere, the one with Ffallow Deere the other with Red Deere, and a lesser park for breeding of Colts, ye Divers very large fish ponds besides great quantities of fishing upon the Rivers of Severne and Avon and other Small rivers …

This was the good news. Taylor went on to express his concern about the dire condition of the agricultural land, which was 'much out of husbandry for want of trenching' and would 'require great charge'. He added, rather pointedly: 'I should leave it much

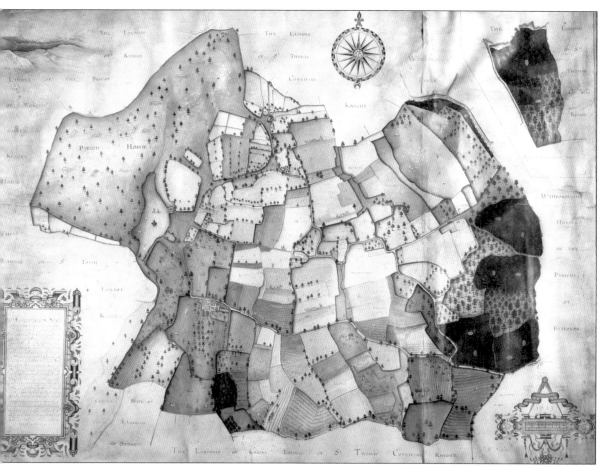

IX A survey of Pirton Parish by Mark Pierce of London, 1623. Pirton Pool, a large medieval fishpond, can be seen to the left of the parish. Croome lies along its southern boundary, Wadborough and Besford to the east, all inscribed as belonging to Sir Thomas Coventry. The view of the Malvern Hills in the top left corner is a rare and particularly fine example of its type for this date.

X The 5th Earl and Countess of Coventry and their family in Croome Park by Charles Phillipps.

XI George William, 6th Earl of Coventry, by Allan Ramsay, *c*.1765.

XII   Maria Gunning, Countess of Coventry, by Francis Cotes.
Pastel, 1751.

XIII   Elizabeth Gunning, Duchess of Hamilton and Argyll, by Francis Cotes, 1751.

XIV *Left*. John Gunning by Sir Godfrey Kneller.

XV *Below left*. Lady Anne Margaret Coventry by Sir Joshua Reynolds.

XVI *Below right*. Barbara, Countess of Coventry, by Allan Ramsay, *c*.1765.

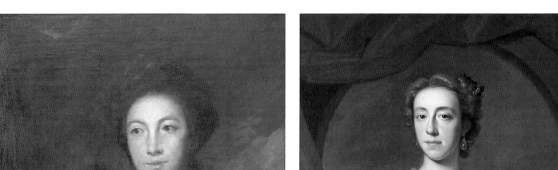

better than I find it'.[21] Taylor also informed Lord Coventry that the rents had been reduced in many parts of the estate since the time of his grandfather and great-grandfather, mainly by around £15-£30 per annum. This was a substantial amount, but a valuation of the estate carried out just after the 4th Baron's death reveals that it was still worth £8,471 19s. 8d. and one farthing per annum. The situation may have been bad, but it was far from desperate.

In March 1681, the 4th Baron granted Taylor a lease of the manor house at South Littleton, together with some of his lands in the parish and the fishery in the River Avon, which had been acquired in 1628 for a fine of £1,872.[22] Additional leases were granted in 1688, and this added considerably to the Taylor family's holdings in the Littletons. It may have been self-interest that prompted Taylor to advise Lord Coventry to purchase additional land around the Littletons. In the report referred to above, he condemned the area with commendable honesty as 'cold naked and starven', with very little timber apart from a few ash trees which are 'not much bigger than ones legg'. But he recommended that Lord Coventry should proceed with the purchase, as he believed it would prove a far simpler transaction than another also under consideration. Taylor was an astute businessman with a sound and practical knowledge of farming, and the Coventry family were wise to heed his advice and nurture their effective working partnership which continued for several decades. Their confidence in his abilities was confirmed by Taylor's appointment as Receiver General of the county and city of Worcester in 1689, by which he became responsible for collecting the levy of one shilling in the pound recently imposed to boost military resources. This was a lucrative post, and also one indicative of Taylor's reputation in the county.[23]

Probably not long after he took up this appointment, Taylor began to extend and improve the manor house at South Littleton.[24] This was then a rambling building of 14th-century origin and built of limestone rubble. It was probably cramped and inconvenient, and Taylor more than doubled it in size with a large new brick addition that presented an elegant and symmetrical brick façade to the village street. It is five bays in width, originally with sash windows, and has a dramatic skyline created by its steep hipped roof rising above a modillion cornice and culminating in a cupola flanked by panelled chimney stacks linked by open arches, which bear a marked resemblance to those at Croome House. Upon the cupola was mounted an iron weathervane inscribed 'FT 1721', which suggests that the work took around thirty years to complete, perhaps as funds became available. Within, the detailing is dis-appointing by comparison, although the surviving portions of the original staircase and the plaster ceiling in the drawing room enriched with fruits and flowers imply that it was once worthy of its distinguished façade. The house, one of the finest of its date in the county, remained part of the Croome estate until the mid-19th century. Since then its condition deteriorated rapidly. An ill-conceived restoration around 1906 and subsequent vandalism and neglect have taken their toll, and the house was in urgent need of repair at the end of the 20th century.

The 4th Baron never witnessed the improvements effected on the estate by the new agent. He died, quite unexpectedly, on 25 July 1687. He was 33, and the cause of his death is

18 Monument of John, 4th Baron Coventry, Croome church.

unknown. He was buried at Croome that August and his mother commissioned a magnificent monument from the workshop of Grinling Gibbons. The articles of agreement between Gibbons and Lady Margaret, the Countess Dowager, confirm that the monument was to be made from white Italian marble, with the effigy 'as big as the life … his Right hand stretched out to catch at a starry crown' presented to him by a statue of Faith.[25] Although executed as instructed and to a predictably high standard, the effigy is unflattering, even repellent. The 4th Baron appears neither 'comely' nor 'gracefull', but lolls dissolutely upon his tomb, and his outstretched arm gropes towards the adjacent statue in an almost improper manner. It is a strange tribute, made all the more unconvincing by the epitaph, which endows the deceased with every possible human virtue, not least his ability to unite the finer qualities of his predecessors:

> The integrity of ye Judge
> The prudence of ye Keeper
> The hospitality of his Grandfather
> The charity of his father

As the 4th Baron had died without issue, the title reverted to his uncle, Thomas, by then a middle-aged politician with extravagant habits, who rose to the challenge with questionable panache.

Thomas, 5th Baron Coventry and 1st Earl of Coventry (1629-1699)

Thomas was 58 years old when he became 5th Baron Coventry, and he was living in some style in the small and pretty village of Snitterfield, or Snitfield as it was then known, in Warwickshire. He had had a reasonably active and successful political career since the Restoration. He became MP for Droitwich in 1660, MP for Camelford in North Cornwall between 1661and 1679, and, finally, MP for Warwick in 1681 and since 1685. A more enterprising and interesting character than his brother, George, he was probably contemplating an agreeable retirement when his nephew died prematurely and somewhat inconveniently.

In 1660, Thomas had married Winifred Edgcumbe, of a prominent Cornish family. She was the youngest daughter of Colonel Piers Edgcumbe (*c*.1610-67) and sister of Sir Richard Edgcumbe (1640-88) of Mount Edgcumbe.[26] (Colour plate VI.) Her family came originally from Cotehele, but in the mid-16th century had moved ten miles south to their imposing new house on a promontory overlooking Plymouth Sound. Charles II and Samuel Pepys were among the many distinguished visitors who stayed at Mount Edgcumbe, and it is likely that it was through his connection with the Edgcumbes that Thomas secured his parliamentary seat for Camelford. Thomas and Winifred had four sons and one daughter, but only the second and youngest sons, Thomas (b.1662) and Gilbert (b.1668), survived.[27]

Not long after his marriage, Thomas purchased his estate in Snitterfield from Lady Elizabeth Hales, whose husband's family had been lords of the manor since 1546.[28] His decision to purchase this estate of around 1,000 acres for £14,500 was an eminently sensible investment. The prospect of him inheriting the Croome estate seemed remote, as his brother, George, the 3rd Baron, was still in good health and had a son and heir. He may have envied his brother's good fortune in living in the fine house their father had built, for he dismissed the idea of moving into the medieval manor house adjacent to the parish church in Snitterfield, and built himself a handsome new house on the fringe of the park. This is now demolished, but several drawings and paintings survive which give a good idea of its general appearance, as do some of the surviving outbuildings and garden walling.[29] Although Thomas was determined to emulate the splendour of Croome House at Snitterfield, his new home was more modest in scale, almost like a dower house, or agent's house, and during the next century Snitterfield House did serve as a dower house of the Coventry family. Its style was typical of the period, a brick block of two main storeys with a hipped roof and tall chimneys. There was a symmetrical main façade of five bays articulated by Ionic pilasters with a dentilled cornice, sash windows with pediments on the ground floor, and the central entrance had an ornate doorcase flanked by Ionic columns. It may have owed more to the design of Croome House than more recent influential buildings in the locality, such as Ragley Hall (1679-83), built by Robert Hooke for Lord Conway. The architect or builder is unknown, although Hooke's name has been put forward on the strength of other designs by him, such as Bethlehem Hospital in London of 1674-6.[30] Alterations were carried out to the house around 1680, but the extent of these is uncertain as, in 1694, the 5th Baron's eldest son, Thomas, remodelled the house and grounds, much to the disapproval of his father.[31]

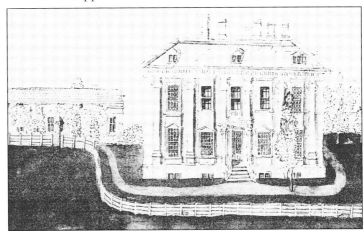

19 Snitterfield House in Warwickshire was built by the 5th Lord, 1st Earl of Coventry, prior to moving to Croome.

After the 4th Baron died in July 1687, Thomas continued to spend much of his time in Snitterfield, despite his additional responsibilities as Custos Rotulorum of Worcestershire, and High Steward of both Worcester and Evesham.[32] One of the first things he did was to buy back most of the 4th Baron's personal estate inherited by his brother's wife, the Countess Dowager. On 27 August 1687, just a month after the 4th Baron's death, the 5th Baron's son, Thomas, wrote to his brother, Gilbert, in Amsterdam, that their father had experienced '... difficulty with affairs at Croome by reason of ye late Lord dying intestate by which means ye personal estate is wholly my Lady Coventrys & will require a considerable sum of money to purchase it.'[33] The 'considerable sum' amounted to a princely £6,000, and the Countess Dowager may not have regretted the transaction. The 5th Baron then turned his attention to the estate and, most probably on the advice of Francis Taylor, he purchased additional land in the parishes of Birlingham and Defford for £2,000 from Sir Francis Russell. It is also likely that Taylor encouraged him to embark upon modest improvements on the estate, as the rental income stabilised over this period, although the emphasis remained on presentation rather than maintenance during his ownership.[34] By the 1690s, Lord Coventry began to complain bitterly to his sons about his lack of funds. This he attributed to the land tax of four shillings in the pound introduced in 1692 to finance the war with France, rather than any imprudent expenditure on his part.

There were other pressures too. Relations between the 5th Baron and his younger son Gilbert became decidedly strained owing to Gilbert's own extravagance, and by 1690 his father refused to have anything to do with him. The situation may have eased slightly by 1692, as Gilbert's personal accounts refer to 'a dead horse for my hounds att Croombe', and 'Running of my horses in ye parke', but father and son never became truly reconciled. After Gilbert married his cousin, Dorothy Keyte, in 1694, he moved to her family estate at Hidcote and Ebrington, in north Gloucestershire, which remained his true home even after he inherited the earldom in 1712.

Gilbert's deteriorating relationship with his father coincided with the death of his mother, Winifred, on 13 June 1694. The cause of her death is unknown, but there is a strange reference to 'the hurry of her Internment', which may imply that it was the result of some highly infectious disease or even that suspicious circumstances made it necessary to dispose of the body as quickly as possible. She had died in London, but her body was not moved to Croome immediately. Instead, she was buried in the chancel of St James's Church in Clerkenwell. George Harris, probably Lord Coventry's secretary, wrote to Gilbert in London on 18 June 1694 to inform him that his father 'wont allow for any Mourning, he is not intending any for himself but wont forbid you if you want some'. He added: '... his lordship says he remembers that you weren't in mourning for the death of your grandmother'.[35] This hints at some difficulties in Lord Coventry's marriage, and it is probably significant that it was not until 1700, after the death of her husband, that Winifred's remains were transferred to Croome by her eldest son, then 2nd Earl of Coventry.[36] A bill survives which details the cost of the removal. This came to a total of £22 12s. 10d., which included a new oak coffin, the loading and carriage of her gravestone, and £6 15s. for a carriage drawn by four horses for the journey to Croome.

The seemingly disrespectful treatment of his deceased wife may have much to do with the 5th Baron's remarriage to one of his servants the following year. On 16 July 1695, he was betrothed to Elizabeth Grimes, or Elizabeth Graham as she chose to call herself.[37] At 25 years old, she was more than forty years younger than him, the niece of Lord Coventry's house-keeper, the sister of a Thames waterman, and the daughter of Richard Grimes, a turner of St Giles, Cripplegate. Clearly, she had much to gain from the marriage and, according to Nash, Lord Coventry's sons were 'disgusted' by their father's behaviour.[38]

Their misgivings were temporarily cast aside by an event of major significance in the history of the family. Thomas's lavish expenditure on inheriting the title and estate had included a generous present of £8,000 to William III. The political implications of this gift were apparent, but the personal gain was more significant. As a Whig, Thomas would have been aware that, since the death of Queen Mary in 1694, the King was in an increasingly vulnerable position as a target of Jacobite opposition. The Tories were gaining strength in the Commons, and the King was dismayed at the ingratitude and inner conflict of the English whom he had attempted to unite and serve following the Revolution of 1688. This gift, therefore, was a valued and well-timed reminder of the Coventry family's enduring support of the monarchy during the past century. On 26 April 1697, Thomas was created Viscount Deerhurst and Earl of Coventry. It was a fitting end to a remarkable century of achievement.

The 1st Earl of Coventry withdrew from public life during the last years of his life. He suffered harrowing attacks of gout, and he died on 15 July 1699, aged 70. His funeral took place at Croome on 2 August and was a truly magnificent occasion. Indeed, such was the pomp and ceremony with which it was conducted that it verged on the vulgar. The new Countess may have felt a need to prove herself, or possibly it was because she now had reason to celebrate. She had inherited her husband's huge personal estate and he had left her as sole executor of his will. The 1st Earl's sons were less than pleased, but it was the funeral itself that twisted the knife.[39]

The invitations were a grisly combination of glorious and ghoulish sentiment, and depicted a somewhat athletic and well-fed Grim Reaper regarding his skeletal recruit with evident distaste. The procession itself was a splendid affair and included 'most of the Persons of Quality and Distinction of the Counties of Worcester, Gloucester and Warwick', among them the pallbearers, Sir Anthony Crowen, Sir Francis Russell, Sir Inigo Packington and Sir Charles Lyttelton. It passed in the customary manner from the

20 An invitation to the funeral of the 1st Earl of Coventry.

21 Monument of the 1st Earl of Coventry in Elmley Castle church.

Dining Room 'through the Great garden and out of ye Gate on ye East side of the Garden to the great gate on ye East side of ye Green Court, and so through the Gatehouse of the Inner Court, and in at ye South Door of ye Church ...'. This is of interest in itself, for it confirms the layout of the grounds immediately surrounding the house at this time, with a 'Great' garden to the south and 'Green' or grassed courtyard to the north. Trumpets sounded and heraldic banners fluttered in the breeze as the long procession wound its way in a stream of rich colour and flashing arms to the church door. The highest ranking estate officials held high their white staves of office and, when the speeches and service was over, they broke the staves symbolically over the 1st Earl's grave. The entire ceremonial took a gruelling five hours, the guests lingered for days, and the legal consequences lasted for years.

The 1st Earl's young widow had commissioned a suitably ostentatious monument in the Gibbons style from the London sculptor, William Stanton (1639-1705).[40] Arguably, this is the best of all the Coventry monuments. Made of black and white marble, the effigy of the bewigged earl, dressed in robes adorned with huge buttons and an opulent lace cravat, reclines beside his coronet. Angels stand at either side of him, and above him soars a canopy with an enormous coat of arms breaking through the pediment. Further angels clasping long trumpets hover above the pediment, and every surface flaunts a crisp collation of classical ornament. This splendid tribute had one vital flaw. The arms of the Coventry family were impaled with those of the Graham family. This was impertinent, but might have been tactfully ignored were it not for the epitaph, which included several lines in praise of the Countess Dowager and claimed she was of the noble Graham or Grymes family from Norfolk.[41] Elizabeth had been assisted and encouraged in this act of deception by Gregory King (1648-1712), genealogist, engineer, statistician and Lancaster Herald, who had presided as Marshal at the funeral. King was a former clerk of the antiquarian, Sir William Dugdale, and was clever, capable and cunning. In 1694, he had been accused of embezzling fees when making the arrangements for Queen Mary's funeral. It was revealed later by the Court of Chivalry that he was a close friend of the Grimes family, and he married Elizabeth's sister, Frances Grattan, in 1702. In the Croome archive is a sketch for the 1st Earl's monument, on the rear of which is scribbled the following note:

Mrs King

Pray send me my Point Crevat I bought last in Holland, or one of the Falls? Of it, for a pattern to cutt my Lord's Crevat by, for they are going to cut it with large gimp flowers which have been out of fashion these 15 years or better.[42]

The Mrs. King in question must be Gregory King's first wife, Anne Powel, soon to be replaced by Elizabeth's sister.[43] King's apparent concern that Lord Coventry should not be immortalised wearing an unfashionable cravat contrasts sharply with his apparent disregard for accuracy elsewhere on the monument. It is also evidence of the extent of his control over the entire proceedings, as the 2nd Earl can have known little about the detail of the monument until it was completed. It is conceivable that King had managed to trace Elizabeth's ancestry back to this Norfolk family, but, on the copper plate inscription on the coffin, Elizabeth aspired to be of the Graham family from Yorkshire instead. Detailed studies have since been carried out to verify these claims.[44] These reveal that Elizabeth's alleged connection with the Graham family from either Norfolk or Yorkshire was purely hypothetical and little more than an informed bluff; but worse was to follow.

The new Countess Dowager spent little time in mourning. Having inherited much of her husband's personal estate, she married Thomas Savage of Elmley Castle in south Worcestershire a few months later. To add further insult, Savage had been invited to the funeral as one of eight assistants to the Chief Mourner, the 1st Earl's son, Thomas, now the 2nd Earl of Coventry. Desperate to take his revenge, the 2nd Earl refused permission for his father's monument to be erected in Croome church so, undaunted, the Countess Dowager arranged for it to be installed within Elmley Castle church, presumably with the agreement of her new husband. The new Earl of Coventry resolved to place the whole unpleasant business before the Court of Chivalry so that the extent of the deception would be made public. King, shamed and excluded from public life, later sought to make amends, and in December 1704 he wrote to William Bromley at Holt Castle, then MP for Worcestershire, to ask him if he would help him to seek Lord Coventry's forgiveness so that the monument might return to Croome.[45] Very sensibly, Bromley would have little to do with the affair. The magnificent monument remained at Elmley Castle as a permanent reminder of the regrettable business.

After King's death in 1712, Gilbert, now 4th Earl of Coventry, seemed keen to restore the cordial relationship between the Coventry and Savage families, possibly for dubious motives. His daughter, Anne, was a regular guest of the Savages at Elmley Castle, and the bond between the two families was strengthened further when Thomas, a great-grandson of Lord Keeper Coventry's youngest brother Walter, married Margaret, the daughter of Thomas Savage and his wife Elizabeth, the Countess Dowager.[46] Following the reversion of the earldom to Walter Coventry's descendants in 1719, and the death of the Countess Dowager in 1724, there was good reason to settle the dispute for good.

But the whole affair had cast a shadow across a defining moment in the history of the Coventry family. It took decades marred by rivalry and mismanagement before the family could channel their energy and resources effectively to build upon the achievements of their 17th-century ancestors.

VI

Debts, Dowagers, Dormice
and Divisions

Thomas, 2nd Earl of Coventry (1663-1710), Anne, Countess of Coventry (1673-1763), and their son, Thomas, 3rd Earl of Coventry (1702-1712)

The early years of the 18th century brought little respite from the problems that had arisen during the first earldom. The incompetence and inertia that had marred the post-Restoration years was replaced by a surge of enthusiasm as the 1st Earl's sons sought to stamp their mark upon their country seat in a somewhat piecemeal fashion. Their ambition was ill-matched by their income, to which they paid scant regard, despite their father's warnings. There was a more pressing problem, too. When George I came to the throne in 1714, the descendants of Lord Keeper Coventry were in urgent need of an heir.

Thomas, 2nd Earl of Coventry, was the second son of the marriage between Thomas, 1st Earl of Coventry, and his wife, Winifred Edgcumbe (colour plate VII). Their eldest son, also called Thomas, died at birth, leaving his name and his inheritance to his younger

brother. He was brought up at Snitterfield and, after the customary spell at Oxford, he travelled to Holland in 1683 with his brother Gilbert. When his cousin John died in 1687, Thomas was only 25 and enjoying the irresponsible and indulgent life of a privileged and wealthy young gentleman. At once, his future became more clearly defined. His marriage to Lady Anne Somerset on 4 May 1691 was a most welcome alliance. That she was a daughter of an illustrious noble family was an undeniable asset, but, more importantly, she was loyal and resourceful, shrewd and intelligent, and, as her portrait by Sir Godfrey Kneller reveals, blessed with the grace and good looks so advantageous to her position.

22   Anne, Countess of Coventry by Sir Godfrey Kneller.

Lady Anne (1673-1763) was the fourth daughter of Henry Somerset, 1st Duke of Beaufort, and his wife Mary, the daughter of the 1st Baron Capel of Hadham and widow of Henry, Lord Beauclerk. The Capel family were famous for their botanical interests and Lady Anne's mother, Mary Capel, was among the most important botanists of her day. Her garden at Badminton was noted for its exotics and she commissioned an outstanding series of botanical drawings of her plant collection. Thomas and Anne moved to Snitterfield, and it was not until after Thomas had inherited the title and estate in 1699, that their two sons were born, Thomas in 1702 and John in 1705, although John died the following year.

The 2nd Earl is said to have been a committed Whig. He was Custos Rotulorum of Worcestershire and Recorder of Coventry from 1706 until his death in 1710. Once he inherited the earldom, he divided his time between Snitterfield and Croome, where he lived the life more of a scholar than a sportsman. His wife was similarly inclined, with an informed interest in a wide range of subjects, notably botany due to her mother's influence, but also in horticulture, architecture and medicine. A catalogue of her library made in 1698 included Culpeper's *London Dispensary*, *The French Gardener*, Rabisha's *Whole Body of Cookery*, *Guide of ye Waters at Bathe etc*, Hughes's *Flower Garden*, Ovid's *Metamorphoses*, Homeck's *Best Exercise*, Stalker's *Art of Japanry*, and Palladio's *Quattro Libri dell'Architettura*. To this list might be added numerous other volumes on subjects ranging from mathematics, classics, navigation and anatomy to astronomy, heraldry, cosmography and horsemanship. In 1708 she added to her library the *Meditations and Reflections, Moral and Divine*, a small but very special volume dedicated to her as a tribute to her 'piety, wisdom and virtue'.[1] It was an enviable and catholic collection, intended for her personal instruction rather than to impress, and her curiosity about the natural world was typical of her time, as scientific advances steadily expanded both intellectual and geographic horizons. In a letter of *c*.1713 she thanked her husband's niece, Lady Anne Carew, for the butterflies which she had sent to her, and remarked: 'I hope you find some amusemt & entertainmt (as I confess I do) in remarking ye vast beauty & variety in nature'.[2] Like many noblewomen of this period, Lady Coventry was a talented needlewoman and collected medical and culinary recipes, many of which survive among the Beaufort archive. Most of the medical recipes are for the treatment of ailments such as gout, colic, consumption and dropsy. More unusual ones include a cure for the bite of a mad dog, 'Great Plague Water', and perhaps the most impractical and improbable of all, a recipe for Swallow Water recommended for convulsion fits. It begins:

> Take ffortie or ffifty swollows when they are ready to fly out of the nest, bruse them to pape [sic] in a mortar feathers and all; then add to them 2 ounces of Castarium beaten to powder, and 3 pints of strong white wine vinegar and mix all very well together and put it into a still and distill it ...[3]

A note at the end recommended that: 'They must not be chimnie swollows'. Presumably the soot might spoil the taste! More appetising are the various culinary recipes, which include instructions for making raspberry, apricot and jasmine water, preserving pomegranates and pistachio nuts, and a more dubious snail syrup.

To Make Swollow water goode agaᵗ convulsion fittes

Take ffortie or fiftie Swollows when they are ready to fly out of the nest, bruse them to pape in a morter feathers and all; then adde to them 2 ounces of Castarium beaten to powder, and 3 pints of strong white wine vineger, mixe all very well together and put it into a still and distill it: You may draw from it a pint of very good water, you may give the patient 2 or 3 sponfulls swetned with Suger they must not be Chimnie Swollows.

23   Recipe for Swallow Water to treat convulsion fits.

24   Posthumous portrait of Thomas, 3rd Earl of Coventry. School of Kneller.

The personal documents, which survive in increasing numbers among the various family archives from around this date, hint at the affectionate relationship that existed between the 2nd Earl and his wife. For example, in 1705 their elder son Thomas, Viscount Deerhurst, became ill when his mother was at Badminton, and the 2nd Earl sent her frequent bulletins on the progress of his illness.[4] In these letters he addresses her as 'My dear rogue', and seems rather pessimistic about their son's condition: 'I coud [sic] wish I were able to give you more hopes or encouragm't as to ye poor child's recovery than indeed, at present …'. He signs himself 'yr disconsolate & melancholy husbd Coventry'. The Countess's little medical knowledge proved potentially harmful, as she became convinced that her son was suffering from rickets, and her criticism of the doctor's diagnosis did little to assist her son's rapid recovery. Despite a disgusting sequence of purges, young Thomas regained his health eventually and soon after was sent away to Eton. A rare example survives of his geometry homework of quite daunting complexity (see no. 26, p.63).[5] There is also a charming nonsense letter among the Beaufort papers from Thomas to his mother, in which he asks her to scold 'Mopsy', possibly a friend, his nanny or even a favourite toy:

> Pray write a scolding letter to my wife Mopsy and reprimand her severely for not keeping up a correspondence with her husband; and if you can force her to a submission and make her promise to be more dutyfull [sic] for the future—you shall (which is the best thing I have to bestow upon you) receive a dormouse as an acknowledgement for so great a favour confer'd upon
>
> Your truly affectionate husband
> T Deerhurst
>
> More I would write but now ye clock strikes three and I must go to school, ah woe is me!

His mother made a habit of berating her various correspondents, notably Lady Anne Carew and Agnes Keyte, if they failed to reply promptly to her letters. Perhaps the Countess should have offered them a dormouse as an incentive.

According to the Antony report, the 2nd Earl enjoyed a greater income than his predecessors. This suggests that the rental income had increased significantly and, as his wife had brought money to the marriage, he felt confident to embark upon a series of improvements at Croome and Snitterfield. The extent of this work is uncertain. Some of it may have been initiated by the 1st Earl, and undoubtedly the alterations at Croome were continued during the 4th Earl's ownership, but the surviving bills and accounts fail to clarify the situation completely.

Snitterfield had been altered and extended during the 1680s by the 5th Baron, but a letter from his secretary, George Harris, suggests that Thomas, his eldest son, made further alterations not long after his marriage in 1694. In this letter, Harris informed Lady Anne that: 'His Lordship is very much dissatisfied with Mr Coventre's pulling down the top of the House and says the house served very well in his time'.[6] The work involved the addition of a new large wing, new outbuildings and a formal garden in the Dutch style. Bills and estimates for the garden work among the Beaufort papers that date from the late 1690s refer to stone for two summerhouses in Snitterfield garden, timber for a greenhouse, mottoes for sundials and a bill for garden tools.[7] The 2nd Earl also donated money to the parish church in Snitterfield, notably in 1710, when he provided funds for a new oak roof in the chancel, new paving, and the removal of the tracery in the chancel windows.

He commissioned the artist, John Wootton (1683-1764), to paint Snitterfield House in the early 18th century, probably to commemorate the completion of the alterations and new garden layout.[8] Wootton, a pupil of Jan Wyck, was closely associated with the Coventry family during the early stages of his career. He was probably born in Snitterfield, studied under Jan Wyck, and under the Duke of Beaufort's patronage, he visited Rome and for several years was page to Lady Anne.[9] Wootton achieved great success for his equestrian portraits and hunting scenes painted in the Flemish style, and the 1st Earl's

25 'The Great Horse' by John Wootton. Believed to commemorate the horse race at Westwood that, according to tradition, led to the founding of the Coventry Hospital in Droitwich.

sons admired his work with an enthusiasm outmatched only by the 9th Earl's passion for all things equestrian during the 19th century.

At Croome, the first task was to refurnish the house, as the 1st Earl's widow had removed much of its contents to Elmley Castle. Then work began on the exterior, probably including the addition of a square porch with a balustraded parapet to the north front of the house, and a clumsy protrusion was of no obvious architectural merit, as can be seen in the *c*.1750 bird's-eye view (illustration 14). It is also probable that the chimneys acquired their familiar profile at this time and work began on the new wings at each end of the south front, which extended and updated this elevation. These were certainly finished by 1714, when Henry Beighton made his drawing of the south elevation of Croome House, and it is likely that Gilbert, by then 4th Earl, laid out the south garden after 1712 to complete the new scheme.

The Household Accounts for this period imply that the 2nd Earl and his staff lived well. Between 25 March and 25 October 1707, the household consumed no less then 3 sheep, 2 lambs, 1 buck, 32 lbs bacon, 21 rabbits, 8 brace of wild fowl, 10 pigeons, several dozen salmon and lampreys, 15 lbs cheese, 28 chickens, 8 ducks, 1 goose, 372 eggs, 112 lbs butter, 44 lbs sugar, 4 oranges and 10 lemons. There were additional supplies of meat from the butcher at Croome, fruit, herbs and vegetables from the kitchen garden, 16 ½ bushels of wheat for the bakehouse and 74 lbs of oats, although some of the latter were probably intended for the horses. Copious quantities of claret, white wine, sherry and sack, and ale provided the necessary liquid refreshment.

This was a happy but brief interlude. The 2nd Earl died on 20 August 1710, after three months' illness. His young son became 3rd Earl of Coventry, only to die at Eton 17 months later, on 28 January 1712, aged 10 years old. No monument to the memory of either the 2nd or 3rd Earls has survived, but a painting of an unidentified child among the collection of the Croome Estate Trust may be a posthumous portrait of the 3rd Earl. Set within an oval frame, the child's face appears unhealthily flushed and behind him looms the brooding features of Father Time. A distressing picture, it well conveys the grief and suffering that accompanied his premature death (see picture 24).

The 2nd Earl had died intestate and left debts of £7,914. Presumably his plans for Croome and Snitterfield were unmatched by his income, although great quantities of timber were sold during this period, which should have contributed significantly towards the building expenses. The Antony report can offer no satisfactory explanation as to the cause of this unfortunate state of affairs:

> … But how it can be supposed the estate can be clogg'd with great Debts without any Mannor of Provisions going out of it for Childrens Fortunes is very misterious, It being well-known to both Town and Country, that my Lord was no ways extravagant or reputed to live above his Neighbours of less Estates, whilst he was Lord Deerhurst, & was possessed of an Estate of £1600 p. ann. and no child till about two years after he was Earl, & enjoyed that Title & Estate upwards of 12 years with a greater Income than any of his predecessors, neither did he keep any Hounds, Hawks, Running Horses, or any ways given to gaming, or going to publick meetings but rather delighted in Books …

During her son's brief minority, and for some time after, the Countess Dowager administered the estate. Some insight into the cause of her husband's financial problems is provided by the various schedules prepared on her behalf, which were delivered to His Majesty's Court of Exchequer in November 1716 in order to discharge the debt.[10] These lay the blame upon the modest allowance given to the 2nd Earl during his father's lifetime, the impact of the land tax introduced in 1692, the minor debts incurred to furnish, alter and repair Snitterfield, and the cost of altering and re-furnishing Croome. More revealing are the repeated references to interest charges. Reading between the lines, the real source of the problem was the 2nd Earl's inclination to borrow large sums of money.

On the death of his nephew, Thomas Gilbert, brother of the 2nd Earl, became 4th Earl of Coventry. His grasp of economics was no sounder than his brother's and it was the Countess Dowager who dealt adeptly with the debts. Taking the wisest

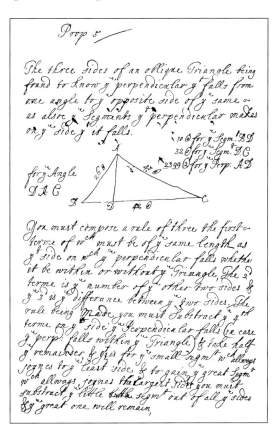

26 The schoolwork of Thomas, 3rd Earl of Coventry, while he was at Eton.

counsel at her disposal, she left Gilbert somewhat bitter and bemused and he continued to feel the victim of a conspiracy for the rest of his life. The terms of the 2nd Earl's will did little to improve the situation between himself and his sister-in-law. The Countess Dowager had inherited her husband's personal estate, the house at Snitterfield, plus the arrears of rent due and 18 months' profits of the whole estate. She received in jointure the manors and lands in Oxendon, Bisley and Hardwick in Gloucestershire, Mitton, Longdon and Feckenham in Worcestershire, and Postlip in Gloucestershire, which was exchanged for Snitterfield. The personal goods included considerable presents of plate and money given to her husband by his father, and there were a number of reversionary leases, which had been granted for her benefit prior to her husband's death. 'Unusual and dark proceedings' are said to have surrounded the details of these leases, which were alleged to be 'kept concealed above a year after her son's death' from the 4th Earl.[11] Possibly these proceedings were a necessary part of her plan to pay off her husband's debts without Gilbert's unwelcome interference. This plan involved a major sale of goods and chattels from her husband's personal estate in 1711, which raised £1,653 10s. 3d., and the felling of further large quantities of timber on the estate; the timber taken from the Fallow Deer Park alone in 1711 raised £45 17s. 8d. The remaining debts were paid out of the rental income which amounted to £2,526 1s. 9d. for the half year to Michaelmas 1712, including her jointures.[13] It was typical of her compassionate nature that the Countess Dowager made sure that the money owing to the tradesmen and servants was paid first, and the larger debts owed to her husband's wealthy financiers were left till last.

Much interesting information emerges from the various inventories of Croome that were drawn up during this period.[14] These conjure a reasonably detailed image of the interior of the house in the early 18th century. The scale of the building is apparent from the references to the Hall Chamber, the Great Hall, my Lord's Chamber, the Withdrawing Room, the Great Parlour, and the Best Parlour, which would conform with the building contracts of 1640-2 among the Beaufort archive. The offices were clearly extensive and included accommodation for the butler, the steward, the bailiff, and the porter, together with every facility for a self-sufficient household, including several pantries, a laundry, brewhouse, granary, dairy, wash house and still house. The main house had evidently been re-furnished well; for example, the Withdrawing Room included such refinements as 'a teatable, a japan'd cabinett, a "prcell" of china, nine chairs with silk covers, two pieces of tapestry and two large looking glasses'. Upon the Great Stairs were hung a series of seven paintings brought to Croome by the 2nd Earl, the finest of which was one of *Samson and Delilah*, and the Countess Dowager argued at length with Gilbert about who was the rightful owner of this valuable work.[15] The longest entry of all in these inventories relates to the contents of the kitchen, equipped to provide the most sumptuous of feasts and fitted with shelves that gleamed with an impressive collection of 46 pewter dishes and nine dozen pewter plates.

The Countess Dowager did not return to live at Snitterfield on a permanent basis till 1726, when the various legal disputes were finally settled. In 1712, she wrote to Gilbert for his assistance in finding a tenant for the house, and it appears that she spent the intervening years in the Duke of Beaufort's Chelsea home or at Badminton.[16] Her jointure was valued at around £1,600 p.a. and enabled her to live in considerable comfort until her death in 1763. Her charitable and philanthropic deeds won her immense popularity among the people of Snitterfield and, following her late husband's example, she gave generously to the parish church. She donated funds for the new north porch in 1723 and for an elaborate three-decker pulpit some years later. She also gave a chalice, a paten and a flagon to the church, and embroidered an altar frontal and a pulpit tabard. The hatchments on the walls of the church tower serve as an additional reminder of the Coventry family's links with Snitterfield, and show the arms of Thomas, 2nd Earl of Coventry, impaling those of the Beaufort family.

During these years, the Countess Dowager had time to develop her creative and literary interests. Her collection of sea shells grew steadily, and were made into pictures and panels which encrusted the walls and fireplace of her square parlour. Sitting in her mahogany 'Easy Chair', an elderly nymph in her enchanted grotto, she entertained a wide circle of wealthy and influential friends, among them the young curate, Richard Jago. Jago (1715-81) was the son of the rector of Beaudesert, Warwickshire, and he became curate of Snitterfield in 1737, and vicar in 1754. He was well-known for his topographical poetry, and his friendship with the Countess Dowager was probably founded as much on her interest in religious philosophy as their shared love of gardening, landscape and poetry. Jago introduced her to a number of important contacts, among them the poet William Somerville, who was sufficiently inspired by the molluscs on her fireplace to compose an enthusiastic tribute to her skills. The closing lines of this poem are as follows:

> You, madam, sprung from Beaufort's line;
> Who, lost to courts, can in your closet shine,
> Best know to use each blessing he bestows,
> Best know to praise the pow'r from whence it flows,
> Shells in your hand the Parian Rock defy,
> Or agat, or Aegyptian porphyry
> More glossy they, their veins of brighter dye.
> See! Where your rising pyramids aspire,
> Your guests surpriz'd the shining pile admire,
> In future times, if some great Phidias rise,
> Whose chissel with his mistress Nature vies,
> Who with superior skill can lightly trace
> In the hard marble block the softest face;
> To crown this piece, so elegantly neat,
> Your well wrought busto shall the whole compleat;
> O'er your own work from age to age preside,
> Its author once, and then its greatest pride.[17]

Jago was at school in Solihull with the poet and gardener, William Shenstone (1714-63), and had accompanied him to Oxford to study poetry. Shenstone had taken on the lease of The Leasowes in Halesowen, Worcestershire in 1745, where he spent much of the remainder of his life improving the grounds into an influential garden, following the example of Philip Southcote at Woburn Farm, near Weybridge, Surrey. It is likely that Jago introduced him to the Countess Dowager, who shared his enthusiasm for botany and horticulture. She planted the elms, limes and cedars in the park at Snitterfield, which were admired by another of her friends, George Lucy, who later employed Capability Brown to improve his parkland at Charlecote in Warwickshire.

Brown embarked upon the transformation of Croome for the 6th Earl of Coventry during the Countess Dowager's lifetime, and she must have eagerly awaited an invitation to view the work in progress. Since the title had reverted to William Coventry, who became the 5th Earl in 1719, she had had little to do with the new breed of Coventrys at Croome.[18] There is no doubt that the legal and financial entanglements which followed the death of the 2nd, 3rd and 4th Earls obliged her to keep her distance but, after the 5th Earl's death, the 6th Earl made a concerted effort to heal this rift. He began to send her regular gifts of venison, and in a letter of 1752 he expressed his wish that Snitterfield were closer to Croome so that they might see more of each other.[19] However, the 6th Earl's intentions may not have been entirely honourable. His kind enquiries usually developed into requests for an invitation to Badminton on behalf of his new wife, or for the support of the Duke of Beaufort on behalf of his brother, John, who was standing at the forthcoming general election.

The Countess Dowager died on 14 February 1763 in her ninetieth year. According to her obituary, she remained in the best of health until two years before her death and expired 'without the least emotion', at about nine o' clock in the morning after a particularly good night's sleep.[20] She had hoped to be buried at Croome, next to her husband, but such was her longevity that when she died the old parish church at Croome had been demolished and the new church was not yet complete. On 17 February 1763, the Beaufort family wrote anxiously to the 6th Earl to enquire whether the new vault was ready.[21] When they learned that it had not been consecrated, they tried to persuade Lord Coventry to induce the Bishop of Worcester to undertake an impromptu consecration as a special favour.[22] This proved impossible, and so the Countess Dowager's body was conveyed to Badminton for burial instead. Was it really impractical to consecrate the church at such short notice, or was the 6th Earl simply being awkward? It seems unlikely that he would disrupt his plans even for the sake of a distant relative, and the timing was hardly tactful. He was still waiting to put the body of his young wife in the new vault.

Richard Jago was invited to preach at the Countess Dowager's funeral at Badminton, and he also gave a sermon in her honour at Snitterfield. This was printed in Oxford later that year and was entitled *The Nature of a Christian's Happiness in Death*: presumably there was no irony intended.

Gilbert, 4th Earl of Coventry (1668-1719)

Gilbert was 44 when he became 4th Earl of Coventry. As a young man, the chances of his inheriting the title seemed slim, and his wilful and disruptive behaviour did little to inspire the respect and affection of his immediate family. When his young nephew died at Eton, Gilbert was mellowing into middle age at Hidcote, riddled with gout. Although he had never spent much time at Croome during the ownership of his father and brother,

XVII   A watercolour of Pirton Castle by James Wyatt, 1801.

XVIII   A watercolour of the Panorama Tower by James Wyatt, 1801.

XIX Croome Court by Richard Wilson, 1758.

XXI   A design for the east window of Croome church by Robert Adam.

27 'Rover' by Gilbert, 4th Earl of Coventry.

he appears to have welcomed the opportunity to exercise some control over his inheritance at last. He had only nine years left to live, but during this period he stamped his imprint on the place with commendable energy and enthusiasm. The place thronged with builders, gardeners, upholsterers, artists and craftsmen, but it was typical of Gilbert that he paid equal attention to the comforts of his dogs and his horses. One of the first things he did at Croome was to build new stables and kennels, and several of his favourite animals were immortalised on canvas, notably by his sister-in-law's former page, John Wootton. Gilbert was a competent artist himself, as witnessed by his painting of his favourite spaniel 'Rover', its collar inscribed with the words 'NARIBUS UTILIS' ('Good with his nose'). Praise indeed, and at the foot of the painting was another Latin inscription, a line from Virgil: 'ET GROSSUM CANES COMMITANTUR HERILEM ('the dog accompanies his master's steps').[23] It is an affectionate portrait by a man, whose commitment to pleasure was such that his relatives could only express their relief that the 4th Earldom was mercifully brief.

He had been brought up at Snitterfield with his elder brother, Thomas, and in early 1683 they had travelled to Holland together. Following the conclusion of the Second Dutch War in 1673 and the marriage of William of Orange to the king's niece, Mary, in 1676, their father believed it sensible to educate his sons in Dutch commerce and culture. Gilbert was nearly 15, and it was intended that he would become apprenticed to a Dutch merchant.[24] Not long after Gilbert arrived in Amsterdam, his father, later 5th Baron and 1st Earl, sent him the following paternal advice:

> ... keep yourself constantly very warme cloathed.. be sure to say your prayers morning and evening, strictly observe the Lord's Day by going to Church ... [and] always to shunne idle drunken lying or swearing company.[25]

All perfectly reasonable and sensible, but wasted words on Gilbert. He loved the freedom and conviviality of Holland, could speak and write Dutch fluently, took music lessons and

soon forgot the more serious purpose of his trip. By the end of the year his father refused
to correspond with him, and his brother Thomas wrote to warn him that their father
'… does expect you shall performe yr promise of being a merchant …'. Gilbert's allowance
of £20 p.a. was stopped and in a letter of 11 October 1684, his brother wrote to tell
him that their father suspected that he was drinking his money away. This was probably
very close to the truth, and eventually Gilbert did become apprenticed to an Amsterdam
merchant, a Mr. Nicholas Andrea Vanderlan, in 1685, but the harsh warnings from his
brother continued. Even the news of the death of the 4th Baron Coventry, and of his
father's consequent financial and legal difficulties, had little affect on his extravagant
behaviour. By 1690 he had left Holland for Paris. His father was furious, and, on 31 May
1690, George Harris informed Gilbert that all communication with the family must cease
altogether. Fearing a permanent rift, Gilbert returned to England later that year but, as
he was refused permission to visit Croome or Snitterfield, he stayed with his mother's
family at Cotehele. At a safe distance from Worcestershire, he wrote apologetic letters to
his father begging for more money. His father attempted to reason with him:

> … you cannot yet be in want of money: … Taxes &c make money scarce with me, which you would
> do well to consider, & ye debts also which your M [other?] and B[rother] & selfe have occasioned; you
> … take no notice of my Dignity as a Peer of the Realm which ought in the first place to be supported.

It is signed 'yr kinde & loving (tho unfortunate) father Tho Coventrye', and it seemed
that Lord Coventry wished to end the quarrel with his son. For a few months, Gilbert
began to consider his future a little more responsibly. Living in Cornwall gave him the
idea of taking a command at sea, but by early summer he was abroad again in Flanders.
That autumn, he returned to Croome, as his personal accounts refer to such items as 'a
dead horse for my hounds att Croombe'.[26] There is also a bill of expenses for a visit
he made to Cornwall in September 1691. The one-way trip of a week's duration cost
a substantial £17 15s. 3d., which included the cost of food, lodging, horses, ostlers, servants,
etc. Admittedly there were a few extra purchases, such as wig oil, stockings, a new hat,
and the most expensive item of the entire trip, a new nightgown for £1 9s., but this still
seems an astonishingly high price.[27] On the rear of the bill are a number of sketches,
probably made by Gilbert at an inn where he was staying on his journey. The Bruegelesque
characters may be anatomically inept, and the table liable to collapse, but the faces are
drawn well and the mood and character of the scene is conveyed most successfully. The
woman's face to the right of the sketch may be that of a serving girl who caught Gilbert's
eye. A sketch of horses and hounds made by Gilbert in 1699 on the back of another
letter is drawn with much greater skill and accuracy. It is interesting to speculate whether
Gilbert was offered any advice from John Wootton on animal anatomy.[28]

In 1694, Gilbert's mother, Winifred, died, and his father's second marriage did little
to improve the difficult relationship between father and son.[29] It didn't help that Gilbert
and his elder brother had fallen out, as Gilbert suspected that he had contributed to
their father's antagonism to him for his own personal gain. It was probably to the great
relief of all when on 30 November 1694, Gilbert married his cousin, Dorothy Keyte

28 & 29   Sketch of a couple and a horse and rider by Gilbert, 4th Earl of Coventry.

(1667-1705) the daughter of Sir William Keyte, 2nd Baronet of Ebrington in north Gloucestershire, and his wife Elizabeth, the Lord Keeper's grand-daughter. He was 26, she was a year younger, and they were well-matched. Dorothy, was an attractive young woman with a mane of thick light-brown hair, a long face with a prominent nose, and a liking for dogs. Their marriage helped strengthen family ties, not least because Dorothy's brother William, later 3rd Baronet, was married to Agnes Keyte, the daughter of Sir John Clopton of Clopton, who became a good friend of Lady Anne, wife of the 2nd Earl.[30] The Keytes had lived in Ebrington for over three hundred years, and in 1663 Francis Keyte had built another fine house, known as Hidcote House, at Hidcote Bartrim, nearby.[31] As Gilbert's accounts and correspondence invariably refer to Hidcote rather than Ebrington, it seems probable that he and Dorothy lived at Hidcote House. This picturesque building remains much as it was in Gilbert's time, a classic Cotswold composition of steep, shaped gables and mullioned and transomed windows, all expertly carved and detailed in honey-coloured limestone.[32]

Extravagant as ever, Gilbert replenished his wardrobe in honour of his new wife, and among the long and detailed list of garments he acquired, three splendid new coats took pride of place:

One fine cloath coate with silver triming & rich pair of breeches ye Ground Silver Brocard & Wastcoate of White Brocarded Silke with Gold & Greene flowers.

One fine Cloath Cate [coat], pocketts & sleeves embroidered with Gold, wastcoate & breeches of brocarded Violett, coloured silks with silver & greene flowers.

One fine cloartth coate trim'd with silver, wastcoate, of blew brocarded Silks with silver flowers and blew silk breeches.[33]

There were also various pairs of gold fringe and silver lace gloves, two Black Beaver hats, 12 day shirts, six nightshirts, four 'leaced' caps, six flowered muslin neckcloths, and

30   Dorothy Keyte, Countess of Coventry by Sir Godfrey Kneller.

endless pairs of stockings. Predictably, Gilbert considered his marriage settlement quite inadequate, but complaints to George Harris had little effect. On 21 January 1696, Harris informed him that his father sent his very kind respects and that he was to content himself with 'what he hath & give him no further trouble …'.[34] After his father's death in 1699, Gilbert tried to badger his brother for money. Thomas, now 2nd Earl, complained to him that he found the cold and distant tone of his letters most distressing, and at the foot of one of his replies to Gilbert he wrote, somewhat wistfully: 'PS. I wish you would treat me with more freedom, giving titles which I don't expect or desire so I can't think it in ye least proper.'[35] Gilbert continued to harbour resentment towards his brother for the rest of his life.

In 1696, Dorothy gave birth to a daughter, Anne, who lived at Hidcote with her parents until she was around nine years old. When Dorothy died in 1707, Lady Coventry appears to have taken Gilbert's daughter under her wing and, as the Beaufort family's London home was in Chelsea, it is almost certain that it was Lady Coventry who arranged for her niece's private education in Chelsea. A Mr. and Mrs. Amand ran the school, and they kept Lady Coventry well informed of Anne's progress.[36] Apparently, she withstood a rampant outbreak of scurvy with admirable resilience, but on 14 December 1707 Lady Coventry was horrified to learn that her niece had contracted smallpox. Young Anne must have had a remarkable constitution, as by Christmas there was a distinct chance that she would recover. By 1 January this had become a certainty, and Lady Coventry was advised that although her niece's face was still swollen, 'it will not be pitted'. Anne was back at her lessons by 16 January, and on 12 February she wrote the following formal note to her father: 'I shall goe to scoole when the wather is better ware I shall indever to improve myself.'

Gilbert showed far more interest in his animals, his business ventures and his building projects than in his daughter's welfare. During the 1680s, his father had purchased some coal workings in Warwickshire, and he inherited these on the death of the 1st Earl in 1699. The demand for coal was increasing at an incredible rate by this time due to the shortage of sea coal and the scarcity of timber. Landowners were sacrificing lawns and parkland in the search for new seams, and the surface workings that Gilbert owned were a potentially lucrative investment. These delphs, as they were known, were run in partnership with the Newdigate family of Arbury, and in particular Sir Richard Newdigate, 2nd Baronet. A 21-year contract had been drawn up between the Coventry and Newdigate families between 1684-6, whereby the Newdigates leased the larger portion of the workings and dealt with the general administration and labour involved. The arrangement had never been entirely satisfactory, and in 1707 Gilbert had asked his friend Henry Beighton (d.1743), the eminent surveyor and engineer, who owned land adjacent to the workings, to draw up a plan so that the contract could be renewed on better terms. From this time onwards, Gilbert decided to place further restrictions on the workings and he demanded that the Newdigates pay him and his heirs £20 for each and every new pit of coal that was sunk other than the original seven-foot delph.[37] Despite a total annual income of £5,000, the workings ran at a loss, and they were finally abandoned in the late 18th century.

The bills and accounts suggest that Gilbert's improvements at Hidcote continued till his death in 1719, and, consequently, it can be difficult to ascertain whether some works apply to either Hidcote or Croome. For example, the accounts for 1707 refer to work at the new Banqueting House. This was most likely intended for Hidcote, or possibly Ebrington Manor, where there is a splendid summerhouse of this date. However a 'Summer House' is referred to in the Inventory of Croome of 1719, which housed a dining table and chairs and may be the same building or one of similar design.[38] It was constructed of whitewashed brick, but references to gilding 'the Weathercock, Pineapple and Pedestal' imply that it was lavishly detailed. It is tempting to believe that Gilbert drew inspiration for these garden buildings from the splendid little banqueting houses at Campden House in Chipping Campden, a Jacobean mansion built for Sir Baptist Hicks not far from Hidcote.[39] Other improvements at Hidcote of this period include the purchase of elm trees, referred to in a letter to George Harris of 26 June 1707, and new outbuildings. On 2 August 1712, the Countess Dowager wrote to her friend, Agnes Keyte: 'I hear Lord Coventry is building a barn at Hittcourt and stable where servants rooms are to be over them.'[40]

31   Gilbert, 4th Earl of Coventry by Michael Dahl.

With the death of his nephew in 1712, Gilbert became 4th Earl of Coventry, and he became increasingly irritated and suspicious by his sister-in-law's failure to consult him about the debts and legal complications that followed the death of his brother and nephew. On 17 November 1711, he wrote to her in Chelsea: 'I am injured & kept in ye Darke for want of those writings & surveys belonging to ye estates in my present possession …'. A series of letters from the steward, John Turner, to the Countess Dowager, that date from March 1710 to September 1715, reveal that the dispute between herself and the 4th Earl persisted for several years.[41] Fortunately for the Countess Dowager, Gilbert was easily distracted. On 12 August 1712, she informed Agnes Keyte: 'I finde by my brother that Lord Coventry is going in to ye west to view ye estate of Mr Carew, and his daughter goes to Mr Savages to stay till he returns'.[42] Gilbert's daughter, Anne, had been sent to stay with the Savages at Elmley Castle, while he went to Cornwall to pay a visit on Sir William Carew (1689-1744), 5th Baronet of Antony and a distant relative of his mother, Winifred Edgcumbe. The Carews were an ancient and distinguished family, who had settled at Antony in the 15th century.[43] The 4th Earl and his daughter knew Sir William well from their frequent visits to Mount Edgcumbe, and it appears that Sir William had begun to view Anne in a fresh light now that her father was 4th Earl of Coventry. His offer of marriage probably delighted Gilbert, as it strengthened the bond between the Coventrys and his mother's Cornish connections. The trip also had an additional bonus. The Countess Dowager, always to be relied upon for gossip, informed the Duke of Beaufort in a letter of 7 October 1712 that 'Lord Coventry has met with a West Countrye widow, and will marry himself before his daughter …'.[44] Nothing came of this brief affair, but the visit to Antony was, otherwise, a complete success. An annual jointure of £500 was agreed, and the marriage took place at Croome on 4 January 1714, Sir William having arrived in Worcestershire the previous Christmas Eve.[45] It was a small and private wedding, but Lady Anne was suitably attired for the occasion. The bills for her wedding trousseau amounted to around £200 and included yards of silk, lace, muslin, cambric, silver and gold brocade and ribbons, numerous pairs of stockings, gloves, and a generous supply of whalebone to give shape to the entire ensemble.[46] Gilbert was certainly intent upon impressing his in-laws, and it seems the feeling was mutual.

Sir William had been making tentative efforts to improve the old house and grounds at Antony in the years prior to his marriage, but his marriage galvanised him into action. There was probably another reason too. As a Tory and active supporter of the Jacobite cause, the Hanoverian succession offered him little chance of political preferment and this must have been a further incentive to concentrate his attentions on his home improvements. In 1718, John Moyle, the Exeter master-builder, was contracted to build the shell of the new house and the work was completed in 1724.[47] Its elegant, if old-fashioned, design of two storeys and nine bays, with a broad string course and hipped roof, derives much of its beauty from its silver-grey local stone which glows creamy-white in the Cornish light. It is interesting that the double-pile plan of the house, with its central corridor, is very similar to the plan of Croome House as built by the 2nd Baron. Possibly it was a

32 Sir William Carew, 5th Bt, MP, by Michael Dahl.

33 Lady Anne Carew by Michael Dahl.

34 Antony House in Cornwall.

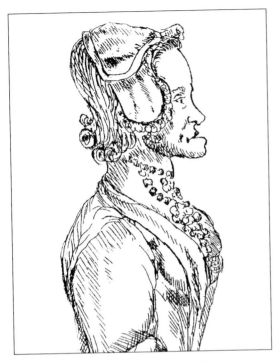

35 Caricature of Lady Anne Carew.

nostalgic reference by a Jacobite to the great houses built during the heyday of the Stuarts, or perhaps Lady Anne expressed a wish to be reminded of her family's Worcestershire home? Sir William later added a forecourt and pavilions onto the south front to embrace the parkland on that side of the house, while, to the north, magnificent views lead the eye across the wooded landscape towards the Tamar estuary. Lady Anne could not fail to love the place, and she filled it with paintings and furniture from Croome to make her feel at home. In 1714, the 4th Earl commissioned the artist Michael Dahl (1659?-1743), to paint a portrait of himself, Sir William and Lady Anne Carew. These splendid paintings still remain at Antony, and show Gilbert posing proudly in his long wig and robes, evidently delighted with the improvement in his fortune. Sir William appears haughty and uneasy as any suspected Jacobite might in 1714. Anne's portrait is painted with great sensitivity and conveys her youthful modesty. It contrasts well with a cruel caricature of her among the Antony archive, which shows her as a gruesome hag, the equine nostrils inherited from her mother are coarsely emphasised and the prominent chin of the Coventry family stretched to its limits. Could her father have sketched this in one of his irascible moods? Undoubtedly, the 4th Earl disapproved of her close relationship with her aunt, the Countess Dowager. Lady Anne Carew corresponded with her regularly and often went to stay with her in Snitterfield and Chelsea.[48] Her aunt sent to her a constant stream of medical advice in return for shells from the Cornish beaches, and they swapped recipes and sometimes insects for their respective collections. Lady Anne Carew's recipe collection was designed both to amuse and disgust the hapless diner.[49] It included two unappetisingly-entitled desserts, 'White Leech Cream' and 'Hedghog [*sic*] Cream', harmless concoctions of cream, almonds and orange flower water intended to liven up the dreariest of parties. In one letter, her aunt enquires after the health of Lady Anne's 'two young people'. This is strange as she and Sir William had only one son, Coventry Carew (*c*.1716-48), who became the 6th Baronet on the death of his father in 1744. In 1738, he married Mary Bampfylde, (d. before 1762), a Devonshire girl and the daughter of an MP with the extraordinary name of Sir Coplestone Warwick Bampfylde Bt. Ten years later, Sir Coventry Carew died without issue and the baronetcy became temporarily extinct, but it was revived in 1772 when, according to his will, the estate passed to Reginald Pole (1753-1835), great-great-grandson through the female line of the 3rd Baronet, Sir John Carew.

With his daughter successfully married, the 4th Earl concentrated his efforts on securing an heir and, two years after his daughter moved to Cornwall, he remarried. His new wife was 24 and there seemed a good chance that she would produce a son reasonably promptly. Confusingly, she was also called Anne (1691-1788), and was the daughter of Sir Streynsham Masters of Codnor Castle in Derbyshire. Masters had recently acquired an estate at Strensham in Worcestershire, just south of Croome, which had formerly belonged to his mother's family. Presumably this is how his daughter had met the 4th Earl and she was unlikely to decline his offer of marriage. Another lavish wedding was arranged on 27 June 1715, this time not at Croome but at the Guildhall Chapel, London, instead.

By early 1716, Gilbert's hopes of an heir looked promising when his new wife embarked upon her first confinement. Among the Croome archive is the transcript of two fascinating letters sent to Lady Coventry from her father during this time.[50] The source of these letters is more curious still. The transcript was sent to the 9th Earl of Coventry in 1888 by a Mr. R. Duke, who lived at Birlingham Rectory, nearby in Pershore, Worcestershire. He claimed that the letters had been published by the Hakluyt Society as part of the Diary of Sir William Hedges, Agent of the East India Company in Bengal from 1681-87. This is quite possible, as Masters had gone to India when he was 15 to work for the East India Company. There he must have met Hedges, and on his return from India 12 years later he was knighted on 14 December 1698. The first of his letters to his daughter was written from his house in Red Lion Square, London, on 4 February 1716 and he informs her that:

> yesterday I delivered to your grandmother Legh an Eagle Stone in an Indian silk bag and paper,—upon it No.21,—and in it a paper wrote upon 'Eagle Stone, good to prevent miscarriages of women with child, to be worn about the Neck, & left off 2 or 3 weeks before the reckoning be out'. I had another of them which was smooth, having been polished, which I believe was that which you write to your grandmother, [which] was lent to Sir Francis Leicester's Lady—I desire you will, if you can, tell me where it is, that I may have it again, and this also I wish to have returned to me, when you have made use of it for this occasion, which I pray God send you happily over …

This was followed by a letter on 25 February 1716, in which Masters told his daughter: '… according to Lady Dawes, during labour one of the stones should be tied to the thigh to cause an easy delivery'. He added:

> the belief in the virtue of Eagle Stones is very ancient—and is alluded to by Pliny and other old writers—The Stones (of a round or oval form) were so called from an idea that the eagle carried them to her nest to facilitate the laying of her eggs …

Lady Coventry had a safe delivery, but the stones were unable to produce a male heir. It seems unlikely that this daughter of Gilbert's second marriage survived infancy, as no reference to her exists within the family archive and histories.

While Lady Coventry was preparing for the birth of her first child, her husband was making plans to alter and redecorate Croome, in hopeful anticipation of the imminent arrival of an heir. His wife had brought a welcome £10,000 with her as part of her marriage settlement, and Gilbert would have had few doubts about how to spend the money. On 14 April, he signed an agreement with George Chine of Warwick to 'Wainscot the Red Room' with 'very good well-seasoned clean white English oak at 4/6 per yard', to lay new oak floor boards, and to install sash windows in 'as many windows as his Lordship will be pleased to have'.[51] Whether these were new or replacement sashes is hard to tell, but sashes are shown in Henry Beighton's bird's-eye view of Croome of 1714. By July, the redecoration was well under way, and Gilbert received a bill for £269 18s. 3d. from Mr. Wood the Upholsterer to refurnish the Damask Room, plus an additional £48 15s. for a piece of tapestry to hang in the room. This must refer to the Yellow Damask Room mentioned in the 1719 Inventory, which also lists the contents of the New Parlour, the Chince Room and new apartments upstairs.[52] Croome House had been refurnished during his brother's lifetime and, by the time of the 4th Earl's death, the house boasted some of the most sumptuous interiors in the county. The Great Parlour was resplendent with gilt leather hangings, while the Best Parlour was crammed full with three large marble tables, two Japan tea tables, two tapestries, four Indian hand screens, two oval tables and 'an additional square table'. Each of the 19 main bedrooms was filled with similarly large quantities of furniture, hangings, Turkey carpets, pictures and plate; the plate alone was valued at £944 11s. 00d.

Meanwhile, the 4th Earl's plans for the gardens and grounds were nearing completion, which was commemorated by Beighton's bird's-eye view of the house of 1714. Interestingly, the new formal south garden appears to have mirrored the geometric

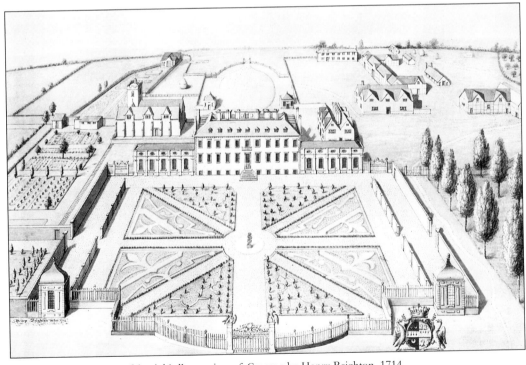

36   A bird's-eye view of Croome by Henry Beighton, 1714.

layout of the formal garden recently completed at Hampton Court Palace.[53] As Beighton was renowned as much for the accuracy as the elegance of his drawings, it seems probable that his drawing of Croome is largely correct. However, the omission of the Jacobean gatehouse from his drawing (evident in the 1750 view) and the inclusion of the statue and gates, which were completed after 1714, would suggest that some artistic licence was employed. Beighton's drawing reveals the new wings attached to the southern corners of the house with pleasing precision, each of five bays articulated by Ionic pilasters and with arched windows. Probably completed during the ownership of the 2nd Earl, little attempt was made to relate them to the original building. Even the levels are different, and steps must have led from them up into the ground floor of the main house. Although unity of composition was evidently not the primary object, the wings succeed in their aim of increasing the apparent size of the building and relating it to the new formal garden with its quartered parterre, grass walks and pavilions. Two further pavilions and a circular lawn are shown on the north side of the house, with other formal and kitchen gardens to east and west.

Work must have begun on the south garden in 1712, when a large supply of plants was delivered to Croome from George Adams, a nurseryman of Stokes Croft, Bristol. This included quantities of carnations, pyramid yews that were five and three quarter feet high, and globe hollies with full heads and three feet stems. In a letter associated with this delivery, Adams boasted: 'I am positive I can furnish my Lord with all sorts of plants boath Domestick and Exotick upon better termes and better success than any other man in England …'.[54] Adams also enquired whether Lord Coventry had 'resolved on a designe' and added that he would be willing to assist in its execution, 'having had great and Long Experience, and have saved some hundreds of pounds in carrying on large designes'. The appointment of a new gardener in 1713, a Mr. Cooper, would also suggest that most of the major garden alterations were instigated by the 4th Earl rather than his brother. It is a little curious that the only other documents to survive that relate specifically to the details in Beighton's drawing occur among a series of letters of 1716-17, which chiefly concern work at Hidcote. Among them is a description of screens with iron gates, fifteen feet high with a coat of arms, and with piers surmounted by eagle finials: 'These eagles I presume ought to be in proportion with ye pillars 2 foot and 10 inches high, the Pedistoll they are to stand upon being 2 foot 5 inches square, so [that] they may be sent without any Pedistoll if carefully packed up … .[55] These gates could have been intended for Hidcote, but they sound too similar to those in Beighton's drawing of Croome for coincidence. It appears that an agreement to make these gates and gate piers was drawn up with Benjamin Taylor of Warwick in 1716. There is also a reference to a lead statue of Hercules by the sculptor, John Van Nost (c.1686-1729), which was bought in May 1715 for 50 guineas. This is referred to in the Croome Inventory of 1719 as being 'Gilt with Gold', and is almost certainly that shown at the centre of the garden in Beighton's view.[56] By 1719, the design of Gilbert's new garden was neither rare nor novel, but it would have been among the best of its type in the county, and possibly further afield.

Gilbert's love of hunting also brought about significant changes to the parkland at Croome. From Michaelmas 1712, he began to rent land from Croome rectory, and this was enclosed within the 'home park' immediately south of the house beyond the new formal garden; this is the first specific reference to the Home Park.[57] Further additions occurred in 1714, when Richard Goodall, a local landowner, died and Gilbert acquired his estate to the north-west of the park, all or part of which may have been rented to Samuel Gold.[58] These additions made up for the loss of the Red Deer Park in 1717, much of which had to be ploughed and kept in tillage in order to clear it 'of thorns and hillocks it now abounds in'.[59] The 4th Earl owed these significant improvements to the careful management of his Park Keeper, William Thorneloe. He had renewed his contract in 1713, but had reduced his salary from £40 p.a. to £30 p.a. in return for certain privileges. These included permission to keep his two horses and other animals in the Fallow Deer Park, and a supply of coal to ensure that he would not cut timber for fuel from the parks without permission.

The 4th Earl made various plans to ensure that his animals' accommodation was refurbished along with his own. The first design for a new stable appears in the Accounts for 1714, and, in 1716, a second design was submitted by Francis Smith of Warwick, although no reference to their construction appears in the accounts. A grand new dog kennel was built north-east of the house and, according to the 1719 Inventory, it was a substantial and well-equipped building. It included a 'Copper' (for heating water), feeding troughs, two meal tubs, a chopping block and 52 iron hooks for hanging flesh. Other payments included those for 'a draught of Park House' to a Mr. Chinn, muscovy ducks, and wild sheep, a vine tree 'of an extraordinary kind' and orange and myrtle trees for the greenhouse. Yew trees were taken up from Hidcote and replanted at Croome, and a green or alley may have been laid out or re-laid, as the 1719 inventory refers to a Bowling Green House.[60]

The 4th Earl's recurrent attacks of gout grew increasingly severe after his second marriage. Visits to Bath on the advice of his physician had little effect and, on 27 October 1719, he died at Croome aged 51, following a particularly severe attack of gout in his stomach. With his death the Barony of Coventry became extinct, and the greater part of the estates devolved upon William Coventry, the lineal descendant of Walter Coventry, brother to the 1st Lord Coventry, according to the limitation of the patent. Aware of the severity of his condition, the 4th Earl had made his will a short time before his death. He left his wife £3,000, all the silver plate at Croome, jewels and pearls of unspecified worth, and all the furniture, pictures and glass bought since their marriage, together with the furniture from Hidcote and everything she brought with her on their marriage.

Lady Anne Carew was appointed sole executrix of her father's will, and she received many paintings, books and some items of furniture from Croome that predated her father's second marriage, among them the portraits by Dahl referred to earlier.[61] She also took to Antony all the family papers that she could find. Her father had left unpaid debts of £2,172 3s. 7d., including such tiresome details as an unpaid bill for eight pairs of satin and lace shoes bought by the 4th Earl's widow in London the previous year.[62] She and her husband managed to pay off most of the debts by selling some of the contents of Croome House to the 5th Earl for £1,451 17s.[63] Sir William Carew and the 5th Earl of Coventry continued to argue about the division of the estate until 1734, although this became a mere side issue compared with the unseemly dispute with the 4th Earl's widow.

The young new Countess Dowager was far from content with her seemingly generous inheritance, and the lawsuit she brought against the 5th Earl was not resolved till 1724.[64] Apparently, in return for the £10,000 and innumerable goods she had brought with her on her marriage, she was to receive a jointure on the 4th Earl's death of £500 per annum. An argument had arisen over the manner in which the settlement was to be drawn, and the 4th Earl's steward, John Turner, was given the task of resolving it. Unfortunately, Turner died and his replacement was unaware of the settlement until a week before the 4th Earl died. Before he could make the necessary arrangements, he was sent on a forty-mile trip and he took with him the key to his office where the settlement was locked up. By the time he returned, the 4th Earl was dead. This implausible story appears to have convinced the jury, if not the family. The whole affair had prompted a heated correspondence between Agnes Keyte and the elder Countess Dowager in Snitterfield. In a letter of 10 February 1720, Agnes, weak from her diet of asses' milk, confided to her friend that the 4th Earl's widow was also after a £1,200 bond that she had been given by the 4th Earl for a diamond necklace. As if to give weight to her argument she added with all the force of a seasoned gossip: 'I hope yr Laspp will be interly easy for ye future who have been a persicuted Lady for some years: & marked more from ye family you came in to then was in their power to do.'[65]

Having secured a substantial portion of the 4th Earl's wealth, his young widow married Edward Pytts, a Tory MP, from Kyre in north Worcestershire in 1725, and they had four daughters, only one of whom survived. At this point she could be dismissed from the story were it not for a series of letters among the Hardwicke Papers in the British Library. These were written between 1718 and 1737 to Sir Hans Sloane (1660-1753), the physician and avid collector of coins, medals, books, and botanical specimens, which became the basis of the British Museum's collection. He may have advised her on her own collections, including her Eagle Stones, and a letter thanking him for a present of a book would imply that it was a close as well as a long-standing friendship.[66]

After Pytts's death in 1753, she went to live at Holt Castle, high on the western bank of the River Severn, a former home of the Bromley family who were related to the Pytts family by marriage. Nash, the county historian, recorded that 'This Lady I saw enjoying perfect memory & good health, approaching fast to ninety years in the year 1779.'[67] She died at Holt on 21 March 1788, aged an astonishing 96, and is buried in the churchyard opposite the castle. Her Eagle Stones have not been traced, and it is interesting to speculate whether they might be credited with her longevity.

VII

The Grave Young Lord and his Grand Design

William, 5th Earl of Coventry (1678-1751)

The major rift in the direct line of succession was well-timed, as it enabled the family to confront the fresh challenges of the Hanoverian age reinvigorated. For too long it had rested complacently upon the power base it had established under the Stuarts, and it was appropriate that the line should now revert to the descendents of Sir Thomas Coventry's youngest son, to acquire new direction and purpose. He had inherited the largest estate in Worcestershire, and as cultural life began to drift away from the capital under the later Georgian regime, Croome established an increasingly dominant role as a symbol of achievement, a source of wealth and power and a statement of cultural erudition and agricultural improvement. Like many aristocratic families, the Coventrys were eager to reap the benefits of the industrial and agrarian revolutions, but they remained essentially conservative in outlook and always defiantly independent in practice. Although they toyed with politics with varying degrees of commitment, from this time onwards it was as patrons and benefactors that they asserted the greatest influence both on their estates and further afield.

Walter Coventry's descendents adapted to their new role with admirable coolness and commonsense to effect a seamless transition; this was all the more commendable as it was not anticipated. Gilbert may have thought it unlikely that he would inherit the earldom, but he probably entertained the idea. The possibility may never have occurred to William. As Nash, the county historian, pointed out: 'from his birth … near forty persons died, any one of whom would have inherited before him'.[1] Actually 38 persons died, but it was still an improbable number. Forty years old, with a flourishing parliamentary career, he promised to be equal to the task. William proved a successful administrator, rather than a visionary, but he brought three sons to Croome, three potential heirs, all of whom showed promise, and one of whom was destined to transform the place into one of the most celebrated country seats of its day.

William Coventry was born in 1678. He was the second son of Walter Coventry of St Peter-le-Poor in London, a merchant and either son or grandson, the dates remain unconfirmed, of Walter Coventry, youngest brother of Lord Keeper Coventry. The family were wealthy and owned land in Oxfordshire and Lincolnshire, which they may have inherited through Sir Thomas Coventry. Walter was married to Anne, daughter of Humphrey Holcombe, also a London merchant, and they had eight children, four sons and four daughters.[2] (Three daughters died unmarried, but the eldest daughter, Ann, married Sir Dervey Bulkeley from Burgate, near Southampton, who became an uncle of some significance. The eldest son Walter died an infant on 5 April 1677, so that William became the heir. The third son, Thomas (d.1751), married three times. His first wife, Mary, was the daughter of John Green of Hambledon in Buckinghamshire, and they had five children. Thomas (d.1797), the second son, married Mary Savage of Elmley Castle, Worcestershire, a distant relation through marriage, and was a successful lawyer. He followed his uncle's lead as MP for Bridport in Dorset and was later appointed a Director of the infamous South Sea Company. The eldest daughter, Mary, married twice and her second husband, Philip Bearcroft, was a Doctor of Divinity and Master of Charterhouse. By his second wife, Gratia Maria Brown, Thomas, had another five children, of whom the eldest was the Rev. Francis Coventry, a poet and author, who lived in Cambridgeshire. His uncle, the 5th Earl, appointed him to the perpetual curacy of Edgware, and he died at Whitchurch of smallpox in 1754.[3] William's youngest brother, Henry, inherited much of the Lincolnshire estate. He lived at Bery Stead house in Lincolnshire and married an Oxfordshire woman, Anne Coles. He was declared a lunatic in 1741 and died c.1750. His son, also called Henry, was a flamboyant intellectual who merged comfortably into Horace Walpole's circle. He became a writer and fellow of Magdalene College, Cambridge, where he was renowned for his prominent Roman nose and his striking outfits, which were 'remarkably gay, with much gold lace'.[4] His most famous work, *Philemon to Hydaspes*, was republished by his cousin, the Rev. Francis Coventry, in 1753. After his death, on 29 December 1752, part of his estate was left to the 6th Earl, his cousin and heir, who paid off the considerable debts that he had accumulated.[5]).

Little is known of the 5th Earl's career before 1717. He evidently took up politics as a young man for he was MP for Bridport in Dorset in the last three last parliaments of Queen Anne and in the first parliament of George I. Although a Whig in the Commons, once he inherited the earldom he consistently opposed Walpole and voted with the Tories. Yet despite his support of the Tories, he maintained Hanoverian favour and on 15 April 1717 he became Joint Clerk Comptroller of the Board of the Green Cloth, and he attended George I to Hanover in 1718. This appointment brought him an additional income of four or five hundred pounds a year, and an invaluable opportunity for further advancemernt, so that on 22 March 1719 he became a member of the Privy Council. Opportunities of a more personal nature followed swiftly behind. Later that year he married Elizabeth, the dark-haired and graceful daughter of John Allen of Westminster, and they moved into his house in East Street, near Red Lion Square in Holborn. Within a few months, any thoughts of further promotion were abandoned, when news reached him in July of the death of his distant cousin Gilbert.

As 5th Earl of Coventry, new responsibilities were immediately thrust upon him. In 1720 he was appointed Lord Lieutenant of Worcestershire and Custos Rotulorum, but less pleasant was the task of unravelling the Coventry family's legal and financial affairs and dealing with various obstreporous Countess Dowagers. The 5th Earl's wealth immediately cushioned the estate from impending disaster and through a combination of good luck and prudent administration the financial pressures and legal complications eased considerably after 1724. The dispute over the jointure of the 4th Earl's young widow was resolved, but the longevity of the other two surviving Countess Dowagers remained a drain on family resources until the second half of the century.

From the start, the 5th Earl embarked upon a sequence of modest improvements to his new estate. Much of the land at Croome had been deemed 'unfitt' in the 1719 Inventory, and extensive work was required to improve productivity. In 1720, he moved a barn and built a new house for a tenant farmer in the Red Deer Park, and he planted trees which his gardener, a Mr. Davison, had bought in Bristol.[6] Within a few years, the 5th Earl had proved himself a competent landlord, and the annual rental income rose from £6,355 9s. 0d. in 1720-1 to £7,733 7s. 7 ½d. in 1722-3 and just over £10,554 in 1736-7, no small achievement, and the additional income allowed for more ambitious improvements to be put into operation. In 1726 a payment was made to a Mr. Colles, who held land at Cubsmoor, for 'Damage done him by rutting trees to make ye Vista through his grounds'. This indicated that he had embarked upon a more ambitious approach to his surroundings, and almost certainly relates to new avenues of trees, which ran south of the house and westwards towards Cubsmoor, shown in John Doherty's survey of Croome of c.1751. There was also important capital expenditure on new and bigger farm buildings. For example,

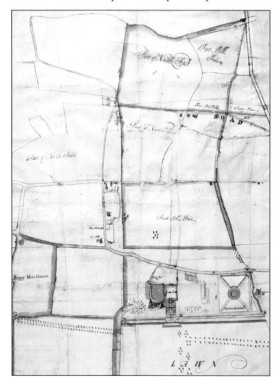

37   Map of Croome by John Doherty, c.1751.

the accounts record a purchase of 83,000 bricks in 1723-4, and 45,513 bricks in 1727-8. A new barn was built at High House in Severn Stoke and repairs to the Pigeon House, seen in the various bird's-eye views of Croome, were undertaken in 1733. From the mid-1730s, the initial agricultural improvements were evidently well in hand and attention became focused upon establishing a new park around the house, which for the first time lay at the centre of the estate. It was at this point that a group portrait was painted of the family by Charles Phillipps (colour plate X). They pose within a wooded corner of the park, and the naïve style, rich colours and informal composition anticipates the work of Gainsborough. The charming setting conveys not a glimmer of the changes that were to transform the scene in the following decades. The reorganisation of the pattern of land tenure was fundamental to these later changes. In 1738, Lord Coventry exchanged lands in 'Crome Common Field' for further land at Cubsmoor with John Thorneloe, son of the 4th Earl's park keeper. This was an early indication that he had plans to extend his parkland westwards towards Severn Stoke.[7] Another important change occurred between 1741-4, when the Red Deer Park was refenced with palings. This is likely to relate to the Agreement of 1717 to plough up the Red Deer Park, then in poor condition, and the decision to partition it into fields. Clearly, Croome was beginning to conform with the growing popularity for enclosure in the cause of greater efficiency and profit.[8] Drainage and planting continued elsewhere, and after 1744 increased dramatically owing to a sudden and tragic change in circumstances from which the 5th Earl never fully recovered.

His three sons had been born in quick succession: they were Thomas Henry, Viscount Deerhurst (1721-44; colour plate VIII); George William (1722-1809), who became 6th Earl of Coventry; and John Bulkeley (c.1723-1801). John was named after his uncle, Sir Dervey Bulkeley, who stipulated in his will that if John took his name he would inherit the Bulkeley estates in Somerset and elsewhere. Later John, also known as Buntling or 'Bunnie' in family correspondence, changed his name to John Bulkeley Coventry-Bulkeley. This rather overstated his claim and may imply that his affections and loyalties inclined towards his uncle's side of the family.[9] It cannot have helped that Thomas Henry and George William appear to have shared a particularly close relationship.

It is probable that the family still spent much of their time in London where the 5th Earl had a long-established network of friends and contacts and the Countess was born and bred. The house near Red Lion Square was exchanged for a more prestigious residence in Grosvenor Square, and the family also retained homes in St James's Square as well as the less fashionable Margaret Street, north of Oxford Street, which may have been let during this period. In 1725, Lord and Lady Coventry took the precaution of inoculating the two elder boys against distemper, showing admirable faith in current medical advances, and it appears that the boys suffered no ill effects. The children were sent to Winchester School and from there Thomas and George moved on to University College, Oxford, apparently inseparable. They revelled in the heady atmosphere, studied diligently and established close and lasting friendships. New ideas were absorbed with insatiable enthusiasm, which sought expression in reams of indifferent adolescent poetry. A bundle of well-preserved and amusing correspondence from this period survives among the family archive, most of it from Deerhurst to his friend Thomas Walter Yonge, who had been at Winchester with him and had moved on to Merton College.[10] The letters are precocious and full of cheerful gossip; for example, when Younge was in Paris staying with Lord Waldegrave in 1739, Deerhurst wrote to him on 13 May to tell him about his recent trip to Amersham to stay with a mutual friend. There he had been particularly impressed by the new library:

> The Wainscot is mahogany and all the other Furniture answerable to the grandeur of it. In short, nothing is wanted but a curious collection of Books; this perhaps you will say is a great deal; but when a man has a taste to make a proper choice and Money enough to answer the demands, that design may be soon put into execution.

This remark proved prophetic in relation to his brother's work at Croome. It may also imply that he had plans for Croome too.

On 23 November 1738, the Countess of Coventry died of dropsy in Grosvenor Square. The shock of her death may have brought the two brothers even closer together, and their studies provided a welcome distraction. The following year, on 20 November 1739, both were awarded their MA degrees. George William was still only seventeen. After Oxford, the two brothers planned a political career, and in 1741 the opportunity arose for Thomas to stand as Tory candidate for Worcestershire, but he was defeated at the election. The 5th Earl regarded this as a personal slight, and when the Prince of Wales made kind enquiries about the result he warned him: 'Sir ... the Tories have betrayed me, as they will you, the first time you have occasion for them.'[11] No doubt by some careful manoeuvring, Lord Deerhurst was elected MP for his father's former seat at Bridport in April the following year, and by 1743 he had been appointed High Steward and also Freeman of Tewkesbury. This was some compensation for the premature death of the Countess, but in 1744 a further and harsher blow was struck. Lord Deerhurst died suddenly and unexpectedly on 20 May from an unspecified illness; he was only twenty-three. The family was devastated. Innumerable tributes to this promising young man from friends such as Sir Edward Turner, and in the newspapers, indicate that he had made a considerable impression during his brief adult life. The *London Evening Post* was particlarly generous with its praise:

> His temper was humane, gentle and good beyond Description; rather graver than is usual at his Age, yet he was never seen but cheerful, and gay as good Sense and good manners would admit of. He had not the least Turn for Satire in himself, nor was he ever entertain'd with it in other People, and certainly he would not have said a thing he thought could have given any one Pain to have been esteem'd as great a Wit as Mr Pope. He had a pleasing Diffidence in his Nature ... And he was never known to contradict but when truth and Virtue demanded it of him ... He did not make a Business of Diversions, as too many do, but partook of those which were innocent and rational with the same Judgement and Moderation, as govern's every other Action of his Life ...[12]

It is interesting that this tribute could have been applied equally well to George William, whose personality and temperament so closely resembled that of his brother. Two days after his brother's death, George William expressed his grief in a letter to one of his closest friends from Oxford, the dilettante-architect, Sanderson Miller:

> My dear Miller, I am so shocked that I know not what I say or do. If I could be severd into two and one part left alive and the other part taken away, the separation could not be greater. He was indeed the better half and therefore God thought fit the worthiest should be removed ...[13]

Similar feelings of inferiority were conveyed in a letter to Miller of 10 June: 'Never can I sign the name without a fresh torrent of grief for the late possessor of it and a bitter remorse that the present one falls so short of his perfections.' This is important as it may help to explain his extraordinary commitment to Croome, a commitment that was motivated in part by an overwhelming sense of duty, a passionate desire to fulfil the expectations of his brother, and compensate for his own sense of unworthiness and inadequacy. It would appear also that his notorious arrogance was but a mask for his own insecurities, although later in life this made him intolerant of his own son's failings.

The 5th Earl was 66 years old when his eldest son died and he never fully recovered. In his letters a year later, he refers to the date of Thomas's death as 'my Black day' and 'that unhappy day, which is always working in my mind'. From this time onwards George William, now Viscount Deerhurst, became actively involved with the estate. After 1748 when the estate was settled on him, the early tentative but effective improvements instigated by his father snowballed into a far more ambitious scheme that was his lifelong obsession.

One other important incident marked this period, which had repercussions on the future career of George William. Since the Jacobite uprisings in 1708, 1715 and 1719, it had become common to consider Tory and Jacobite synonymous. The Coventry family, like many important Worcestershire families, may have nurtured sympathies for the Jacobite cause. The 4th Earl's son-in-law, Sir William Carew, was known to be an ardent Jacobite and had been imprisoned for his beliefs shortly after his marriage, and in 1729 the Countess of Coventry was even obliged to sign an oath of allegiance to the Crown at the Quarter Sessions at Croome.[14] Such sympathies, however, were abandoned by the 1740s, as French support for Bonnie Prince Charlie, 'the Young Pretender', and the War of the Austrian Succession gave rise to serious alarm about an imminent French invasion. George William had every reason for concern. On 22 February 1744, he sent Sanderson Miller a 'dark and suspicious letter' that he had received, which he wished him to deliver to the Secretary of State on his behalf. He told him that in this letter there was a reference to the 'letting of King's blood which has strongly the air of Treason, and may possibly be stretched into a *Hanging Matter* ...', adding 'As to the Spaniards landing at Southampton I don't think it at all impossible.'[15] The letter had apparently proposed that the French and Spanish were to land in Northampton—an unlikely geographical occurrence—which Coventry rightly assumed to mean Southampton. Why the letter was sent to George William remains unclear, but it evidently upset him. On 28 April 1744, he wrote anxiously to Miller about the current proposals in parliament to make any correspondence with the 'Sons of the Pretender' an act of high treason, and noted that even Lord Carteret believed an invasion was possible. Some months later he informed Miller that he was reading Mezeray's *History of France* on the grounds that 'one should know something of the annals of a country that bids so fair to be our mistress and ... I sincerely think the prospect not very distant ...'. He almost certainly mentioned his fears to his father, as Lord Lieutenant of the county. The 5th Earl's correspondence with Richard Coote, Earl of Bellamont, in connection with the '45 rebellion survives within the family archive.[16] Coote was staying at his wife's family home at Birtsmorton Court in south Worcestershire at the time. The letters are frustratingly illegible, but it appears that, once the Young Pretender reached Edinburgh, Lord Coventry arranged a meeting with the various Justices of the Peace and Deputy Lieutenants of the County at Moore's Coffee House in Worcester on 17 September 1745 in order to raise a County regiment. These plans had been abandoned by the end of October, when Lord Coventry informed the King and his ministers:

> It is the unanimous opinion of the gentlemen in Town that the state of affairs is so altered at Worcester by the arrival of so many troops from abroad [from Flanders] ... that it is unnecessary to lay that contribution upon the County which they have so loyally and so cheerfully laid upon themselves ...

This seems irresponsible, almost suspiciously so, but he was spared any embarrassment when the Jacobite rebellion was brought to a conclusion by the defeat at Culloden Moor in April 1746. The whole affair had shaken George William's youthful confidence, and it undoubtedly shaped his attitude to foreign policy later in life.

The 5th Earl died on 18 March 1751. He left money to every member of his staff, but the most interesting bequest in his will is the annuity of £200 from the rent of the the house in Grosvenor Square which he left to Diana Bertie (1709-54). She is referred to in his will as the daughter of Elizabeth Allen, possibly born illegitimately prior to her marriage to the 5th Earl or perhaps a daughter from a previous marriage. No reference to Miss Bertie appears within the family archive until around 1748, when she was invited to join the Coventry household, possibly as a companion to the grief-stricken earl, and she is referred to with considerable affection in much personal correspondence from this time. It seems probable that she was the subject of an enigmatic portrait of a lady painted for the 5th Earl by Allan Ramsay in 1749. No great beauty, the sitter appears to be in early middle age and clasps a cameo of an unidentified man. The resemblance to her half-brother John Bulkeley, also painted by Ramsay, is particularly striking. In 1752, Diana Bertie married George 'Gilly' James Williams (1719-1805), ten years younger than herself, a successful politician, wit and great friend of Horace Walpole.[17] It was an unlikely match, and the marriage was cut short by Diana's death in 1754. Significantly, she was buried at Croome. Not strictly a Coventry by birth or marriage, this would confirm that she was held in very high regard by the family.

John Bulkeley was left the more isolated portions of the Coventry estate, including Bampton and other property in Oxfordshire, and Wiveliscombe and Fitzhead in Somerset to add to the Bulkeley estates.[18] As for George William, the seeds of his grand design which had been nurturing long in his youthful imagination, plans which may have originated and were undoubtedly discussed with his late brother, could now develop unchecked. Croome was his own. Now he was free to sweep away the piecemeal porches, parterres and pavilions of his predecessors to make a serene and sylvan parkland, among the most admired of its time.

George William, 6th Earl of Coventry (1722-1809)—The Grave Young Lord

As the achievements of the Lord Keeper and his children began to pass into distant memory, the aspirations and abilities of George William, 6th Earl of Coventry, gathered momentum. Horace Walpole summoned sufficient generosity to describe this extraordinary young man as a 'grave young Lord of the remains of the Patriot Breed'.[19]

38 Diana Bertie by Allan Ramsay, 1749.

39 John Bulkeley Coventry by Allan Ramsay, *c.*1740.

He was born on 26 April 1722. He and his elder brother, Thomas Henry, were very much alike, studious, even-tempered, polite, but Thomas was the more affable and George the more ambitious. After his brother's premature death, George William's intense grief and sense of inadequacy developed into a steely determination to fulfil the expectations of his brother. His ambition was complemented by his innate taste, a connoisseur's enthusiasm for the rare and unusual, and an informed interest in the arts, architecture, landscape, agriculture and gardening. Immensely proud and rather pompous about his excellent taste, he abhorred vulgar extravagance and could change his mind with wilful regularity, revelling in his role as patron. These interests were cultivated alongside his official and social duties in the county and the capital, and demanded admirable energy and commitment. When Allan Ramsay painted his portrait in early middle age, *c.*1765, he was fashionably dressed in scarlet velvet and carefully posed between a classical urn and a pile of leather-bound books. A handsome, erudite and polished figure, he appeared every inch a man with the world at his feet, a goal in sight, and the means and discernment to attain it (colour plate XI).

40   George William Coventry, later 6th Earl of Coventry, by Allan Ramsay, *c*.1740.

After he left Oxford with his MA at 17, George William spent a few years contemplating a career in politics and enjoying London life. The war in Europe prevented travel abroad and he probably spent much of his time in the company of friends and acquaintances such as Sanderson Miller at Radway, Warwickshire, or Richard Bateman of Shobdon, Herefordshire, where architecture and gardening cannot have failed to be a favourite topic of conversation. Thomas's premature death in 1744 suddenly gave shape and form to his ambition. As trees arrived and turf was dug at Croome, he also launched his political career, replacing his late brother as Tory MP for Bridport and, in 1747, he succeeded in winning the Worcestershire seat that his father had formerly sought for Thomas. This was an important coup, which nurtured his interests in county issues and allowed him to spend more time at Croome, which was settled upon him the following year. He was 29 when his father died, and already in control.

The redesign of Croome was the 6th Earl's outstanding achievement, but it should not be allowed to obscure his other interests and successes, for he executed his duties to the county, country and crown with characteristic diligence, while still finding ample opportunity for the pursuit of pleasure. Like his father, he was appointed Lord Lieutenant and Custos Rotulorum of Worcestershire, a position he held for over fifty years till his resignation in 1808, and he was Recorder of Worcester from 1774 till his death in 1809. He excelled in his role as local benefactor. His friend Judge George Perrot, a landed lawyer and a baron of the Exchequer, claimed that the 6th Earl brought millions of pounds into Worcestershire by his exertions in the improvement of public roads and buildings, and by his encouragement of its public institutions. Many of the benefits he brought to the county were related either directly or indirectly to the massive programme of works at Croome. The 6th Earl's interest in county affairs was genuine, most notably his interest in the development and administration of the Worcester Infirmary. In October 1747, when still Lord Deerhurst, he and the Bishop of Worcester had been appointed the first co-presidents of the

Infirmary, and for the next twenty years he chaired the annual meetings without fail. He remained president of the Infirmary until his death in 1809, when he left it a legacy of £200.

Swift to recognise the commercial and economic advantages of contemporary developments in transport, he resolved to adopt these to good effect on his estates and elsewhere in the county. During the latter half of the 18th century, the work of the turnpike trusts and the development of improved, better-sprung coaches had cut the time of jouneys to the capital in half. The administrative and economic benefits were vast. The introduction of the mail coach in 1784 meant that both letters and passengers reached Croome from London in less than two days. Fresh and exotic produce from the hothouses at Croome were a permanent feature of the Coventrys' dining table in London. Improvements to minor roads on the estate were essential to take advantage of these changes. Several turnpike roads passed through the Coventry estates in Worcestershire and elsewhere and there is considerable evidence of sustained investment in road improvement throughout the 6th Earl's lifetime. Lord Coventry also invested in new roads further afield, around Powick and Upton Snodsbury, for example, and he paid various fees and expenses of over £277 towards the passing of an Act of Parliament for the repair of several roads in the Evesham area between 1756-7.

Road improvements were stimulated by the competition from the new canals. The River Severn remained the main highway to the industrial Midlands and the 6th Earl actively supported the current efforts to improve its navigation. In 1771 he laid the first stone of the new bridge across the Severn in Worcester, which was opened to the public 10 years later.[26] Canal links to the Severn were springing up throughout the county and, aware of their implications, Lord Coventry became involved with the construction of the Staffordshire and Worcestershire, the Birmingham and Worcester, and the Droitwich Canal companies.[21]

His interest in the Droitwich Canal probably owed much to the Coventry family's investment in the salt works at Droitwich. The 6th Earl held 2,000 shares in the Droitwich Salene [sic] Bath Company Ltd., which brought in a modest but reliable source of income. The salt springs at Defford were geologically linked to those at Droitwich and he decided to investigate the possibility of opening his own salt works. Analyses of the brine at Defford were carried out from around 1770, but it was found to be so dilute that 19 hundredweight of coal would have been required to produce just 19 bushels of salt. The watercourse from the salt working was deepened in 1783 but with no improvement to the quality of the brine and the project had to be abandoned.[22] Not to be outdone, the 6th Earl turned his attention to coal instead. In 1797 he agreed to lease part of Defford common to a certain Thomas Telford and two other gentlemen from Shrewsbury on the understanding that he received royalties of one shilling on every ton of coal or ironstone extracted. Again nothing came of the scheme, but the mineral resources at Defford were not forgotten entirely, and were reinvestigated by the 9th Earl a century later.

Despite his responsibilities and interests in Worcestershire, the 6th Earl was still obliged to spend a large proportion of his time in London. This was particularly the case between

1752-70 when he served as Lord of the Bedchamber to both George II and his grandson, George III. He admired George II, as he wrote to Miller in 1752:

> Great as the honour is, I should not have accepted it without the best opinion of my Royal Master which I assure you is not lessened by acquaintance. I have not been long enough a Courtier to flatter and yet I declare in Private Life I never saw a greater assemblage of Virtue than in the Person I have the Happiness to serve.

His serious approach to duties and conventional outlook often made him the subject of ridicule. As a pillar of the establishment, he became a prime target for the scathing pen of Horace Walpole, who seized with delight upon news of a cruel trick played on Lord Coventry by a mutual friend George Selwyn.[23] On 18 December 1765, Selwyn sent Lord Coventry a letter on which he forged the signature of the Duke of Grafton, to inform him that George III had no further use of his services. Lord Coventry, to whom the possibility of such a prank was inconceivable, was completely taken in by the letter. Immediately, he wrote to the Duke of Grafton to demand an explanation. The Duke was equally puzzled by Lord Coventry's news and showed the letter to the King, who recognised the hoax at once and was furious at such impertinence. When Lord Coventry discovered that Selwyn was responsible for the forgery he was deeply hurt and angry, and he and Selwyn were not reconciled until the following September. The episode may even have been to Lord Coventry's advantage, as he remained on most cordial terms with the King even after he resigned his post in 1770. The royal family spent an enjoyable day at Croome in 1788, much to the excitement of the locality and the benefit of Lord Coventry's reputation. As Walpole remarked to Selwyn later: 'nothing is so dangerous as joking with a fool ...'[24]

As previously mentioned, unnerved by the threat of invasion as a young man, the 6th Earl maintained a keen interest in foreign affairs. His political sympathies were ambivalent like those of his father and, during the last years of George II's reign, so dominant were the Whigs that it became more a question of which Whig faction he should support rather than which party. Among the archive at Croome are numerous letters from leading contemporary political figures, such as Chatham, Newcastle, Pelham, Sandwich and North. Some are little more than curt instructions or efforts to solicit his support, but a few include more informal discussions of topical events.[25] Three letters, in particular, are of special interest. These were written to the 6th Earl by the Earl of Essex between the 15-17 October 1759 and concern the capture of Quebec by General Wolfe.[26] The capture of Quebec was deemed essential in the bid to take control of the Canadian trade in fur, fish and naval supplies. The daring and resourceful Wolfe, then still only 33, was chosen by Pitt the Elder, later the Earl of Chatham, to carry out the attack. Wolfe resolved to approach the town unobserved by scaling an almost perpendicular cliff face, the Heights of Abraham, to reach the high tableland on which Quebec is situated. In the first letter, the news is brief. Essex informs the 6th Earl that Quebec has been bombarded and the whole town 'almost reduced to ashes', although the French had not surrendered. The second letter is more detailed and contains a transcript of the dispatches of Vice-Admiral Saunders, which describe the events leading up to the assault on the town:

June 26 and 27.	Landed the troops on the Isle of Orliens without any loss.
28.	Seven fireships were sent down the rivers by the enemy but were towed ashore without their doing any harm.
29.	General Monckton took post on Point Levi.
July 8.	Covered the landing made on the North Shore.
17.	Capt. Rous in the Sutherland (of 50) with some Frigates & small Vessels went above Quebec, & General Wolfe reconnoitred these.
July 20.	A fire Raft of 100 Bateaux [?] was sent down the river with as little success as the fireships.
31.	An attack was made upon the Lines of Montmercency which proved ineffectual.
Aug 5.	Twenty flat-bottomed Boats with 1200 Troops supported by some Frigates were sent up river with an intent to destroy the Enemy's Ships consisting of three Frigates.
17.	Transports which was supposed had the provisions they were laden with still on board.
25.	They returned without being able to effect it. They proceeded 10 or 12 leagues up the river, & destroyed a Magazine.
Sept 1st to 6.	General Wolfe quitted Montmercency camp, & measures were taking [*sic*] when the Lieutenant came away to land the troops above the Town of Quebec. Another attempt was also preparing to destroy the Enemies shipping above mentioned. The Admiral takes notice that the town was not habitable from the ravages made by the Shells & Shot that had been thrown into it. But that the French troops were numerous & strongly entrenched.

He adds that General Wolfe, renowned for his bouts of ill-health, had been extremely ill and then refers to other fields of warfare, notably to the movements of the Russian army, and ends with a request to Lord Coventry: 'I hope you will not forget to send me my tulip trees & Newfoundland Spruce etc for I am since I saw your nursery grown Planting mad …'. It would appear that the horticultural delights of Croome had become a source of admiration and inspiration already.

The third letter brings news that the French had surrendered on 18 September, but that General Wolfe had been killed in the attack:

Our troops landed with incredible difficulty two miles above the town, & having scrambled up precipices they found a plain on which they formed, as did the French under the Wall of the town. The Enemy it is said were about 10,000, and we hardly 5,000. They attacked with great impetuosity, but were beaten, & drove into the town.

In 1760 Montreal was also taken and the Canadian trade was securely in the hands of the British.

During the 1760s, colonial affairs continued to dominate political debate and Lord Coventry began to voice his opinions more forcefully. In 1763, Lord Bute had been replaced by George Grenville as Prime Minister, a sound economist, if uncharismatic leader, who turned his attention to the escalating national debt which had almost doubled from £70m to £130m during the Seven Years War. Among the measures introduced by Grenville was a stamp duty imposed on legal transactions in America to contribute towards the cost of colonial defence. This blatant example of the pamphleteers' phrase 'No Taxation without Representation' created such an outcry that in July 1765 Grenville was replaced by the Marquess of Rockingham, who hastily repealed the Act, but the damage had been done. Alternative measures enforced in 1767 in the form of American import duties outraged the colonists still further. Relations with America began their steady drift into anarchy, which culminated with the Boston tea party of 1773 and finally the outbreak of war.

Lord Coventry was among the minority who supported Grenville's policies and the economic argument that Britain had a sovereign right to tax her colonies. By 1770,[6] 'already more than waivering towards the opposition', he resigned his post as Lord of the Bedchamber, an act typical of the integrity of his ancestry and by then rather charmingly old-fashioned.[27] Coventry could now express his views as freely as he wished and, as the American War dragged on, due as much to George III's influence over Lord North as the general incompetence of North's government, he did not wait long to voice his opinions. By 1779 the war had become international, the costs were crippling and France, Spain and the Dutch had command of the sea. This was particularly galling to Lord Coventry, whose patriotism did not blind him to common sense, and in 1778, 1779, 1780 and 1781 he voted against North. In 1782 he gave a powerful speech in the Lords which underlined the folly of continuing the war with America:[28]

> There is not a Country gent., there is not a Manufacturer, there is not a tradesman, there is not a farmer who does not condemn, shall I say, who does not ? every idea of the American war. They speak of it with one Voice as the Consummation of all Folly, Obstinacy and Madness.

Having stressed its general unpopularity, he then answered the three possible motives for declaring war in the first place, namely taxation, trade and the desire to respect the sovereignty of Great Britain and her colonies. He argued convincingly that the trade and commercial advantages were actually more consistent with peace, that taxation was notoriously unpopular and that war would only bring disgrace and disappointment to Britain. Cost was also a serious consideration and he argued:

> I do most seriously recommend it to his majesty's Ministers to advert with all their Wisdom now while Time is to that great and important object. If they do not I will be bold to say that America dependent or independent will equally be the Bane of Great Britain.

The 6th Earl was neither a great nor eloquent politician, and this was possibly his finest political hour in the Lords. But the speech served its purpose. It represented well the general shift of opinion in Britain, and by the following year the war was at an end and Britain had to acknowledge the independence of the United States of America.

The humiliations of the American war had been alleviated by success in India. In 1783 Lord Coventry voted with William Pitt the Younger, the precocious second son of the Earl of Chatham, against the India Bill introduced by Charles James Fox, to give the government control over the East India Company's immense civil and military powers. Warren Hastings (1732-1818), the first governor-general of India, had been largely responsible for transforming the Company into a successful civil administration, despite opposition from his council in Calcutta. On his return to England, his various opponents contrived to have him impeached, a trial which lasted 145 days, spread over seven years from 1788-95, and concluded with his glorious acquittal. Coventry was a keen supporter of Hastings, probably for personal as well as political motives. He had known the Hastings family, if not personally at least by reputation for many years, for Warren Hastings' father had been the rector of Daylesford, then part of south Worcestershire. Hastings used the money he had made in India to buy back the family home where he retired, and he renewed his friendship with the 6th Earl. Their correspondence is full of requests to convey the 'kindest compliments' to their respective wives, and Hastings was evidently keen to secure Lord Coventry's support in parish affairs.[29]

After Pitt the Younger became Prime Minister in 1784, the 6th Earl appears to have been content to support the pragmatic policies of his government for the next 18 years. Not that all the 6th Earl's time in London had a serious purpose. Although Lord Coventry began to tire of London and became more reclusive with age, as a young man the attractions of the capital were irresistible. He was even moved to write an effusive poem on the subject:

> Led by curiosity and Fame,
> A stranger to this town I came,
> To see the Lions, and St Paul's,
> The parties, Masquerades and balls,
> Banquets so costly and fine,
> That some have thought without a mine,
> Such charges could not be defrayed
> But all is for the good of trade ...[30]

He socialised not only with his fellow peers and politicians but with fashionable artists, architects and playwrights, among them Sheridan and his wife, who were invited to call at Croome in 177[?] on their way to the Three Choirs Festival. The glamourous appeal of contemporary London, its cultural life and popular entertainment in particular, was nurtured by the rapid growth in the newspaper industry, mass publicity and literacy.[31] Lord Coventry received more than his fair share of literary abuse. He was dubbed Peeping Tom of Coventry after a savage article appeared in the *Town and Country Magazine* in 1775. According to this report, one night, after a trip to the theatre, he visited a tavern where he spied through a peep-hole in the wall 'a very intimate acquaintance' in uncompromising circumstances. This acquaintance had later accused Lord Coventry of being a 'Peeping Tom', and so apt was the nickname it inevitably stuck.[32] The article then made reference to his amorous adventures, not least his encounter with a Miss Williams on a park bench. She was said to be the daughter of a clergyman from Brecknockshire, 'remarkably handsome' and well-educated, but abandoned in London by her former lover. Lord Coventry apparently 'beheld her disconsolate situation with a feeling heart, which so justly characterises him, and which excited his curiosity to hear her story, when he relieved her present wants, and has ever since

41 Peeping Tom of Coventry from the *Town and Country Magazine*, 1775.

supplied her not only with the necessaries but the conveniences of life'. The implication that she became his mistress is quite plausible, and the whole affair would be of little interest if it were not for her surname. Could she have been related to George Williams, husband of the mysterious Diana Bertie, the 6th Earl's half-sister? It is quite likely that *Town and Country Magazine* might deliberately misconstrue their relationship to embellish their scandalous article on Lord Coventry. (To further confuse matters, one of the favourite mistresses of the 8th Earl was called Miss Williams. She lived in some style at Severn Bank House in Severn Stoke and inherited Coventry property in Clifton. Their son, George Williams, is buried in the churchyard at Severn Stoke.)

London may have provided the 6th Earl with a heady mix of politics and popular culture, but during the 1750s one of the biggest distractions to be found within the capital was the Gunning sisters (colour plates XII and XIII). Maria (1732-60) and her younger sister Elizabeth (1734-90), were the daughters of John Gunning of Castle Coote, Co. Roscommon, and his wife, Bridget Bourke, the daughter of the 6th Viscount Mayo, and they were declared to be the handsomest women alive (colour plate XIV). They were undeniably pretty. Their fine Celtic colouring, pale complexions, large dark eyes, and rosebud lips accorded perfectly with contemporary ideals of beauty, and both were slender and shapely of figure. Crowds gathered around them wherever they went. People flocked to the roadside to catch a mere glimpse of 'the Beauties' through a carriage window. Today this seems less strange but, at that time, for two girls of relatively obscure origin to cause such a stir was adulation indeed. Horace Walpole delighted in the sheer absurdity of it all. He attributed the excessive public attention to the rarity of seeing such a double vision of perfection rather than to their individual charms. Maria was the more beautiful of the two, but sadly it was a case of beauty without grace. She appears to have been ludicrously self-centred and so socially inept that Walpole was able to lace his letters with innumerable amusing accounts of her idiotic behaviour.

According to tradition, the Gunning sisters were brought to London by their mother in 1751 in the hope that they might become actresses. There they were presented with a forged invitation by a practical joker to a ball given by the Duchess of Bedford. When the fraud was discovered, either their mother or a friend prevailed on the Duchess to issue a genuine invitation and she obliged, no doubt eager to entertain her guests.[33] Their impact on society was immediate, and offers of marriage followed swiftly behind. After a momentous January evening at the King's Theatre in the Haymarket, Elizabeth surreptitiously married James 6th Duke of Hamilton at half-past twelve at night on 14 February 1752 at St George's Chapel, Hyde Park. Such was their haste, that a bed-curtain ring was employed for the purpose, and so great was the attachment between the Duke and his new Duchess that they sat beside each other at table, ate off the same plate and agreed to drink to nobody beneath the rank of earl.[34]

The 6th Earl of Coventry was determined to marry Maria. As Walpole elegantly phrased it: 'Lord Coventry, a grave young lord of the remains of the patriot breed, has long dangled after the eldest, virtuously with regard to her virtue, not very honourably with regard to his own credit.'[35] Their marriage took place six weeks later, on 5 March, a more dignified affair at St George's, Hanover Square. A great rivalry had existed between the Coventry and Hamilton families for generations and one of the few advantages of the Gunning marriages was that it helped to effect a reconciliation.

On 22 June Lord Coventry and his new wife set out for Paris. Lord Downe met them at Calais and offered Lady Coventry a tent bed so that she need not suffer bed bugs at the inns on her journey. She flatly refused, claiming she would 'rather be bit to death, than lie one night from my dear Cov'.[36] But in Paris tempers began to fray. Her naivety, broad Irish accent, inability to speak French, and general lack of refinement were not well received. Lord Coventry refused to allow her to smother herself in rouge and white powder like the Parisian women. At a dinner, he suspected that she had disobeyed him and chased her round the table, seized her and scrubbed the powder off her face with a napkin.[37] The entire visit was so humiliating that they decided to return home early. Lord Coventry apologised to the Duc d'Orleans for not staying for the fête at St Cloud as he had to return to Worcester for the Three Choirs Festival. Feebler still was Lady Coventry's excuse for not attending Madame du Pompadour's firework party. She claimed it was 'her dancing-master's hour'.[38]

Back in England the new Countess of Coventry's popularity persisted. A Worcester shoemaker earned two and a half guineas just by charging a penny apiece to see a shoe he was making for her. However, her behaviour failed to improve. At a private ball in 1753 she affected an 'outrageous passion' at a harmless reference to the Song of Solomon, accusing the speaker of being blasphemous and impious. This caused considerable amusement among the assembled company, including Lord Coventry, whom she scolded vehemently and sulkily accepted the invitation of Lord Holderness to be her paramour for the evening, much to the discomfort of everyone concerned.[39] When she tired of her husband's reprimands, she flirted openly with Lord Bolingbroke. By November 1756, Bolingbroke's aunt, the Countess of Guildford, was 'in terrors, lest Lord Coventry should divorce his wife, and Lord Bolinbroke [sic] should marry her—'tis a well-imagined panic!'.[40] She also flirted with the King's younger son, William Augustus, the Duke of Cumberland or 'Butcher' Cumberland of Culloden as he became known. On 20 April 1756 Walpole noted:

The Duke has appeared in form on the causeway in Hyde Park with my Lady Coventry; it is the new
office, where all lovers now are entered. How happy she must be with Billy and Bully (Cumberland and
Bolingbroke). I hope she will not mistake, and call the former by the nickname of the latter.[41]

George II found her a highly decorative and amusing addition at court and, in 1759,
after she had been mobbed one Sunday evening in Hyde Park, he provided her with
a guard. The following Sunday she spent the entire day walking round the park with
two guards in front of her and 12 soldiers following on behind. When the old King
asked her if she was sorry that there were no masquerades that year, she made the
famous reply that there was only one sight left that she wanted to see—and that was
a Coronation![42] Fortunately, the King thought this was hilarious and told the anecdote
to his family at supper that evening.

By the end of the following year, both Maria and George II were dead. The king
was 77 and Maria only twenty-eight. With uncommon tact and good manners, Maria
was the first to die. During the winter of 1759 she had experienced her first attack
of consumption, her constitution already weakened by the toxic effects of the white
lead in her cosmetics. She appears to have rallied during the summer, but by August
she returned to Croome for the last time and died on 30 September 1760. Her personal
appearance remained her chief concern during her illness. She is said to have spent the
days on her couch clasping her pocket glass as the ravages of tuberculosis took their
toll. During the last two weeks of her life she allowed no light in her room except
for the lamp of a teakettle, and would not permit the curtains to be drawn.[43] When
she died, Croome church was still far from complete, so she was buried at the small,
medieval church on the hilltop at Pirton, to where around ten thousand people are said
to have travelled to pay their final respects.

On 8 August 1761 the following verses appeared anonymously in the *London Chronicle*,
occasioned by the approaching coronation of George III:

1. On the banks of the Styx as a beautiful ghost,
In resemblance the shade of the goddess of Love,
Was revolving the days when a Countess and Toast
She flaunted about in the regions above.

2. News arriv'd which made all Elysium to ring,
That the fates a great monarch had summoned to rest,
In calling great Britain's late father and king,
To a crown of reward in the realms of the Blest.

3. My lady was nettled to miss the occasion,
By dying before him so *mal a propos,*
Of seeing his gracious young heir's coronation,
And making a party herself in the show.

4. But to stop at no point she might hope to get over,
She boldly determined to venture for life;
And tho' Styx was as wide as from Calais to Dover,
Resolv'd to appear again C——y's wife.

5. She therefore in haste skipt away to the ferry,
Where—'Charon-you're empty come take over me:
I'm resolv'd to go back to the world in your wherry:
The only fine sight I ever miss'd of, to see.'

6. Old Charon most civilly bow'd to my Lady,
Stept out of his wherry, and handed her in:
But, finding he wanted a pass, was as ready
Her Ladyship roughly to turn out again.

7. Then sending to Court in a hurry
For a passport, directly to Pluto she ran,
And put Madam Proserpine quite in a flurry,
Thinking Venus was come to seduce her good man.

8. Gloomy Dis only smil'd at the fair one's request,
But more at her Ladyship's whimsical reason;
And having malignly a mind for a jest,
Represented her suit as quite out of season.

9. 'We never (says he) at the instance alone
Of the ghost that may ask, such a favour and grant;
But if for their sake Wife and Husband come
We then may restore them such souls as they want'.

10. 'Since Orpheus, however, in risque of his life,
Long ago made us stare at his musick and passion,
Not a soul has been call'd for by husband
So that journeys of this sort are quite out of fashion'.

11. 'Yet as for your beauty a passport I grant you.
But wherefore again shou'd you covet on earth
To mix with a crowd who perhaps do not want you,
But make you the theme of impertinent mirth'.

12. Besides, pretty lady, you're greatly mistaken,
If pleasure you promise yourself at the sight:
For unseen by your friends, by admirers forsaken,
There's no one will mind an impalpable sprite'.

13. 'Nay, nay', quoth the countess,'if that be the case,
I will stay where I am—here's your passport,
A fig for fine sights, if conceal'd one's fine face,
I had rather see nothing, than not to be seen'.[44]

It was a cruel indictment of her vanity. The 6th Earl still loved her dearly despite their disagreements and sought solace in verse. Several of these poems survive, most of them lamenting the frailty and transience of beauty. One in particular deserves quoting in full:

1. Why Libitina to the Silent Tomb
Consign a form to make a thousand sighs
Ah! Chill'd by Death's cold hand Maria's bloom
And closed, for ever closed the brightest eyes

2. Did Jealousy inflame the Paphian Queen
Say was her bosom filled with fierce alarms?
Did Venus envious of her Peerless Mien
Wish from the world the Rival of her Charms?

3. How frail is beauty what a transient flower
Come a sharp frost it kills the tender bloom
The splendid wonder of a little hour
How soon it blushes vanish and perfume

4. In vain the sons of Esculapius tried
To give to distant days her fleeting breath
This to the worlds warm wish fate denied
And doom'd her to the solitudes of death.

5. Her noble Partner 'midst his Mansion Mourns
Now treads at Evg the dusky Vale forlorn
Like Philomela pouring Plaintive Tones
At nights pale Moon upon her lonely Thorn

6. The muse no farther can her strain prolong
Deep in the floods of sorrow quench her fire
Thus in life's shadowy close upon her song
Dirge of sweetest melody the swan expires[45]

(Maria's sister, Elizabeth, lived for another 30 years. On 18 January 1758, her first husband, the Duke of Hamilton, had died from a cold caught out hunting. Later that year, she became briefly engaged to Francis Egerton, the Duke of Bridgewater (1736-1803), who disapproved of her sister, and so she decided to refuse him and she married John Campbell, Marquess of Lorne on 3 March 1759. Her husband succeeded to the Dukedom of Argyll in 1770, and six years later Elizabeth was created Baroness Hamilton of Hambledon in Leicestershire. She is said to have remained remarkably beautiful for the rest of her life and she died in London on 20 May 1790.)

Maria Gunning produced three daughters before she finally fulfilled her dynastic obligations and gave birth to a son and heir. The eldest child, Maria Alicia, was born on 9 December 1754.[46] She married Andrew Baynton Rolt, son of Sir Edward Baynton of Spy Park, Wiltshire, but the marriage was a disaster and was dissolved in 1783, and the sordid and unpleasant events that accompanied the breakdown of the marriage soon destroyed her health.[47] She died not long after her divorce on 8 January 1784. The second daughter, Elizabeth Ann, died an infant in 1756. The youngest daughter, Anne Margaret, was born on 18 March 1757 (colour plate XV). She inherited her mother's looks, but also her temperament, which was a mixed blessing. On 20 October 1778 she married Edward Foley, second son of Lord Foley of the wealthy Worcestershire family of ironmasters, but the marriage ended in divorce in 1787 and she married Captain Samuel Wright of the Dragoons on 15 July 1788. She appears to have always been of a somewhat weak and neurotic disposition, which developed into full-blown hypochondria later in life. Between 1811 and her death in 1822 she kept a diary.[48] This uninformative and dreary sequence of notes is really rather sad. Debilitated by severe attacks of gout, she became obsessed with her deteriorating health, and she forced herself to follow a rigorous and joyless routine. When not confined to her bed or couch, she punctuated her day with walks in Hyde Park or around the lake at Croome, and only invitations to dine at Coventry House were anticipated with something approaching enthusiasm. George William, the youngest child, was born on 28 April 1758. The focus of his father's hopes and ambitions, possibly the strain proved too much. He quarrelled bitterly with his father as a young man, which scarred him for life.

On 27 September 1764 the 6th Earl remarried. The previous year the Treaty of Paris had brought an end to the Seven Years War and, like many English aristocrats, the 6th Earl had rushed off to Paris with his friends to do some shopping prior to his wedding. According to George Selwyn, selecting new furnishings was not the only thing on the Earl's mind, for he observed that 'His preparation here has been the most extraordinary that ever was made for any sacrament whatever.'[49]

His new wife, Barbara (1737-1804), was the daughter of John St John, 10th Baron of St John of Bletsoe, and his wife, Elizabeth, the daughter of Sir Ambrose Crowley (colour plate XVI). Her brother was the Dean of Worcester, and it was probably this local connection that brought the couple together. Barbara was a lady of remarkable qualities, and she worked tirelessly to reunite the family. Beautiful like her predecessor, but less obviously so, her abundant grace and charm soon stilled the social ripples created by Maria. She shared her husband's interest and involvement in developments at Croome, she loved the countryside, she was fond of animals and she was interested in horticulture. She also brought with her a substantial dowry at a time when Lord Coventry's expenditure was getting a little out of hand: a most happy situation.

Maria had always preferred London to Worcestershire, so the interest that his new wife Barbara showed in Croome must have delighted Lord Coventry. The new model dairy, the menagerie and the model farm at Croome were all gifts to Lady Coventry from her husband, and she received the income from the farm as 'pin-money'. During the 1770s, references to gifts of seeds and plants occur frequently in her correspondence. In one letter she thanks her sister for the latest batch of plants she has sent to her and adds: 'you have made mine the best furnished greenhouse in this country, the seeds from Botany Bay are not yet come. I will send some to you as soon as I have them.'[50] Her menagerie was filled with rare and exotic birds, and her dairy was a model of

XXII   George William, Viscount Deerhurst, later 7th Earl of Coventry, by Allan Ramsay, *c*.1765.

XXIII   The 9th Earl of Coventry and his elder sister Maria outside Severn Bank House, by William and Henry Barraud.

XXIV   The 9th Earl of Coventry by Sir Percy Bigland, 1913.

XV   Blanche, Countess of Coventry, English School, *c.*1915.

XXVI An aerial view of Croome.

elegance and productivity, and it is probable that it was she who ordered the
'Specimens of Petrifition' from Derbyshire for the grotto in 1783 and supervised their installation.[51]

Barbara was a keen collector of the
advertisements for a host of new products
that proliferated in the newspapers. Many
of these, together with the bills and re-
ceipts from her shopping trips to London,
were neatly collated and filed away and these
provide a fascinating insight into her tastes
and habits. They include bills from the
bookbinders, jewellers, haberdashers, drap-

OLYMPIAN DEW;
OR,
GRECIAN BLOOM-WATER:
The beſt and moſt valuable C O S M E T I C,
The Sweeteſt and moſt Refreſhing PERFUME ever introduced;
IS SOLD, WHOLESALE AND RETAIL,
By C. S H A R P,
Perfumer and Razor-Maker to His Royal Highneſs the PRINCE *of* WALES,
No. 1 3 1,   F L E E T - S T R E E T;
And (by Appointment) at HARRISON and Co.'s, No. 56, CORNHILL,
L O N D O N:
In B O T T L E S of 5s. and 15s. each, Stamp included.
No Perfume ſo ſweet, ſo delicate, ſo elegantly fragrant and uſeful, as OLYMPIAN DEW, *ſays her Majeſty of France.*

42   Late 18th-century advertisement for Olympian Dew.

ers, milliners and confectioners, all with attractive letter-headings. There are also advertisements for new medicines and cosmetics, notably one for Olympian Dew or Grecian Bloom-
Water, claimed to be made from fragrant flowers from the fertile valleys near Mount Olympus
and to clear the skin of unsightly wrinkles, freckles and tan.

The Countess also had a great sense of fun. The new garden buildings and parkland
at Croome provided the ideal setting for boating parties, summer picnics and firework
displays. Several bills survive from a firework artist in Holborn, London. They include
such intriguing items as Chinese Trees of Silver Flowers, Italian Suns, Roman Candles
to throw up blazing Stars, Gold Flower-pots and Water Rockets. Reflected in the lake
and exploding high above the new mansion, the effect must have been truly spectacular.
Most exciting of all was the royal visit to Croome by George III and Queen Charlotte
in July 1788, which is said to have engrossed the attention of the entire county. Richard
Cooksey, a local historian and probably connected with the Mayor of Worcester of the
same name, wrote a fascinating account of the visit:

> The King, Queen, three Princesses attended by Lady Beaulieu and Constown and Colonel Guinn arrived
> there at 10 o'clock—breakfasted—saw the dairy and walked around the plantations. The Queen then
> ordered her carriage into which she took the two older Princesses and Lady Coventry. The Youngest
> and attendants … were in the second coach. The King with Lord Coventry on horseback attended by
> his suite and accompanied by the coaches rode over the whole park and Lady Coventry's farm and
> followed by at least 500 horsemen and women on horseback and the most motley group conceivable
> … Dinner [was] served in the saloon, I mean the room which looked due south. The King at first wished
> to dine in the Tapestry Room but altered his choice. Lord and Lady Coventry (his Lordship in Boots)
> had the honour of dining at the same table with the King and Queen and three Princesses. They were
> waited upon by twelve servants out of livery sent by Messrs Lygon and Sandys etc. The King ate some
> salmon, which he said was the best he had ever tasted, some potted lamprey and venison and drank
> two glasses of port. There were a brace of carp each weighing nine pounds … They spent an hour and
> a quarter at dinner took their coffee and went in the coaches to the menagerie and hence to Severn
> Bank and left the Regions of Croome at 6 o' clock in the evening. The King was in remarkable high
> spirits and to use the expression of one who followed him in his ride 'you can't conceive sir how he
> laughed and joked with Lord Coventry'.[52]

The 6th Earl and his second wife had two sons, John (1765-1829), his father's favourite, and Thomas William (1778-1816). There was also a daughter, Barbara, but she died an infant. John married twice. His first wife, whom he married in 1788, was Anne Clayton, and they had two sons and two daughters. Caroline, the eldest, was born in 1789 and married Hugh Mallet. Frederick (1791-1859) married the only daughter of Henry Halford and they had four children. John (1793-1871) settled at Burgate House in Hampshire and was married three times and had numerous offspring, while Anne, the youngest daughter (d.1869), married her cousin Thomas William in 1823. They had seven children but eventually separated in 1834. Two weeks after the death of his first wife, Anne Clayton, in August 1809, John was remarried to Anna Maria Eves (d.1837), the daughter of Francis Eves of Clifford Place in Herefordshire. Thomas William, the second son of the 6th Earl's second marriage, married a Miss Clarke of Evesham in 1801. She died in December 1806 and he died in poverty in 1816. They had five children, the eldest of whom, Thomas William (1800-82), married his cousin Anne.

Lady Coventry endeavoured to unite her husband with his eldest son for much of their marriage and it appears that the 6th Earl depended on her increasingly in his old age as he became more reclusive. When she died on 25 November 1804, he lost much of his former enthusiasm for life. Even his interest in Croome faded visibly. As he withdrew into himself, around him family life disintegrated into a sequence of bitter squabbles, elopements and divorce proceedings.

The Grand Design

The 6th Earl of Coventry may have lacked the legal and political acumen of his more celebrated ancestors, but as an improver, cultivator and, above all, patron, he surpassed them all. Croome now appeared inadequate and old-fashioned, certainly not fit for an Earl who prided himself on his taste. The changes wrought by Gilbert, in particular the new formal garden and the rearranged and consolidated deer parks, had left Croome a place notable within Worcestershire. No longer was the estate characterised by dilapidation and decline. But the 6th Earl was preparing to implement changes which would revolutionise the landscape, be celebrated for their vision and which would make the efforts of his ancestors pale by comparison. He planned a scene of pastoral perfection, in the midst of which would stand a new house, furnished with fashionable discernment to dazzle his guests.

It was now that the 6th Earl's ability to recognise exceptional talent became crucial to the development of his enterprise. Lancelot, not yet 'Capability', Brown, recently embarked upon a career as an independent architect and designer was to prove equal to the task of realising the 6th Earl's vision. The introduction, by Sanderson Miller, of Brown to Lord Coventry was momentous. At Croome, Brown rose to the notice of men whose power and means could ensure that his new landscape style flourished, changing forever the scale and extent of landscape design.

Lord Coventry was also among Robert Adam's most valued, if not most co-operative, clients, and he employed many more of the most distinguished artists, designers and craftsmen of his day; among them Richard Wilson, Allan Ramsay, Reynolds, Sefferin Alken, Joseph

Rose, John Cheere, John Wildsmith, Joseph Wilton, and Antonio Zucchi.[53] He went to Paris to acquire furniture, artefacts and tapestries for his new house and developed an enthusiasm for French neo-classicism. His library was indicative of his wide-ranging interests. He subscribed to the *Vitruvius Britannicus* (the fifth volume of which featured Croome), Leoni's *Palladio*, and various works on Greek and Roman antiquities by authors such as Dalton, Hamilton, Desgodetz and Le Roy. Less predictable were the conspicuous number of horticultural items, such as Dodart's *Memoires pour server a l'Histoire du Plants* of 1676, and Baxter's *The Nature of the Soil* (1745). He was an early, immensely enthusiastic and assiduous plant collector, and gathered specimens from the most remote corners of the world, including Russia, South Africa and the South Pacific. He was also an agricultural improver, proud of his model farm and dairy, and had a passion for Holderness and Alderney cows. According to the 1809 inventory of Croome, the revitalised pastureland supported 140 cattle, over 1,000 sheep, and 33 pigs in addition to the large herds of deer. From the start, the earl oversaw his estate with a vigilance, which was later to provoke the description of Croome as, above all, 'a seat of prudence and order'. In December 1753, his agent Thomas Harbutt noted that he was 'extremely angry' that the estate workers were behind with the maltmaking and brewing, that the brickmaking failed to meet the current demand and that the supply of bacon was far from adequate.

The image of Croome as a former morass was a popular one. It was used by the 6th Earl himself when he composed the inscription on Brown's memorial in 1797, and it was used by John Darke in 1794 and William Dean in 1824. Much of the Croome landscape had, indeed, been marshy and infertile and of little agricultural value. The contrast with the ordered and fertile parkland of the later 18th century underlined Brown's achievement. It gave almost heroic status to the venture, a revelation of mankind's ability to triumph over natural adversity, and, on a more practical level, demonstrated the virtues of progressive agricultural methods. The Earl was proud of his superb system of drains, which were very largely the work of Brown. Indeed his ambitions for Croome relied almost entirely upon the remarkable drainage system that was installed and perfected in

43　The south elevation of Croome Court, from *Vitruvius Britannicus* vol. V.

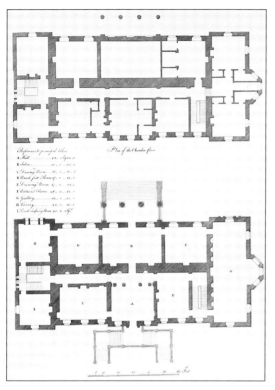

44   Plan of Croome Court from *Vitruvius Britannicus* vol. V.

five phases between 1747 and 1847. The drains reached out beyond the perimeter of the parkland, and huge brick culverts were constructed to channel the surplus water into the river and lake to create a virtue of practical necessity. Where open ditches were needed, these were given a gentle profile to allow them to be grazed flush with the level of the water.

Ambition on this scale required vast investment. The project at Croome is said to have cost a staggering £400,000, around £28,000,000 today. On average around £10,000 was spent each year, rising to double that amount towards the completion of the project. This mostly covered by the cost of the craftsmen's wages and the purchase of materials, notably Bath stone, Westmorland slate, Forest marble from Oxfordshire, and stone from Painswick, Bibury, and Bredon. Lord Coventry even rented a quarry on Bredon Hill, Worcestershire, for a short period. His second wife brought a new source of wealth on their marriage in 1764, and it was no coincidence that in the same year Lord Coventry acquired a new London home, Coventry House in Piccadilly, to complement his prestigious country seat. Shortly afterwards, he also commissioned Brown to build Springhill House on his Broadway estate in south Worcestershire as a place to retreat from his arduous social and official duties.

The importance of Croome, its buildings, landscape, furnishings and plant collection, is now widely acknowledged by scholars of Capability Brown and Robert Adam, and by historians of 18th-century furnishings and landscape gardening. Recent work by the National Trust continues to provide further insight into the creation of the landscape. There is space here only to summarise this remarkable achievement, a triumph of perseverance, imagination and skill.

Croome

No writer conjures up a better picture of the contemporary excitement and wonder provoked by the transformation of Croome than William Dean, the last head gardener to the 6th Earl of Coventry. A combined eulogy and gazetteer for horticulturalists, his description of the place in 1824 captured eloquently the 'finely picturesque and powerful effect' of Brown's design. He completes his general account with a quote from a correspondent to the *Gentleman's Magazine* of August 1792. The writer has just returned

from Croome and describes how he was charmed, 'in the highest degree, as to the
gratification of my eyes':

> for never did I see a more beautiful spot; nor any kept in such perfect order ... A vast extent of ground,
> formerly a mere bog, is now adorned with islands, and tufts of trees of every species; and watered round,
> in the most pleasing, and natural manner, possible ... In short, Mr Urban, if there be any spot on the
> habitable globe to *make a death-bed terrible*, it is Lord Coventry's at Croome, Worcestershire.

Such was Croome's contemporary impact. The reference to the 'natural manner' of the
park is significant. For although Croome was a collective achievement, it was a milestone
in the career of its chief designer, Capability Brown, the embodiment of English 18th-
century landscape gardening, the serene English Landscape style. Croome was his first
independent design of any scale, a work of vital importance, that made his reputation,
spawned a host of imitators and left an enduring impression on landscape throughout
the western world.

Brown had been head gardener at Stowe in Buckinghamshire for 10 years before his
arrival at Croome. There he had witnessed William Kent's contribution to the steady
transformation of the hitherto geometric characteristics of most English garden design.
The angular and formal designs of Bridgeman, Vanbrugh and Switzer had gradually
responded to the discovery of curvilinear beauty, described by Pope and Hogarth. Kent
had, in turn, allowed a looser composition of 'natural' elements. But nowhere had designers
entirely relinquished the desire to contain and regulate the topography. Kent's clumps of
trees were 'puny' and his rills of spring water made to flow in rigid stone meanders. Brown
was overwhelmingly a practical man, with little interest in intellectual artifice but, crucially,
he had grasped the power of using topography rather than suppressing it. His early years
at Stowe had taught him the limitations of human endeavour in landscape works and
his interventions encouraged to perfection the existing accents and characteristics of a place.
His more naturalistic style took advantage of the special qualities of the landscape, concealed
or improved its defects, and thereby revealed the 'genius of the place'.[54] Brown introduced
large clumps and belts of trees into his landscapes to control views, screen less desirable
elements, and manipulate the spaces within his landscapes. Water in the form of sinuous
lakes enlivened the middle distance, and all was set among acres of green turf, whose
levels were carefully managed to give subtle elevation. The smooth fluid lines are believed
to have been influenced by William Hogarth's *The Aesthetics of Beauty* (1753), which emphasised
the merit of gently curving Lines of Grace and Beauty. The desired effect was, to mid-
18th-century eyes, uncontrived, but required massive drainage systems and earthworks.
Croome provided the template for this radical approach.

Not long after his elder brother's death in 1744, George William began to put his
plans for the estate into action. Survey work was carried out, more fields were exchanged,
divided and enclosed, and there was a reduction in leaseholders between 1749-50 made
possible by doubling the rent. The formal gardens were really swept away, unlike so
often where this description is an unjustified exaggeration, and work began on the artificial
river, south-west of the house. Much of this work was supervised by John Phipps, who

was taken on in 1747 and remained at Croome till 1753. George William was evidently eager to begin but no major plan had yet formed in his mind. His friend, Sanderson Miller, provided invaluable advice and encouragement during this early period. Miller was an amateur architect with a taste for the inventive Gothick of William Kent, for ruins, castles and cascades. He had built himself a picturesque thatched cottage at his estate in Radway, Warwickshire, in 1744. Then he altered his house in the Gothick style and erected a sham castle and massive octagonal tower nearby, with painted glass in the windows, which Coventry had found for him in a farmhouse near Malvern. He built another sham castle for Sir Thomas Lyttelton at Hagley, Worcestershire, and produced work in a similar vein for Lord North at Wroxton in Oxfordshire and Sir Roger Newdigate at Arbury. Best of all was the Gothick hall he designed at Lacock Abbey, Wiltshire, in 1753-5. Another friend of Coventry's, Richard, Lord Bateman, remodelled the church on his estate at Shobdon, Herefordshire, into an elaborate Gothick confection. Their experiments fired the new Lord Deerhurst with enthusiasm. In 1747 Miller wrote to him:

> As Mr Talbot [John Ivory Talbot of Lacock] tells me your Lordship's spirit of improvement begins to exert itself. I have no idea how you can live within a day's ride of two such places as Wroxton Abbey and Hagley. Were you to see them but once you would return with Ideas as much enlarged as a Poets would be the first time he reads Homer and Virgil.[55]

The artificial river was complete by 1748, the first major new feature of which George William was particularly proud. In its early form it lacked any naturalistic meanders and curved round towards the house to terminate in a grove of trees. That August, Sir Edward Turner complimented him on his achievement,[56] and on 20 September another friend, the wealthy and good-humoured Roger Nugent, who served as Lord of the Treasury and Vice-Treasurer for Ireland, gave him some practical advice on making the river watertight and warned him: 'In making your Piece of water you should be mindful of my Lord Granville's maxim, rather more than He was, Take and Hold …'. Lord Bateman was equally complimentary, writing on 17 April 1750: 'I dare say Croomb is in great beauty … You have made a River where no water ever ran before ...'.[57] A Chinese bridge was designed by the architect and carpenter William Halfpenny (d.1755) and built along the line of the avenue south of the house to link the areas of parkland bisected by the river.[58] New hot houses were also constructed during this period for which Lord Deerhurst received a gift of pineapple plants in 1750.[59]

As Doherty's survey of c.1751 revealed, this initial activity was executed in a desultory fashion, and the place appeared a jumbled mix of old and new elements. A radical overview was required and, fortunately, the necessary help was at hand. In November 1749, Miller visited Stowe and was shown round the gardens by Brown. The following August, Brown was invited to Radway, and it was probably at this point that Miller introduced him to Lord Deerhurst.[60] As his period of employment overlaps with that of John Phipps, it is likely that he was brought in originally to work on the house in 1751. The close resemblance of Croome Court to Miller's later design for Hagley, and Miller's early involvement in the project, including his designs for a stables and lodge of 1750, have given rise to the suggestion that he was the architect of Croome.[61] This idea was supported by a much-quoted but misleading letter from Lord Coventry to Miller of 1752 in which he states: 'Whatever merits it [Croome] may in future time boast it will be ungrateful not to acknowledge you the primary Author … It was owing to your assurances that nature had been more liberal to me than I apprehended …'.[62] This clearly refers to the scheme as a whole, not just the house, and Lord Coventry was expressing his gratitude to Miller for his vital inspiration and advice in the initial tentative stages of the project. Having said this, the general profile of Croome Court may have been developed from one of Miller's sketches, but it is evident from the accounts that Brown was responsible for the finished design, which was planned as the restrained and dignified culmination of its surroundings. Further evidence of Brown's authorship can be found in another letter Lord Coventry wrote to Miller in January 1756, in which he remarked: 'Croome … is a good deal altered since you saw it, but I fear will never deserve the encomiums you have so plentifully given.'[63]

Brown was 35 when he started at Croome, and he continued to work for Lord Coventry till his death over thirty years later in 1782. This included two intensive phases between 1751-6 and 1762-6, the second of which overlapped with Robert Adam. He was paid in instalments that totalled around £5,000, and it was possibly because his work was in such demand and his relationship with Lord Coventry on such friendly terms that he tolerated being paid up to two years in arrears.[64] After 1766 he appears to have acted more in an advisory capacity and he visited Croome as a guest rather than as a retainer. Brown brought to Croome a reliable team of master craftsmen, including William Eltonhead, the bricklayer, Robert Newman, the mason, and John Hobcroft, the carpenter and a protégé of Brown's. Other trusted craftsmen included Francesco Vassalli, a decorative plasterer, Benjamin Read, the foreman, who worked for Brown at Blenheim, and William Donn, a surveyor. Brown rebuilt the house, offices, stables and church, but part of the house interior and the church interior was entrusted to Adam. Adam was later asked to alter the offices and stables and he designed the dairy interior. Of the park buildings, Brown designed the Rotunda, the grotto, the dry arch, the island temple and the wooden bridges in the garden; most of these were altered later.

Adam worked for Lord Coventry over a similar period of 31 years. His earliest drawings date from 1760, not long after his return from the continent, and he was still producing designs for him as late as 1791. The majority of the work was undertaken in two phases between 1760-7 and 1779-83, and from the bills, account books and letters that survive, it appears he was paid a total figure of £733 12s.[65] Apart from his work at the house and church, Adam designed most of the important buildings in the park, the Temple Greenhouse, the Alcove or Park Seat, the London arch and the pier gates, and probably Dunstall Castle. James Wyatt completed the work in the park after Adam's death and developed his design of the Panorama Tower from Adam's drawings. Although Lord Coventry was among Adam's most important clients, his reluctance to pay his bills either in full or on time came as something of a surprise to Adam. A memorable incident

45 View of the Temple from the south east from William Dean's *An Historical and Descriptive Account of Croome D'Abitot.*

occurred early in 1764 when Adam submitted his bill to date for £260 8s. 0d. A standard practice and perfectly reasonable sum, but Lord Coventry decided to send Adam just £250 towards it. Perhaps he was wary that Adam might have overcharged him as Henry Holland had done when the house was roofed.[66] Adam regarded the inadequate payment as a personal insult to both his expertise and his honesty. On 3 April he wrote back to Lord Coventry in an injured tone, and informed him that all his other clients generally sent him 'a present over and above the Bill itself', and he assured Lord Coventry that he would exert himself with the other buildings for Croome. Anxious to make amends, Lord Coventry paid the full amount the same day.

Before 1751 the house at Croome, lying within a shallow bowl, did not command the best views over the park. But as it was barely a century old, it was decided not to rebuild from scratch. Brown made the most of the rising ground to the east of the house and used belts, clumps and scatters of trees to enhance its setting and achieve the sequences of controlled views he sought. The old house was partly demolished and remodelled in Bath stone with a roof of Westmorland slate, the latter work supervised by Brown's son-in-law and eventual partner Henry Holland (1714-85). Around fifty tons of slates were required in total, at a cost of £330 16s. 9d. The roofing was complete in 1757, although, as new furniture was delivered prior to this date, it is probable that the house and offices were completed in stages. This would enable Lord Coventry to stay at Croome while work was in progress, or he may have resided at Pirton Court. The plasterers did not finish in the house until late in 1762, and new furniture was acquired and alterations made, notably to the main staircase, 20 years after this date.[67] The house was built not only on the old foundations, but also retained some external and internal walling and the massive central chimneystacks, which ran along the central spine of the house. The chimney-stacks were omitted from the elevation of the house as it appeared in *Vitruvius Britannicus* to give a cleaner profile to the building but, as far as Brown was concerned, their practical merit outweighed such purist considerations.

This meant that it retained the double-pile form bisected by a transverse corridor which was by then distinctly old-fashioned, but it was updated and extended by the addition of four corner pavilions with Venetian windows on the ground floor. Central emphasis was given to the main elevations by the addition of a pediment and a double flight of steps on the north front, and a tetrastyle portico on the south front, later guarded by a pair of Coade sphinxes. Adam did three drawings for the arms within the north pediment in 1761, before Coventry was satisfied with its appearance. A gallery was placed along the entire length of the western end of the building with a central canted bay that projects between the pavilions. This provides views towards the river, balances the proportions of the gallery within and sheds light on Adam's magnificent chimneypiece. A massive range of offices was added at the eastern end, which linked the house to a vast stable quadrangle. According to the 1809 Inventory, this provided accommodation for 45 horses with plenty of room for the grooms and other members of staff on the upper floors. The offices and stables were built in brick with stone dressings. It may have been intended to face them completely or in part, but this idea may have been abandoned on economic grounds or for aesthetic reasons as the different material expressed these buildings' subservience to the whole and did not detract from the simple profile and proportions of the main house.

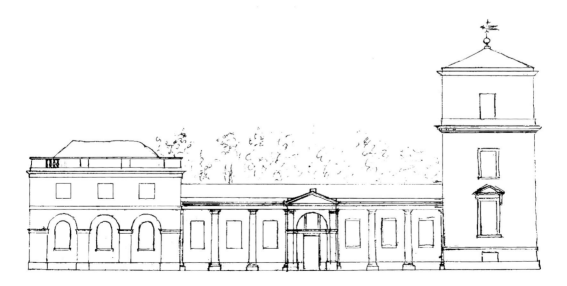

46   A proposal to alter the offices at Croome by Robert Adam.

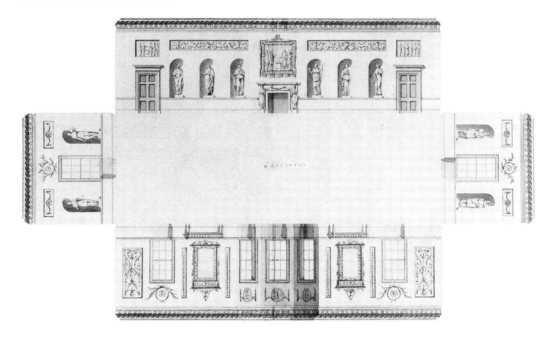

47   Gallery wall elevations by Robert Adam.

48   Gallery chimneypiece by Robert Adam.

The design was dignified but plain, a pleasing but not particularly inspiring exercise in the Palladian manner. Dorothy Stroud observed a close resemblance to other early houses by Brown, in particular Claremont in Surrey.[68] The influence of earlier Palladian palaces, notably Colen Campbell's unexecuted design for Houghton Hall, Norfolk of 1722, is undeniable in terms of its plan and its corner pavilions, which look back to Inigo Jones's design for the south block of Wilton House, Wiltshire of the 1630s. William Kent's Holkham Hall in Norfolk had adopted a similar theme with Venetian windows set in corner towers, and it may be no coincidence that similar towers were adopted at Shobdon Court in Herefordshire, the seat of Lord Coventry's friend Lord Bateman. The chief disadvantage of adding the corner pavilions at Croome was that it gave the building rather elongated proportions. William Dean considered Croome Court 'too low for its extent', but this was a small price to pay for so fashionable and convenient a transformation. Its distinctive new appearance was all the more commendable for its restraint and the artful way in which it was assimilated into the design for the landscape.

49 *Right*. Sphinx on the steps of the south front of Croome Court.

50 *Below*. The south front of Croome Court.

51 *Bottom*. The north front of Croome Court.

Inside, Brown was responsible for the decoration of the hall, with its Doric screen of four fluted columns, the gold and white saloon, the yellow drawing room, the dining room and the billiard room. These are in the splendid but sober style of George II's reign, and there are richly carved and gilded doorcases with fluted half-columns and open pediments, deep moulded cornices and elaborate marble chimneypieces. The rooms were filled with an outstanding collection of furniture, some of it designed by Adam and carved by Sefferin Alken, and all of it supplied by the leading cabinet-makers of the day, including Vile and Cobb, Ince and Mayhew, Chippendale, Pierre Longlois, Gordon and Tait, and France and Bradburn.[69] The competition established amongst these craftsmen for the commissions undoubtedly worked to Lord Coventry's advantage. Many of the rooms have lavish plaster ceilings by either Francesco Vassalli or Joseph Rose, the two most distinguished masters of the day, and on the walls were hung some of the finest items from Lord Coventry's collection of paintings. The family portraits in the saloon had carved and matching frames, and the south wall had pier glasses and console tables with ornate *trompe l'oeil* carving supplied by Vile and Cobb in 1761 at a cost of £206 12s. The 1809 Inventory also refers to bronze figures, two marble urns, mahogany card tables, screens, leather chairs and sofas in the saloon, and, oddly, four fishing stools, possibly to support gouty legs. Festoons of fruit and flowers in moulded plasterwork embellished the dining room walls, and in 1809 the room housed several vast mahogany dining tables and sideboards, which supported a display of six flower pots filled with evergreens and also a painter's easel.[70]

The gallery, library and tapestry rooms were the work of Robert Adam, and are the chief delight of the interior. The gallery was intended originally for use as a library, and the bookcases that Adam designed for the room were installed later in the little library in the south-east pavilion. Adam's first ceiling design of large hexagonal panels and small roundels is dated September 1760 and was not executed. A subsequent design produced the following March was adopted instead, which has elongated lozenges and octagons, comparable to that at Syon House in Middlesex.[71] The walls included niches for statuary by John Cheere (1709-87), as in the dining room at Syon, above which were set panels of arabesque stuccowork. For some reason these were not carried out on the western side of the room, and the full-sized oil sketches for the panels were nailed in place instead. The marble chimneypiece is among Adam's finest. Life-size caryatids, Nymphs of Flora, were carved in superb detail almost in the round by Joseph Wilton (1722-1803) at a cost of £338 1s. 2d. A grisaille overmantel completed the composition. It was finished in 1766 and was such a success that Adam repeated the design in the dining room at Hatchlands, Surrey, and at Harewood, Yorkshire, where it was employed with equal effect. The gallery was furnished with long stools and armchairs designed by Adam, one set made by France and Bradburn, the other by John Cobb, while Alken provided the required carved decoration for both.

The library has an Adamesque ceiling of delicate plasterwork and another fine chimneypiece carved with turtledoves by John Wildsmith, above which hung Ramsay's splendid portrait of the 6th Earl. The room was furnished with pedimented and glazed

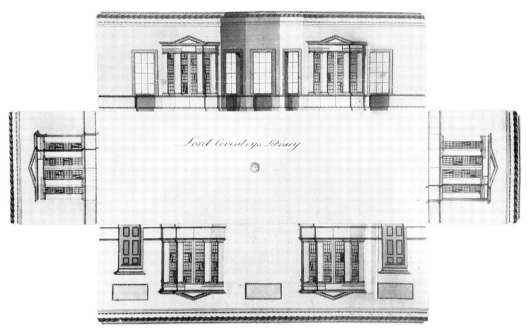

Lord Coventry's Library

52   Library wall elevations by Robert Adam.

mahogany bookcases based on Adam's designs that were made by Vile and Cobb for £260 in 1763 and carved by Alken, now housed in the Victoria and Albert Museum.[72]

The tapestry room was the *pièce de résistance*. Lord Coventry was keen to assert his reputation as a connoisseur by installing a tapestry room at Croome to rival the best in England, not least the tapestry drawing room recently installed at Hagley. During his shopping trip to Paris in the summer of 1763, he visited the Royal Gobelins Manufactory where he acquired a sumptuous set of crimson Boucher-Neilson tapestries depicting scenes of 'Les Amours des Dieux'. These were among the new compositions conceived by the factory's new director, Jean-Germain Soufflot, which incorporated medallions containing scenes by Boucher set within frames that resembled carved and gilded wood. They could be adapted to a variety of subject matter and different sizes of room, and only nine sets of their type were made prior to the French Revolution, five of which went to clients of Robert Adam in England. The following October, Adam was summoned to Croome to design a suitable room setting for them.[73] Adam's initial proposal for a rather rigid neo-classical theme was rejected and altered, and it was also decided to use the ceiling design that he had produced for the library at Croome in the tapestry room, which explains why it appears overscaled beside the intricate detail of the tapestries. The room also included six oval-backed, straight-legged chairs, two settees and five stools, all made by Ince and Mayhew to Adam's designs.

The main staircase is oddly unimpressive and tucked away at the eastern end of the building. Cantilevered with an iron balustrade, it does not relate to the fenestration and appears as an afterthought. A secondary staircase with turned oak balusters in the western

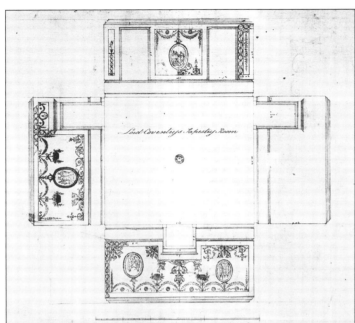

53 The Tapestry Room wall elevations by Robert Adam.

54 The Tapestry Room.

half of the house certainly predates the principal staircase and may have been part of the older house.[74] Adjacent to the main staircase, on the first floor of the Red Wing or offices, is a series of rooms which were altered in 1799 by James Wyatt into an apartment for Lord Coventry. Possibly he required in his old age a more convenient and compact private suite that was adjacent to the main staircase. These rooms include a highly-polished, bolection-moulded fireplace, studded with fossils, similar to that found in Lord Coventry's bedroom at the opposite end of the house, and probably salvaged from the old house. The rooms also contain some fine Jacobean panelling, again either salvaged from the earlier house, or possibly from the former parish church. This may have been installed in Lord Coventry's apartment by Wyatt, and later used to line the new partitions when the apartment was converted into a nursery. A letter dated 1828 refers specifically to the panelling in the nursery and a plan to paint it rather than cover it with wallpaper, 'as the Children could not injure it so much as the Peoperin [papering]'.[75]

Lord Coventry's bedroom, on the south-west side of the house, was distinguished by a large alcove, which contained a magnificent bed designed by Adam in 1763 in preparation for the Earl's forthcoming marriage, and made by France and Bradburn for £50 1s. 0d. It was Adam's first finished design for a bed, and it included a scrolled and carved dome, coved and carved cornices, and posts with spiral fluting and Corinthian capitals, the whole dressed in a fresh green linen.

Other notable items of furniture made for Lord Coventry at this time include Adam's design for 'A Tripod altered from a French design for a Water Stand' of 1767, based on an Athienne or classical tripod.[77] Eileen Harris has identified this with a sketch by Adam, which she believes provides conclusive evidence of Adam's knowledge and use of French neo-classical design, communicated to him by Lord Coventry and other patrons.[78] According to Anthony Coleridge, this was probably made for a basin or ewer of varnished redwood, which the 6th Earl had purchased in 1767 from Ince and Mayhew.[79] There was also a pier table in the Tapestry Room, which incorporated a black marble top supplied by John Wildsmith in 1759, which was inset with stone and marble samples so that it served the purpose of a mineral cabinet. Among the samples was a specimen of plumb pudding stone. The intended function of one other unusual item remains unclear. This is a casket on a stand, to which there is no reference in the accounts, but was almost certainly supplied by a major firm of cabinet-makers. What was it intended to contain? Could it have been a valuable family heirloom? Jill Tovey has suggested that it might be the silver-gilt basin and ewer referred to in the Lord Keeper's will.[80]

With the furnishing and decoration of Croome well under control, Lord Coventry could turn his attention once more toward the outbuildings and grounds. Between 1759 and 1767, Adam produced designs to alter the offices, reduce them in height and face them in ashlar with applied classical embellishments so that they might appear less dominant in profile and more prestigious in appearance.[81] His designs were not executed but, by way of a compromise, Adam designed a clock dial in 1765, and a lamp column in 1766 for the stables to provide some relief from Brown's massive and somewhat austere brick

55-58 *Above*. The stable courtyard. *Below left*. The stable clock and its workings. *Below right*. Adam's design for a stable lamp.

complex. The clock was made by Thomas Mudge of the famous London clockmakers Mudge & Dutton, who was the inventor of the lever escapement. Mudge's unusual design was unlike most turret or tower clocks in that it employed rack striking, a system whereby the same hour might be struck a number of times rather than in sequence. Also, the shaft of the hour hand is not a hollow tube but constructed of three long strips of iron fixed to circular rings to form a cylindrical cage.[82] Adam's stable lamp was placed at the centre of the courtyard within iron railings, and set on a column raised on a square pedestal with a swag frieze. (In his drawing at Sir John Soane's Museum 29(139) it is shown with a circular pedestal.) The lamp was demolished in the 1960s, but the pedestal was saved and relocated north of the stables where it now supports a statue of St Joseph. Adam's designs for the dairy interior of 1763-5 were probably not carried out until 1774-5, when the accounts refer to a bulk purchase of 'best white dutch tyles' to line the interior walls at a cost of £32 8s.7d. A pair of niches was set in the east wall to hold vases, although marble statues of the seasons were later installed instead, and marble tables ran right round the walls to support an impressive collection of Wedgwood china.[83] Little wonder that the Countess included her model dairy as a highlight of a tour round the house and grounds.

Adam produced two designs for a sundial between 1765-7, with a 'triangular pedestal and baluster for the dial'. The earlier design cost £1 7s. 0d. and the later more elaborate one cost two guineas, which was probably the one executed. This has since disappeared, but was originally located in the new kitchen garden, which covers a remarkable seven acres east of the stables on part of the site of the former kitchen garden established

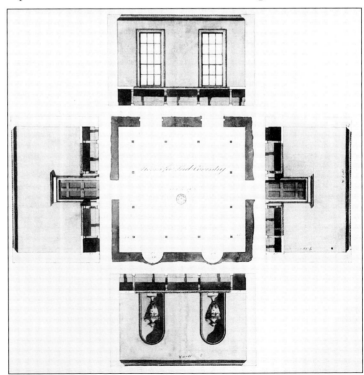

59 Dairy plan and wall elevations by Robert Adam.

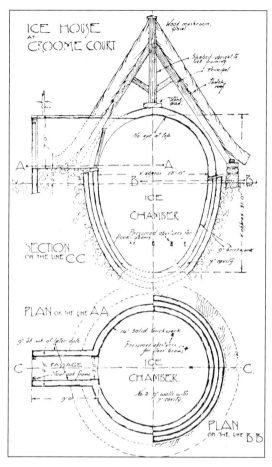

60   The Icehouse at Croome.

61   The Rotunda at Croome.

earlier in the century. North of the kitchen garden was built the icehouse, concealed within woodland beside the new church, while, to the south, a sinuous route led from the south portico past a semi-circular pool, which formed the south side of the stable quadrangle, through the Home Shrubbery. The path led past terms, the aviary and an elegant, ornamental hot-house towards the Rotunda on the ridge. The Rotunda is an endearing little circular and domed garden room, designed by Brown and built between 1754-7. It is framed within a glade of graceful and majestic Cedars of Lebanon, which form an essential element of the overall com-position, and it has superb views towards the Malvern Hills and Bredon. The door and windows are pedimented and set beneath panels with swags, and inside there is a coffered ceiling and stuccowork by Vassalli of 1761, which supplemented the original carved decoration by Alken.

Shrubberies, tree belts and clumps were planted to the north and east of the house, notably around the new lake and site of the Temple Greenhouse. The river was extended to trace a meandering course and its upper end now curved west to meet the new lake. It reflects the curving course of the River Severn a mile or so to the west as a complement to this important natural feature of the local landscape. Work also began on the inward-facing ha-ha, which ensured uninterrupted views from the house, and a 'scoop' was taken from the hill north-east of the house in preparation for the construction of the church.

In 1758 Richard Wilson (1713-82) com-memorated the completion of the house and initial stage of the landscape in his celebrated painting of Croome (colour plate

62   The elevation of the Temple Greenhouse by Robert Adam.

63   The Temple Greenhouse.

64 A preliminary sketch of Croome Court by Richard Wilson showing the new church on the hill in the distance built to a classical design as originally proposed. This sketch is in the possession of a private collector who has not been traced.

XIX). It shows Halfpenny's Chinese bridge and also the new church on the hill in the distance, built as an eye-catcher against a backdrop of dense woodland. A little artistic licence was applied here, as the church had not yet been built, but the site had been prepared and plans for the church were under discussion. A sketch by Wilson for his painting shows the church built in a classical style with a portico and dome, as was originally proposed.[84] The 6th Earl may have opted for a Gothic design as the height and vertical dimensions of the west tower would serve the purpose of an eye-catcher most effectively. The new church was dedicated to St Mary Magdalene rather than St James the Apostle, possibly in memory of the 6th Earl's first wife. It incorporated masonry from the demolished church, and comprises a three-bay, aisled nave with embattled parapets and two-light windows, a long chancel to house the monuments removed from the old church, and a prominent west tower. The tower has a pierced parapet with corner pinnacles, and at its base a fine pair of iron gates lead into the porch, which has a vaulted ceiling and side niches with hoodmoulds in the Gothick style. Tall, carved entrance doors lead into the main body of the building.[85] The gates, mouldings and doors were all designed by Adam, who appears to have taken over from Brown in 1761, probably before the building was complete, which may explain why two columns on each side of the nave are too wide for the entablature they support.[86] Robert Newman, John Hobcroft and Joseph Rose all contributed their expertise to the building, and Sefferin Alken was responsible for some of the plasterwork details. Adam's drawings for the interior were modified considerably in execution. He had planned imitation fan vaulting in the nave and aisles. The effect would have been a trifle overwhelming, a true rival to Shobdon church perhaps, but instead the 6th Earl opted for a more restrained scheme with an elliptical vault to the nave, a centrepiece to each bay, and plain, flat ceilings to the aisles (colour plate XX). The panelled dado rail was also omitted, but the ceiling mouldings, cornices and fine plasterwork detail, especially around the windows, entrance and chancel arch, partly compensate for this loss. Possibly the most regrettable omission was Adam's design for a splendid stained-glass east window, which would have cast a jewelled glow across the monuments and given the necessary definition to the eastern end.[87] (Colour plate XXI.) Adam also designed the limestone pavement, the iron altar rails, mouldings for the pews, a superb hexagonal pulpit with a gabled and pinnacled tester, reading desk and a 'fount', most probably the remarkable font, intricately carved by Alken for £11 14s. The rearrangement of the interior has since detracted from Adam's scheme. The pews were intended to be grouped in the corners of the nave, and the pulpit to be set high up against the north-eastern column with the reading desk below. All six bells were transferred from the old church, one of which was inscribed in memory of the 1st Earl.

The church was consecrated on 29 June 1763. From the porch and, especially from the roof of the tower, there are panoramic views across the park which convey the true extent of Brown's talent. Numerous members of the Coventry family have carved their names on the doors and walls of the tower stairs as they have climbed up to the roof to admire the view after a service. This graffiti makes an absorbing study in itself.

The land that had become the inner park, surrounded by the shrubbery belt, and church had been divided from the house by the original public road running from Pershore to the Severn. An important part of the recomposition of the landscape was the removal of the public road to the north of the inner park, where the natural curve of the eastern ridge of the park could conceal the road surface and mute the effect

65 Croome church doors by Robert Adam.

66 Croome church from William Dean's book, 1824.

of traffic. The old alignment became the eastern and western drives, which swept to the north façade of the Court in carefully controlled curves.

Road building was a significant element in the design of the wider landscape too. In 1782, for example, the road from Cubsmoor to Severn Stoke was lowered, widened by 15 feet, and laid with over ten inches of gravel to improve access to Severn Stoke and the Worcester/Tewkesbury road. The new village of High Green was also linked to Severn Stoke by a new carriageway that ran alongside Knight's Hill Pool, now much overgrown and partly disappeared.

From the 1760s the expenditure on the park increased considerably as both Adam and Brown were working for Lord Coventry, and significant additions were made. Brown completed the grotto beside the lake, built of tufa and spar; he also designed the dry arch, the boat house and the wooden bridges in the lake gardens, and was responsible for further levelling, planting, etc. in the park as it was steadily expanded. Lord Coventry owned just over 1,216 acres of land in Pirton. In 1762 the Enclosure Act for Pirton was passed and the Award followed in 1763. The necessary surveying work was undertaken by John Broome, and Brown probably drew up his plan for Pirton Park of *c.*1763 from this survey, which introduced islands into Pirton Pool and extensive planting, including a planted ride which linked the park with that at Croome. Additional areas of land were added to the east and west of the park at Defford and Cubsmoor, although Cubsmoor was not acquired altogether until 1773.[88] As planting continued apace in the park, Adam was commissioned to punctuate it with the necessary focal points.

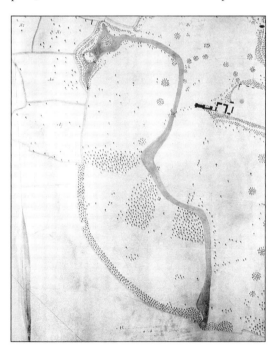

His earliest park building was the Temple Greenhouse or conservatory, designed in 1760 for the sum of 15 guineas.[89] Later a bothy was added to the rear, and Adam designed scroll stools for the interior in 1765. The building faces south towards the north front of the mansion and provides an important feature among the belt of trees, which run from the lake around to the foot of Church Hill. The design is similar to the conservatory at Osterley Park, with its central Doric portico, originally glazed with large sash windows. The flanking niches once contained painted lead statues of Flora and Ceres, supplied by John Cheere for £50 8s. 0d., but these niches are now glazed. In 1765 Sefferin Alken carved the final flourishes for the Greenhouse, a beautiful basket of flowers and festoons set within the pediment, and horns of plenty that decorate the panels of the end bays.[90]

67   Broome's survey of Croome drawn in 1763 but updated in 1768.

Adam's next project was Dunstall Castle. In a letter of 19 September 1765 to Lord Coventry he refers to a 'Drawing of the Ruin for a visto from your House. I think it might be built to have a good effect at a Distance at no great expence, as there does nor require much delicacy in the workmanship.' He was paid five guineas for his drawing, and from the accounts it is clear that the ruin was built between 1766-7. It is located about one mile south of Croome Court on Dunstall Common and was once clearly visible from the court. L-shaped in plan, it is a whimsical combination of Gothic and Romanesque detail, with a square tower at one end, and a round one at the other end and at the angle. The towers have blind round-arched openings, and there is one pointed and one round arch in the connecting masonry, the former designed

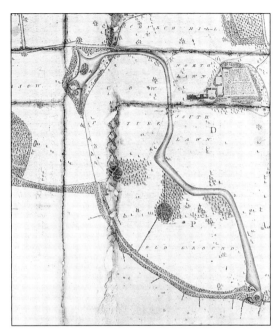

68   Snape's survey of Croome of 1796.

69   Dunstall Castle by E.F. and T.F. Burney. Pen and wash, 1781.

70   The Park Seat or Owl's Nest.

to appear as if it once incorporated tracery. Despite the documentary evidence
available, some Adam scholars dispute his
authorship on stylistic grounds, as nothing
comparable occurs within his other designs
of this period. Unfortunately, Adam's
drawing has not been traced, and the only
record of the ruin's original appearance is
the small sketch in the border of Snape's
map of Croome of 1796 and another
larger sketch, probably by Robert
Newman.[91]

Adam's design for the Alcove or Park
Seat, now referred to as the Owl's Nest
owing to a former occupant, dates from
1766.[92] Lord Coventry was charged six
guineas for the drawing but he paid a
further three guineas for a revised and
simpler version. The Seat was not built until 1770-2, and it stands on an elevated site
at the southern tip of the river with views towards Croome Court. It forms a small,
rectangular building with apsed ends, with an arched opening on small Tuscan columns.
These are flanked by larger columns, which support a pediment. Adam had intended
there to be an apse on the rear wall too, and the frieze, string course and fluted detail
on the columns were also omitted from the executed design, possibly to reduce costs.

Another important design of this period was for a 'building between the woods',
which was planned to stand on Knight's Hill at Cubsmoor at the western extremity of
the park. Adam provided at least three different versions of his design, one of which
was for a square building with a domed roof, while the other two incorporated a flat
roof with an observation gallery and a small central, domed room to contain the staircase.
There was a semi-recessed, semi-circular porch at the centre of each elevation, with niches
set behind a three-bay Corinthian screen, and each of these porches was also flanked
by niches set beneath relief panels. The Panorama Tower, as it became known, was
eventually built under the supervision of James Wyatt, who based his design on Adam's
ideas. It was not finally completed until after the 6th Earl's death, probably in 1812,
when the estate began to pay Window Tax on the building.[93]

Some uncertainty has arisen over the identity of the designer of the Island Temple
of 1776-8. Brown is the most likely candidate, but Adam's bills of 1771 refer to a design
for a Garden Seat and a bench for it, which could mean either the Alcove Seat or
this small temple building with Corinthian columns on one of the islands in the lake.
In 1778 several Coade plaques were installed inside; the larger one depicts the Aldobrandini
wedding, and there are two decorated with griffins, and two more with Phrygian
shepherds, all standard items from the Coade catalogue.[94]

As the landscape extended to the north and west, planted rides helped to link the various parts of the designed landscape so that two principal viewing circuits were established: a three-mile walk and a 10-mile ride. On the eastern perimeters of the park, a highlight of the tour included a visit to the Wilderness, noted for its truffles, the Arboretum, which had more than 300 exotic trees, carefully labelled and, above all, the rare delights of the Flower or Botanic Garden. This included a rock-work pool, two exotic houses devoted to East and West Indian plants and Cape plants, root houses and a conservatory for Chinese plants. Most of these plants were collected during the 1760s, 1770s and 1780s by friends and relations of the family and occasionally from more specialist suppliers, among whom was Lord Rochford, Ambassador at the Spanish Court and a friend of Lord Coventry. By 1800, the collection of plants at Croome was second only to that at Kew.[95] On 8 May 1764, Rochford sent Lord Coventry a list of plants that he had received from 'a very great Botanist' from the region around Barcelona, who promised to procure the seed Lord Coventry had requested. He added enthusiastically, 'I have seen two sorts of broom with purple flowers that grow in Galicia; the prettiest shrubs I ever saw. I have sent for some seeds, and you shall have some.' Lord Coventry's contacts from further afield included John Bush, who wrote to him on 20 September 1771 to inform him of his recent arrival in St Petersburg, and that he had already dispatched one box of plants, including ferns, orchids, lilies of the valley, birch, geranium, and rhododendron. He expressed his hopes of finding more in the spring, although it was 'dangerous in these woods to collect plants there being large Bears & Wolves'.[96]

A circuit of the park also promised a visit to Lady Coventry's Menagerie on Cubsmoor. Work began on the Menagerie around 1768, and it was planned initially as a modest

71   The Island Temple.

enterprise, with brick walls enclosing a few acres of grass, a number of pens, sheds and aviaries built against the walls, and a small brick dwelling at the eastern end for the keeper. Lady Coventry supervised the upkeep of her birds herself at first but as her collection increased she employed a Mr. Watmough as keeper.[97] Soon she had 135 birds in total, of 21 different kinds, including silver pheasants, Canada geese, Turkish ducks, Cape geese, white turkeys, Guinea Fowl, 'Sparrows of Paradise', a pair of red-headed parakeets, a 'Nunn' bird, and a 'Snow' bird. The only mammals among her Menagerie appear to have been a flying squirrel, acquired on 27 September 1789, and possibly two American deer.[98] Such was the interest that the Menagerie aroused that in 1780 a charge of five shillings was made by the Mayor and Corporation of Worcester upon the city to pay for their visit. Clearly, it was time to upgrade the place, and it was decided to add a banqueting house where guests might take refreshment and which would lend distinction to the whole. In 1780, Adam provided Lord and Lady Coventry with a magnificent design, which included an imposing banqueting house with an adjoining tearoom and accommodation for the keeper. This was linked to corner pavilions by a balustraded wall with blind arcading which increased the scale and grandeur of the composition. The best birds were to be housed in the pavilions and the rest in a continuous row of aviaries that ran along the walls. Adam charged Lord Coventry £21 for the design, around £2,500 today, but well worth it for a drawing of such quality and detail. It cannot have failed to impress Lord Coventry, but for some reason it was never built. Possibly he decided that it was too large and ostentatious for its purpose, but this must have been discussed at an early stage. Most probably, Lord Coventry had last minute doubts about the expense and sheer vulgarity of it all, and instead Adam designed a new front for the existing keeper's dwelling with large windows facing west from which to view the Menagerie.[99] This cost just £107 4s. 5d. to build, although it was decidedly more dull. At least Lord Coventry's guests could take tea beside the fine Adam fireplace with a fluted frieze, which now graced the interior. Further improvements followed after 1805, when numerous fruit trees were planted that provided welcome shade and softened the stark outlines of the Menagerie.[100]

Up till the early 1780s Brown was still busy in the park. The third phase of drainage works were under way, repairs were made to the head of the lake, and additional plantations were created. The Grotto was completed and its interior studded with fossils and gems. A Coade nymph, Sabrina, the goddess of the Severn, was installed, with water falling from her urn to feed the lake. Recent archaeological work undertaken by the National Trust has unearthed a profusion of fragments of the original decorations and exposed a long buried pool, set with fossils, tropical shells and large rounded pebbles. More work remains to be done. Additional sunk fencing was constructed, and Pirton Farm and the new cottages, farm and inn at High Green were built in lieu of the demolished Croome village that had stood formerly to the north-east of the mansion house. This must have been a satisfying period for both Brown and Lord Coventry, for the early planting began to mature and the landscape began to assume its intended form. The compliments had been forthcoming for years; as early as 1767

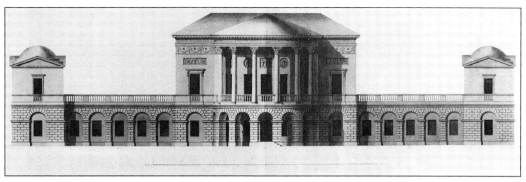

72 *Above.* Menagerie elevation by Robert Adam which was unexecuted.

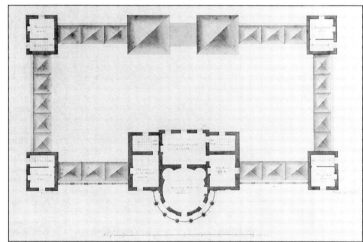

73 *Right.* A plan of the Menagerie by Robert Adam, which was also unexecuted.

74 *Below.* The keeper's house at the Menagerie as remodelled by Robert Adam.

75   The Grotto, *c.*1971.

76   Sabrina, the nymph of the Grotto.

Croome was referred to in an anonymous tribute to Brown in equal terms with Blenheim:

> But your great Artist, like the source of light,
> Gilds every scene with beauty and delight;
> At Blenheim, Croome, and Caversham we trace
> Salvator's Wildness, Claud's enlivening grace,
> Cascades and Lakes as fine as Risdale drew,
> While nature's vary'd in each charming view.
> To paint his works wou'd Poussin's powers require,
> Milton's sublimity and Dryden's fire.

Brown never claimed to be an artist, but Richard Wilson may also have appreciated the compliment.

On 25 August 1771, Lord Temple of Stowe wrote to Lord Coventry:

> I am now approaching those happy territories which are more immediately under the mild influence of your Lordship's Rule and Government. Duty and Inclination lend me to pay my Court to your lordship at your Country Palace at Crome [*sic*].[101]

The following July, Lord and Lady Coventry were invited to Stowe, perhaps to compare notes. Then, in his *A Tour through parts of England, Scotland & Wales* of 1778, Richard Sulivan was most effusive in his praise of Croome:

> The grounds are elegant, and kept in the nicest order. On leaving the house, you turn through a shrubbery, filled with a choice assemblage of plants to a small building on an eminence, called the Rotunda, whence you have a prospect of hill, wood and dale, and of every beauty that can give richness to a scene. Nature has, in this view, poured a profusion of her bounties.

Of course, nothing could be further from the truth. It was Brown that had inveigled Nature into such apparent acts of generosity.

Brown was returning home from dining with the Coventry family in London when he collapsed and died in February 1783. His death was a considerable personal loss to Lord Coventry, as Brown had shared and realised his ideals and ambitions and over the years he had come to value his companionship as much as his advice. In 1793 he wrote to Humphry Repton that he 'certainly held him [Brown] very high as an artist and esteemed him as a most sincere friend'.[102] A series of watercolours of Croome were made by E.F. and T.F. Burney in 1784, initially intended as illustrations for Nash's county history, and these serve as a charming record of the park at the end of Brown's time.[103] A Coade stone casket in memory of Brown was erected beside the lake at Croome in 1797. The inscription on the pedestal read:

> To the Memory of
> Lancelot Brown
> Who by the powers of
> His inimitable
> and creative genius
> formed this garden scene
> Out of a morass.

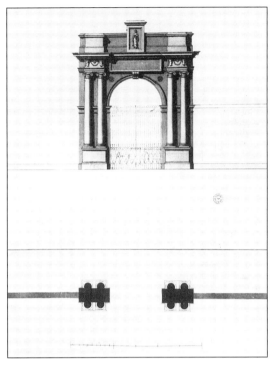

77   Sketch for the London Arch by Robert Adam.

78   The London Arch by E.F. and T.F. Burney. Pen and wash.

Although Adam continued to produce designs for Lord Coventry right up till the early 1790s, many, like the outstanding Menagerie design, were never executed. He produced three designs for bridges across the river, in 1761,1781 and one undated, the best of which was embellished with swags and relief panels. Others include designs for gateways, among them the new Pershore gateway, known as the London Arch, designed in 1779. According to David King, this impressive structure resembles the Roman arch at Pula in the Balkans, which Adam saw in 1757, but it is more widely believed that he sought inspiration from the Temple of the Sun at Palmyra. The archway is flanked by pairs of Ionic columns, which support a frieze enriched with ox skulls, and above this rises a prominent blocking course with relief panels on each face. These represent Night and Day, with Day mounted above the outer face to welcome Lord Coventry

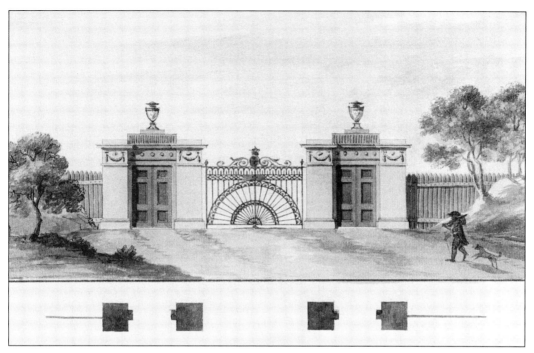

79 A design for the Pier Gateway by Robert Adam.

on his arrival at Croome. Regrettably, this relief panel is now missing. Adam designed gates for the archway with a horizontal top rail, but, as executed, the gates have a curved profile, and, as an afterthought, he sketched in flanking stretches of low walling terminating in a pier surmounted by a lion. The walling was built, but it was decided to top the piers with large Coade urns in 1795. Three designs were made by Adam for lodges to be added to an existing gateway, very probably the London arch, but the lodge adjacent to the London arch was the work of James Wyatt, and it was rebuilt in 1877. In 1791 Adam also made a design to alter the Pier Gates by the lake, which may have been built to an earlier design of his, and which derived its name from the broad piers, which flanked wooden doors either side of the elaborate iron gate in the carriage entrance. After Adam's death the following year the scheme was abandoned temporarily.

One other drawing by Adam in the Croome archive presents a mystery. Adam charged five guineas for it on 14 April 1780, and there seems a strong possibility that it was intended as a new front for Severn Bank House at Severn Stoke, as the plan and dimensions conform so closely with those of its north elevation. Severn Bank was a fishing lodge of probable early 18th-century origin that stood on high ground overlooking the River Severn. It served as a useful 'place of pleasure for fishing parties', but the 6th Earl may have decided to upgrade it with an elegant classical façade in keeping with his other buildings in the park. From Adam's drawing, we can see that the elevation was already bow-fronted and of two storeys, and Adam planned merely to add end pilasters and an arcade attached to the central bow to support a balcony or viewing

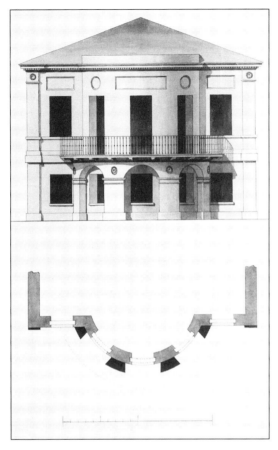

80   An elevation of a house by Robert Adam was probably proposed as a remodelling for the north front of Severn Bank House, Severn Stoke. It was unexecuted.

platform. He also enlarged the upper-floor windows to provide access onto this new balcony.

For some reason, these alterations were never carried out and the building was simply repaired and re-roofed instead. Robert Newman's bills of 1781-2 reveal that the building was already castellated by this time, as he was paid for 'plain work' and 'moulded and sunk work' to the existing battlements. It also appears that it was rough-cast, presumably to give the appearance of stone, and this was replaced with stucco. This suggests that before 1780 the building had already assumed its picturesque Gothick appearance, and Lord Coventry may have decided to retain and enhance its romantic character, which was most appropriate to its setting. A large amount of timber was felled in the surrounding woodland at this time to create vistas through the trees towards the river, and the relevant accounts show that the pleasure boat at Severn Bank was repaired in 1787 and a sunk fence and icehouse were added in 1790. Further alterations occurred around 1820, when the building was occupied by Elizabeth Williams, mistress of the 8th Earl, but these were not completed till after the 8th Earl's death when the house was let to the Dent family, the Worcester glove manufacturers. These alterations included the addition of a third storey that gave the building a more dramatic profile from the river, a large service wing at the eastern end of the building, and, finally, a new driveway, a garden wall with Gothick panelling and an embattled entrance lodge.

In 1792, Robert Adam died, and the 6th Earl was asked to be one of the pallbearers at his funeral at Westminster Abbey. After Adam's death, Lord Coventry commissioned James Wyatt to complete the unfinished projects, which took until 1805. Wyatt produced an altered version of Adam's Pier Gates in 1793, which supported large shallow oval vases of Coade stone rather than the tall, smaller vases proposed by Adam, and earned the gateway the name of the Punchbowl Gates. He also added the lodge to the London arch and designed the Worcester lodge and gates, remodelled the dry arch, replaced the wooden bridges on the lake with iron ones, and added various items of Coade statuary, notably the sphinxes on the south front, the Druid in the Greenhouse Shrubbery, and the Coade stone casket in memory of Brown. However, Wyatt's most important contribution was the eye-catchers, the Panorama Tower and Pirton Tower (colour plates XVII and XVIII).

The Panorama Tower at Cubsmoor was, as mentioned previously, based on Adam's earlier designs. Wyatt painted a beautiful watercolour perspective of his design in 1801, although the work did not start on the building till 1805 and was not complete till 1812. Pirton Tower was another sham castle, set high on Rabbit Bank in Pirton Park among a row of cedars with southerly views towards Croome. Wyatt painted a watercolour of the ruin in 1801, presumably of the completed building rather than a proposal.

Wyatt also designed the famous Broadway Tower for Lord Coventry, high on the Cotswold escarpment, from where his estates in Worcestershire and Gloucestershire could be seen in a single glance. It is said that a beacon was lit on the top of the tower to warn the staff at Croome of Lord Coventry's imminent arrival from London. Wyatt's plan and elevation for the tower date from 1794, and its unusual Saxon or Romanesque design is an important example of the growing contemporary concern for archaeological authenticity. Wyatt may have been influenced by Gibbs's Gothic Temple at Stowe of 1741, by Flitcroft's Alfred's Tower at Stourhead in Wiltshire, of 1765-72, and, more

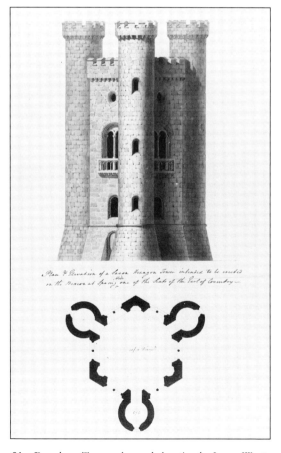

importantly, by his knowledge of original architecture of the period, such as Orford Keep in Suffolk, described and engraved by William King in his *Observations on Ancient Castles* of 1783.[104] The hexagonal tower has three round turrets at alternate corners and is four storeys high, its main storey, at third-floor level, having large round-arched openings of two lights, which lead onto balconies with balustrades of intersecting round-arched arcades on squat columns with cushion capitals. The tower was acquired by Sir Thomas Phillips in 1824, and in 1867 he leased it to Cormell Price, a friend of William Morris. It was while Morris was staying at the tower in September 1876 that he drafted his letter to *The Athenaeum* that led to the formation of the Society for the Protection of Ancient Buildings.

During the early years of the 19th century, the plant collection at Croome continued to increase. Thousands of trees, shrubs and herbaceous plants were supplied in accordance with detailed lists drawn up by William Dean, now head gardener. In

81 Broadway Tower, plan and elevation by James Wyatt.

his *Annals of Agriculture* of 1801, Arthur Young rated Croome second only to Kew as a botanical garden. He observed that 'not a thistle or a weed can be seen, not a single tree or shrub out of its proper place'. Dean notes that among the collection were plants from Otaheite, an island in the South Pacific that had been visited by Captain Cook in 1796. He also listed 27 varieties of oak and pine, 14 species of olive, 26 kinds of acacia, 27 different aloes and an astonishing 191 species of heather.[105] It would be interesting to know whether Dean persuaded Lord Coventry to invest in the 'little wind engine' offered to him by a millwright of Tewkesbury at this time. It was recommended that this be 'Built and put in a floate on your Lordship's Serpentine River to move to any place to water the shrubs or green sward …' and was claimed to be 'the first thought of that kind in ye Kingdom'.[106] Numerous new hot houses and greenhouses were rebuilt and altered during this later period to accommodate the expanding plant collection.[107] For example, in 1805 George Tod supplied a new vinery and shed for £241 12s. 4d., which was described in his *Plans … of Hothouses* of 1812 as being 'constructed entirely upon arches, in order that the vines may not be interrupted in spreading their roots. One fire heats this house; coming in at one end; it goes all round, returns upon itself, and out by a chimney at the other end.' Continual alterations and improvements to the kitchen garden and hot houses during the 19th century have obliterated much of the work undertaken during the 6th Earl's period of ownership.

Towards the end of the 6th Earl's life, the bills for work at Croome had risen to around £20,000 a year. A proportionate increase in rentals accommodated this increase quite comfortably, together with income from sales of timber and livestock, notably the livestock sale held in December 1796, which raised £1,644 9s. 0d. When tax increases threatened to unbalance the accounts, Lord Coventry responded promptly. The Window Tax was a particular problem as there was a total of 167 windows at Croome Court, and he drew up a list of windows 'that might be stopped without prejudice', some of which are still visible on the east elevation of the house.[108]

In his *Views of the Seats, Mansions, Castles etc of Noblemen and Gentlemen in England, Wales, Scotland and Ireland,* of 1822, J.P. Neale wrote of the 'exuberance of timber in full growth' and of 'the rising plantations' at Croome, 'magnificent scenery, where it might have been supposed art was unavailable …'. It has been argued that the design of the landscape did not evolve slowly but adhered to a coherent scheme. Thus both viewing circuits were devised to pay tribute to the elements and the seasons, and to confront the visitor with contrasting images of civilisation and decay, and of wilderness and plenty.[109] This would be hard to disprove, not least because such contrasts are inherent within any artificial landscape or garden where the natural world has been tamed and cultivated by mankind's endeavours. Also, the degree to which the balance between maintenance and natural decay is retained is governed as much by practical as aesthetic considerations. Certainly such a claim has little bearing on the historic and aesthetic value of the landscape park as a major work of art. For over one hundred years the park remained almost unchanged and was allowed to mature gracefully, tended with expert care by the 6th Earl's descendants as a tribute to his achievement.

Coventry House, No. 29 (now 106) Piccadilly

The work at Croome was well in hand by 1764, when the 6th Earl of Coventry embarked upon his new London home. The family still had their houses in St James Square and in Grosvenor Square, so his motive for buying another house in London is unclear, especially as he was laying down so much money towards Croome at the time. Probably, his decision was connected with his second marriage in 1764 to Barbara St John. Not only did she bring a considerable sum of money to the marriage, but it may have seemed appropriate to acquire a new home free of associations with his former wife. Also, as an enthusiastic patron of the arts, the 6th Earl may have welcomed this opportunity to exhibit his excellent taste and exert his influence in a home within the most fashionable part of London overlooking Green Park. In 1759 Walpole had observed twenty new stone houses in the street, certainly sufficient incentive for Lord Coventry to add his name to this exclusive list.

The site of Coventry House was originally occupied by an inn called *The Greyhound*, and was on part of the London estate of the Marquess of Bath. The inn was leased to Sir Henry Hunloke, who came from a Derbyshire family seated at Wingerworth Hall,

near Chesterfield, a classical mansion designed by Francis Smith of Warwick in 1726 and now demolished. In 1759 Sir Henry took out a 99-year lease on the site and built himself a new house, which was completed in 1762. The architect is un-known, but Matthew Brettingham the elder (1725-1803) is a possibility, who worked for Edward Coke, Earl of Leicester, and had supervised the building of Holkham Hall, designed by William Kent. Hunloke married Margaret Coke, a relative of the Whig magnate Thomas Coke of Holkham in 1764.[110]

The house has retained its impressive façade. There is a rusticated ground floor with blind arcading, and the windows of the *piano nobile* have alternate triangular and segmental pediments, the central window emphasised by console brackets beneath the pediment. Originally each of the windows on the *piano nobile* had its own balustrade set into the window embrasure; the present cast-iron balcony across the whole width of the façade is 19th-century. Inside the house there was an adjoining

82 Coventry House, 106 Piccadilly, London.

saloon and withdrawing room on the *piano nobile,* which faced onto the park, and behind the saloon was located the principal bedroom and one of two small octagonal rooms, which formed a dressing room. Hunloke lived at the house for only two years, and in 1764 he assigned the remaining 94 years of his lease to Lord Coventry.[111] Sir Henry's marriage to Margaret Coke may have influenced his decision to sell. The precise figure Lord Coventry paid is unknown, but apparently Sir Henry wanted 'what it cost him [to build it], with the interest of this money'.[112]

At once Lord Coventry commissioned Adam to alter the house to suit his personal requirements. Initial survey work undertaken in the autumn of 1764 suggests that major structural work was proposed, and an undated plan in the Soane Museum shows the first floor with eight principal rooms arranged around two courtyards. As no accounts exist for any structural or exterior work, Lord Coventry must have changed his mind and opted for a more modest scheme of refurbishment, which included replacing plasterwork and joinery and refitting the service quarters in the basement. Work began in late spring 1765 and took around a year to complete. Several of the craftsmen who had worked at Croome were employed at Coventry House, including Sefferin Alken, John Hobcroft and Joseph Rose. Work progressed slowly and, on 19 September 1765, Adam wrote to inform Lord Coventry of the delay:

> I was in hope that the House in Town would have been more advanced than it is. But things go on vastly slow. The relaying of the floors has retarded Mr Rose's people so that the Bed Chamber is the only room that is yet finished … I propose to get the Plasterer sett to work immediately in the Great Rooms & shall do all I can to push them on. But as Rose has been at Margate bathing for his health things move slower in his absence.[113]

Most attention was lavished on the first-floor suite of rooms, the 'Great Rooms' referred to in Adam's letter. Each was provided with a new ceiling and chimneypiece. Adam made six designs for chimneypieces for the house, but none of these survive *in situ*

and may not all have been executed. The finest ceiling was in the drawing room and is still intact. This has a wide border with inset roundels containing busts and urns. The central portion is divided into three compartments; the largest central compartment containing a vast roundel with a painted centrepiece, and there are additional paintings within ovals and medallions incorporated in the side compartments. The paintings are by the Venetian artist, Antonio Zucchi (1726-95), who knew Adam in Italy and had made the drawings for his book, *Ruins of the Palace of the Emperor Diocletian at Spalato*

83 A detail of the saloon ceiling at Coventry House, Piccadilly, London.

(1764). Zucchi charged 10 guineas for the central 'Tableau des Muses', 16 guineas for 'Les Deux Triomphes' in the side ovals, and 12 guineas for all four medallions. The carved detail and stucco decoration in the octagonal dressing room is also quite outstanding. Four walls contained the fireplace, door, window and a mirror, while the slightly narrower walls between them included grotesque panels, now obscured behind protective boarding. On completion, the house boasted one of the finest Adam interiors in London and was furnished with some of the best items from Lord Coventry's growing collection of paintings, furniture and plate.

In 1788 a fire broke out in an adjacent house. According to Berrow's *Worcester Journal*, Lady Coventry had a very narrow escape and was forced to rush out onto the street with 'hardly time to slip on her cloaths'. There she remained 'in much perturbation' till the arrival of Lord Chesterfield, who escorted her to Chesterfield House for the night. Presumably Lord Coventry was not in the house at the time, but his brother John is said to have slept so soundly that he did not wake even when the fire burst into his room and 'communicated itself to his curtains'. A mob gathered in the street eager to assist in the removal of Lord Coventry's furniture, not entirely for Lord Coventry's benefit, and it was left to Lord Chesterfield to resist their efforts. The extent of the fire damage is unknown. No major repairs seem to have been required, but some of the furnishings and decorations must have been lost and had to be replaced at considerable expense. It was possibly on the site of the fire that the Earl of Barrymore began to construct a new house for himself later that year. Adam was consulted to carry out negotiations with him on Lord Coventry's behalf to ensure that the new building would not block light from the Venetian stair window at Coventry House. In 1796, James Wyatt was commissioned to carry out minor alterations and repairs mainly to the offices, including re-paving the kitchen passage.

In 1799 an insurance valuation was made of Croome Court and Coventry House and their contents. The former building was valued at £15,000 and the latter at £8,000, but the contents of Coventry House were valued at around twice as much as the contents of Croome. An Inventory made after the 6th Earl's death assessed the value of the contents as follows:[114]

Furniture, Looking Glasses, China, Glass and Books	2753	15s	0d
Pictures	3892	11s	0d
Plate	459	0s	0d
Wine	1319	19s	0d

In its heyday, Coventry House was among the finest private houses that lined Piccadilly and invitations to a ball or assembly at this veritable treasure house were much sought after. Such a luxurious reputation proved difficult to sustain, and, as is described in the following chapter, by the mid-19th century the family had abandoned the house and removed its contents to Croome.

Springhill House, Broadway, Worcestershire

Croome may have been the 6th Earl's lifelong obsession, but as early as 1750 he had admitted to Miller that the 'Hospitality my Ancestors exercised for some generations at Croomb makes it impossible for me to effect any privacy or retirement there. It has always been an Inn and always must remain so.'[115] At the time of his second marriage, he embarked not just on a new London home but a new house in the country too. Evidently delighted with Brown's exertions at Croome, he commissioned him to build a house on his Broadway estate in 1763, so that he might pursue his sporting and horticultural interests in more secluded surroundings. Brown's design was appropriately understated but sufficiently well equipped to ensure that Lord Coventry need not compromise comfort for seclusion. The house was described in 1819 as 'a mansion beautifully situated on an eminence in the centre of a small park of about sixty acres'.[116] It had a plain ashlar façade of five bays, with a central entrance accentuated by a modest pediment, flanking service wings and ample stabling and outbuildings. Its ample accommodation included seven best bedrooms, a music room, a nursery, extensive offices and an excellent wine and beer cellar. There was stabling for 17 horses, a cottage for the bailiff and the gardener, a summerhouse, an icehouse, and a walled garden with a peach house, a greenhouse, a pinery and a melon ground. Lord Coventry altered and extended it twice, in 1783-4 and 1797, and he described the house to Humphry Repton as being 'without any pretension to architecture' but 'perhaps a model for every internal and domestic convenience'.

After 1809, Springhill became the home of Lord Coventry's second son, John, and in 1824 the lease was acquired by the Lygon family of Madresfield, Worcestershire. The Lygon family had been created Earls Beauchamp in 1815, and were related to the Coventry family by marriage when the 8th Earl married Emma Susannah Lygon, the second daughter of the 1st Earl Beauchamp on 16 January 1808. The house was used primarily by Henry Lygon, a successful politician, and his brother Colonel Edward Lygon. Edward Lygon had joined Wellington's army in 1812 and, after he distinguished himself at Waterloo, he was made a colonel and later achieved the rank of general. To commemorate this epic victory, he spent the next few years planting a complex collection of spinneys on the hillside at Springhill, which were intended to represent the troop formations at the battle.

84   Springhill House, Broadway, from a 19th-century drawing.

* * * * * *

The 6th Earl of Coventry died at Coventry House on 3 September 1809. He was 87. His body was taken to Croome and met at Evesham by the whole body of his tenants. His funeral procession was said to be a mile long, and a simple and elegant wall memorial was erected in the new church at Croome, designed by Bacon Junior, with a relief of a kneeling woman beneath an urn on a pedestal.

Lord Deerhurst did not attend the funeral. Towards the end of his life, the 6th Earl had made a concerted effort to improve his relationship with his eldest son, who was invited to Springhill, and received the usual placatory gifts of venison from Croome; but he left it far too late. Such gestures merely irritated old wounds, and Lord Deerhurst valued his integrity too much to play the hypocrite as chief mourner at the funeral. His son sent him a detailed account of the sombre but magnificent occasion.[117] He wrote of 'the grandeur with which the proceedings were conducted', the 'respect shown by every class of people', but most significantly he added:

> whatever his private faults may have been, he certainly possessed to an eminent degree the admiration of people in this county with regard to the upright and sensible part taken in his public situation— few men indeed have died more honourably than Lord Coventry—& as (if I know you at all) you possess as well as myself a tolerable share of Family pride, the reflection of my humble description of the general feeling exibited [sic] must afford you as it does me the highest satisfaction and gratification ...

A monument was erected in memory of the 6th Earl in the park at Croome on 25 October 1809, the jubilee of George III. He had died within weeks of the King's jubilee, just as his first wife, fifty years earlier, had much to her regret died within weeks of the King's coronation. The inscription on the monument was composed with admirable care and sensitivity:

Sacred to him the genius of this place
Who reared these shades and formed these sweet retreats
With every incense breathing shrub adorned
And flower of faintest hue
His cultured tastes and native fancy bathed the scene around
Rise perfect and amuse who much he loved
Still joys to haunt it
Crowned with length of days
He lived one wish alone unsated
Much his loyal heart had cherished
Fond hopes to hail the day of Jubilee
And close his earthly course in Britain's hour of joy.

Not far from the monument, the 6th Earl's great-grandson planted an acorn. The gesture was moving in its simplicity, and the metaphor would have been much appreciated by his great-grandfather.

VIII

Blind Heirs and Disgraces

George William, 7th Earl of Coventry (1758-1831)

The will of the 6th Earl of Coventry was cleverly contrived and pointedly phrased to deal a final reprimand to his eldest son.[1] He did not disinherit him, as this would have gone against the grain, but with pedantic precision he made sure that even death would not heal their deep-seated resentment of one another. As the 6th Earl had left such a glittering fortune, his ruthless selectivity was all the more pertinent. At the time of his death, his estates were worth around £35,000 per annum, and he owned property worth over £120,000. Croome, its contents, and the remainder of his estates in Worcestershire and Gloucestershire, were inherited by Viscount Deerhurst, now 7th Earl of Coventry. Springhill, his retreat, and his other property in the Cotswolds and in Somerset, he left to his second son, John, the only one of his sons referred to as 'my beloved son'. The youngest son, Thomas William, earned hardly a mention, and his inclusion in the will appears a necessary formality and nothing more. Thomas's marriage to an obscure woman from Evesham, possibly a servant at Croome, sealed his fate as far as his father was concerned, and he died in obscurity and poverty in 1816, suffering from some mental disorder, 'a sad and melancholy instance of the effects of indiscretion & imprudence'.[2] His brothers shared his funeral expenses and he was quietly forgotten.[3]

The division of the estate was quite proper and predictable with the exception of the leasehold mansion in Piccadilly. The 6th Earl left this to John, on the strict instruction that the contents were to be sold to cover his funeral expenses and to discharge his debts. He knew perfectly well that this would be a major disappointment to his eldest son, so he included a clause in his will calculated to place him under considerable pressure and inconvenience just when his sense of indignation would still be running high. Under this clause, George William, now 7th Earl, had the right to purchase both Coventry House and its contents for £14,000 from his brother, provided that he signified his wish to do so in writing within three months of their father's death. John, of course, was appointed as sole executor of the will.

Thus John was very well provided for, Thomas virtually ignored, and George William inconvenienced as much as possible. It was to the credit of the two elder brothers that they handled a potentially difficult situation with such amicable and dignified discretion that any devious intentions their father might have had were neatly swept aside. The 7th Earl wrote the required letter to his brother and, by 1810, he had moved out of his home in Devonshire Place and was making plans for the refurbishment of Coventry House. Furthermore, he made sure that the necessary £14,000 was raised in a way of which his father would have totally disapproved. Over 2,000 oaks and 150 elms were felled on the Croome and Pirton estates.[4] The 6th Earl must have guessed that his trees were at risk, for in his will he had made it clear that his eldest son would inherit Croome as a tenant for life 'without Impeachment of Waste', that is, without the authority to fell any tree other than those that were dead, dying or for thinning purposes. Felling such vast quantities of timber must have stretched this legal loophole to the limits but, if Dean and other contemporary guides are to be believed, the task was executed in such a way as to have minimal impact upon the Croome landscape.

The remaining and larger proportion of the money was raised by a sale of much of the 6th Earl's cherished collection of paintings 'by Mr Christie at his Great Room, Pall Mall' on 16 and 17 February 1810. Over two hundred items were included in the auction, many of the highest quality, including work by Holbein, Rubens, Veronese, Tintoretto, Caravaggio and Canaletto. The departure of this valuable hoard from the walls of Croome Court and Coventry House was a regrettable loss, but perhaps the 7th Earl derived some sense of personal justice by their disposal, not least because he spent most of his adult life blind. Indeed neither sale appears to have been conducted principally for financial gain.

Only weeks after his father's remains had been placed in the vault at Croome, the 7th Earl placed a stream of orders for jewellery and plate with Rundell, Bridge & Rundell, the royal jewellers and goldsmiths. These purchases continued unabated for the next few years, costing on average several thousand pounds per annum, and included a set of diamond and turquoise bracelets and earrings worth over £900, and a necklace of 61 diamonds, which cost £274. There were also four magnificent ice pails of chased silver with grapevine borders deco-rated with the family coat of arms, bought for £747 14s., and a splendid pair of chased silver candlesticks decorated with female heads and a honeysuckle pattern that cost £442 11s. 6d. Evidently, the 7th Earl was determined to enjoy his inheritance, albeit in a more tactile form.

George William, the youngest child of the 6th Earl's marriage to Maria Gunning, was born on 28 April 1758.[5] (Colour plate XXII.) He left Christchurch, Oxford on

85 A Christie's sales catalogue from 1811.

5 January 1776 to become an Ensign in the 64th Foot Regiment and by the following
year he had risen to the rank of lieutenant in the 17th Light Dragoons. His relationship
with his father began to deteriorate not long after he had left home, when he acquired
friends of dubious reputation eager to take advantage of his generous allowance. Clearly
his conduct gave genuine cause for concern, as his father soon banned him from both
Croome and Coventry House. Probably, the high-spirited young viscount was too much
like his mother for his own good. When, at the age of 19 he eloped to Scotland with
Lady Catherine Henley (c.1760-79) during the winter of 1776, he finally overstepped the
mark. Under different circumstances, the match might have met with Lord Coventry's
wholehearted approval. She was the fourth daughter of Robert Henley, 1st Earl of
Northington (d.1772), a former Lord Chancellor, and the last person to hold the title
of Lord Keeper, a title deeply ingrained in the Coventry family history. It seems that
her excellent credentials only intensified Lord Coventry's anger and embarrassment and,
with necessary haste, he arranged for the errant couple to be remarried some weeks
later on 18 March 1777, in Worcestershire rather than London, away from the public
gaze. Scandal was neatly averted, but Lord Deerhurst was made to pay for his wilful
behaviour. Immediately after his marriage, he promised his father he would set sail for
America to fight for his country in the American War of Independence. In view of
the 6th Earl's views on the war, this seems somewhat hypocritical. When Deerhurst's
ship was detained in Portsmouth harbour by a contrary wind, he took the opportunity
to write to his stepmother, Lady Coventry, on 24 March 1777, to enquire whether his
father's anger 'was so far mitigated as to flatter me with a possibility of a reconciliation
…', he added:

> I shall leave this Country with that only Comfort and will improve it by a strict Alteration to my
> Conduct … If I should on my Return find his Resolutions unalterable (which God forbid) I must live
> a victim of my own Indiscretions.[6]

The voyage appears to have weakened his own resolution, for only a few weeks after
his arrival he sold his commission for £500 and returned home. Maybe he regretted
leaving his new wife so hastily and had no wish to endanger his life in a vain attempt
to mollify his father. The 6th Earl was not impressed, and for the next two years Deerhurst
strived to secure his forgiveness with Lady Coventry's assistance, but to no avail. By
17 December 1777, he wrote to his stepmother that: 'Time appears to wear my Father
of every spark of paternal affection', and, more desperately, that he would 'willingly enter
a dungeon' to recover his father's favour.

On 9 March 1779, Lady Deerhurst died in childbirth in Ledbury, Herefordshire. For
the next 18 months, Lord Deerhurst drifted aimlessly through the houses of his friends
and relatives. Much of the winter season was spent with the Foleys in Herefordshire,
and during the summer he stayed on the Isle of Wight. Towards the end of the following
year, further misfortune befell him when he was blinded in a hunting accident. Reports
differ as to the precise location. Some accounts state that he was hunting with the King
in Windsor forest, while others claim he was many miles away in Oxfordshire accompanied

by the Duke of Beaufort. With characteristic imprudence, he forced his horse to jump a five-barred gate. The horse slipped, and fell on him with such force that his right eye 'was beat into his head, his nose broke and laid flat to his face', and he was 'much mangled'. Probably he was lucky to survive at all, and he seems to have been remarkably accident-prone, for the *London Chronicle* reported that he had shot himself in the leg just a month before this accident took place.[7] Recovery was slow, but by 27 January 1781 he could tell light from dark and there was a possibility that his left eye might be saved. But this hope dwindled as the months past, and by 1785 he had taken to wearing a green silk patch over the remains of his right eye, while his left eye, yellowed and sightless but not deformed, he kept exposed.

To his credit, Lord Deerhurst appears to have resigned himself to his predicament with admirable fortitude, and for the next twenty years his father's lack of compassion gave him far greater cause for discontent than his injuries. He carried out his official and social duties with enthusiasm and commitment, he continued to ride and breed horses and was considered an excellent judge of horseflesh. He was noted for his regular attendance at his box at the Theatre Royal, Drury Lane, and he engaged in building projects and similar enterprises with all the energy and enterprise of his father.[8] Only his hesitant signature with its uncrossed 't' served as a reminder of his disability. Tributes to his courage appeared in the press, among them the following sonnet composed by a family friend, the newspaper proprietor and poet, John Taylor:

> No more to view the glorious Orb of day,
> Ah! COVENTRY, the fate of MILTON thine!
> Yet, not like him, in sorrow dost thy pine,
> Resign'd with firmness, with discretion gay;
> Like him hast thou beheld the Dawning ray,
> The glowing Zenith, and the mild Decline,
> Directing MAN to trace the source benign,
> And grateful homage from reflection pay.
> Then, while thy mental vision, clear and bright,
> Can Human Life through all its maze explore,
> By Wisdom guided with internal light,
> And Mem'ry shall retain thy classic store;
> How poor, my Noble Friend, mere outward sight
> To Thee, whose mind to loftiest heights can soar.

The porcelain works at Worcester also paid tribute to his bravery many years later, although there were undoubtedly commercial motives behind their concern. Lord Deerhurst's interest in porcelain increased after his accident, and he began to collect a popular dessert service known as 'Chelsea Rosebud', which the Chelsea Porcelain Factory had started to produce around 1760. The service consisted of various serving and sweetmeat dishes, bowls and plates, oval, square and shell-shaped in form, some with scalloped rims, and all decorated with a robust relief design of rose leaves and buds. Its tactile quality was obviously most appealing to Lord Deerhurst. The Chelsea factory had gone out of business by 1768, but by this time the design was also being produced by the Worcester

86 'Blind Earl' dessert dish. By courtesy of The Museum of Worcester Porcelain.

porcelain factory, which had either acquired the moulds or made copies of them. But when the design went out of production in the 1770s, it became increasingly difficult for Lord Coventry to supplement and replace items from his collection. In 1820, he decided to commission a complete new set of the service from the Worcester factory, by this time the Royal Worcester Porcelain Company, for £47 5s. 0d. On the invoice from Flight, Barr and Barr, then owners of the factory, of 17 June 1820, the words 'modelled on purpose' were underlined.[9] This has given rise to the misconception that the design was originally created specifically for the 7th Earl, rather than as a revival of the 'Chelsea Rosebud' pattern. It is most likely that new moulds had to be made to meet the Earl's specific requirements, and this prompted the factory to produce the new version of the service under the new name of 'Blind Earl' in his honour. The design has continued to be produced in small quantities ever since, notably during the Edwardian period when there was a resurgence of interest in this type of china.

The optimism and lack of self-pity with which Lord Deerhurst faced his disability owed much to the attentions of Margaret 'Peggy' Pitches, the daughter of Sir Abraham Pitches, a wealthy brandy merchant from Streatham in Surrey. They met some time in 1782, and soon resolved to marry, but Lord Deerhurst was very anxious to gain his father's approval so as not to strain family relationships even further. In November 1782, he wrote the necessary brief and formal letter to Lord Coventry:[10]

> I have lately been in the house of Sir Abraham Pitches at Streatham, whose Daughter's person and Character have long been known to me. It has been my good fortune to obtain her affections, and your consent is alone requisite to my possession of her.

The question of her dowry, probably the chief subject of concern to his father, was mentioned as a postscript and left deliberately vague. Deerhurst estimated Miss Pitches' 'Fortune' to be 'five thousand pounds and I believe eventually more', a sum sufficient to honour the occasion, but modest enough to imply that his intentions were entirely honourable. He even ventured to express some hope that he and his future wife might rely upon the goodness of his father to supplement their income. To his immense relief, the 6th Earl gave his consent, and the marriage took place on 10 January 1783 at St George's Church in Hanover Square.

It seems doubtful that Lord Deerhurst's marriage improved the situation with his father. Still unwelcome at Croome, it became necessary for him to establish a new base in the country for himself and his new family. It is possible that Lord and Lady Deerhurst stayed at Severn Bank on their infrequent visits to Worcestershire, and it may be no coincidence that the alterations to the fishing lodge were completed just after their marriage. This would also account for their eldest son's affection for the place, and his decision to move into Severn Bank when he came of age. However the close proximity of the house to Croome and its modest size were unlikely to have provided a satisfactory long-term solution to Lord and Lady Deerhurst's needs. As their family increased, they started to look elsewhere, and the obvious place was Streatham, close to the home of Lady Deerhurst's family.

Around 1800, Viscount Deerhurst purchased an estate at Streatham of around eighty acres from Lord William Russell, who had acquired it from his brother, the Duke of Bedford, a few years previously. The estate included Streatham Manor, an old Jacobean manor house at the corner of Streatham Common, formerly the home of the Howland family. Lord Deerhurst demolished part of the house and commissioned James Wyatt to build him a fashionable villa to incorporate part of the former offices, later known as Coventry Hall. Work on the villa must have started around 1803, according to the date on the bills and vouchers in the Croome archive.[11] These are for small amounts of only a few hundred pounds, so work evidently progressed tentatively at this stage. In the archive there is also a copy of particulars of a freehold estate at Streatham, to be sold by Christie's in 1806, and noted to be 'One of the most enviable Residences in the Vicinity of the Metropolis.[12] The house is described as a 'substantial brick messuage ... lately erected at great Expence', which 'may at moderate Expence be finished in the

87   Proposed elevation and plan of Coventry Hall in Streatham.

Manner proposed'. There is also reference to extensive offices, hot houses, a cottage ornée, gardens and also meadowland, which might provide 'a charming spot for the erection of villas in beautiful paddocks' and 'ample opportunity for lucrative speculation'. This would suggest that Deerhurst decided to sell Coventry Hall to raise funds prior to its completion. Alternatively, the particulars could refer to an adjacent estate, possibly that belonging to his father-in-law, that he was considering buying and reselling for speculative development. The former possibility seems most likely, as there is an undated letter in the archive, which reveals that Lord Deerhurst had discussed selling his Streatham estate with Mr. Christie, who had suggested that he divide it into small lots to benefit from the contemporary demand for modest suburban villas.[13] Despite the tempting profits to be made from such a sale, Lord Deerhurst was reluctant 'to do anything injurious' to the place, and must have changed his mind. Between 1807-8, further vouchers and bills from Wyatt appear in the archive, again for relatively small amounts, then in 1811, after he had come into his inheritance, the 7th Earl commissioned John Nash (1752-1835), an expert at rebuilding and altering houses, to remodel Coventry Hall on a grander scale. This may have been due to the influence of his eldest son, now Viscount Deerhurst, as Nash was a friend of Lord Deerhurst's and both frequented the Court of the Prince of Wales. Nash, among the most fashionable architects of his day and a master of the 'picturesque' style, was the obvious choice to breathe life into the project, for too long subjected to indecision and inadequate investment.[14] He drew up detailed proposals for the partial reconstruction and redecoration of the house, and by using salvaged materials he reduced his estimated costs to approximately £4,000. How far Nash's plans strayed from Wyatt's original proposals is unknown, but a principal feature of his design was the addition of a conservatory onto the drawing room. This was 'to be formed by Trellis or openwork Therms supporting an openwork Cornice … and covered with a painted awning or canopy and a glass dome', and the walls were to have removable glazing, 'so as to exhibit an open Temple' during the summer months. The additional cost of this ingenious structure was £713. Nash also provided separate estimates for stuccoing the house, and for a veranda supported with 'openwork trellis therms', similar to those on the proposed conservatory.

Unfortunately, Nash's imaginative scheme was rejected. Possibly it was too whimsical for the 7th Earl's conservative tastes. Wyatt died in 1813, but the villa was completed according to his original proposals under the supervision of his nephew Jeffry Wyattville.[15] An unidentified elevation and plan in the family archive, which do not relate closely to each other, and descriptions in various 19th-century historical and topographical accounts of Streatham help to create some idea of the villa's appearance. It was built of stuccoed brick to a symmetrical design and its rectangular plan measured approximately 85 feet long and 50 feet wide. There was one principal storey on a rusticated basement, and the main elevation was distinguished by a central Ionic portico flanked by pedimented windows on the *piano nobile*. The interior was similarly grand, and richly decorated with carved doorcases and fireplaces, some of which had been removed from Coventry House to lend the required quality and distinction to the villa.[16]

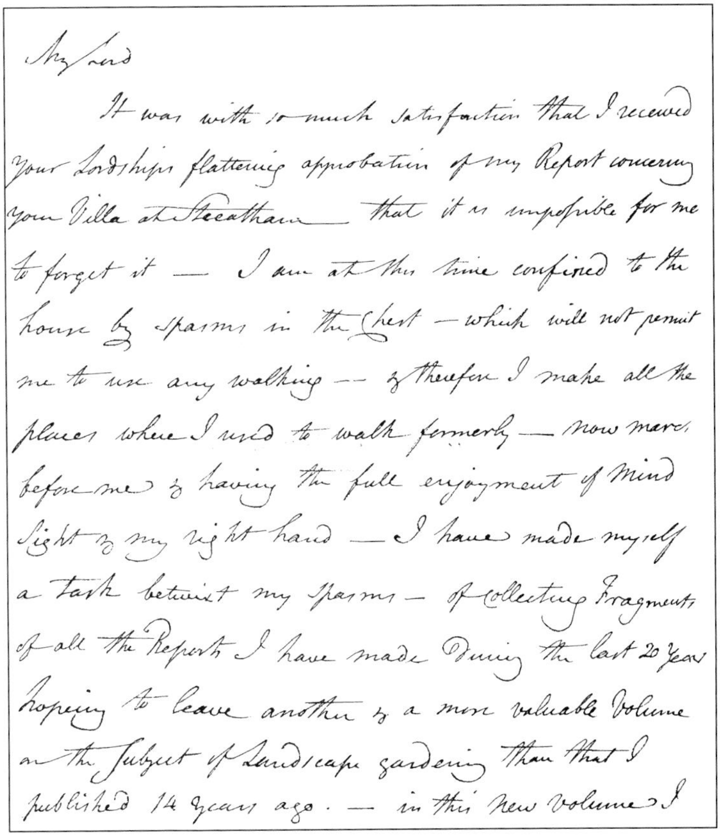

88 Extract from a letter from Humphry Repton to the 7th Earl of Coventry, 9 January 1815.

[handwritten letter]

> My Lord
>
> It was with so much satisfaction that I received your Lordships flattering approbation of my Report concerning your Villa at Streatham — that it is impossible for me to forget it — I am at this time confined to the house by spasms in the Chest — which will not permit me to use any walking — & therefore I make all the places where I used to walk formerly — now more before me & having the full enjoyment of Mind Sight & my right hand — I have made myself a task betwixt my Spasms — of collecting Fragments of all the Reports I have made During the last 20 Years hoping to leave another & a more valuable Volume on the subject of Landscape gardening than that I published 14 years ago. — in this new Volume I

Humphry Repton (1752-1818) was asked for his advice on laying out the grounds, and on 9 July 1815 he wrote to Lord Coventry to thank him for his 'flattering approbation of his report' which he had received with so much satisfaction 'that it is impossible for me to forget it'.[17] Repton's health was failing by this time, and he was confined at home with spasms in the chest. Having spent the past sixty years without even an ache, he believed it was only right at his age to 'expect a squeeze in the trap door thro' which I am to slide the Stage of Life'. Not a man to remain idle, he was now 'collecting fragments of all the Reports I have made during the last 20 years hoping to leave another and more valuable volume on the subject of Landscape Gardening than that I published 14 years age'. He added that:

> I shall have much to say on the subject of Villas and may wish to mention Streatham as furnishing some general useful matter ... There may be some vanity in this supposing my works to go down to posterity-but if your Lordship's praise will not call forth vanity—it will call forth my thanks.

Repton did indeed publish the advice he had given to Lord Coventry in his *Fragments on the Theory and Practice of Landscape Gardening* of 1816. In this he wrote that the design of villas was much underestimated 'by those who value a place by its size or extent, and not by its real importance, as it regards beauty, convenience, and utility'. Using Coventry Hall as his example, he explained in some detail why he believed that the scale and semi-rural location of grounds surrounding villas demanded a different treatment than a landscape park, something that ardent followers of Capability Brown's often failed to comprehend.

> The art of landscape gardening is, in no instance, more obliged to Mr Brown, than for his occasionally judicious introduction of the Ha! Ha! Or sunk fence, by which he united in appearance two surfaces necessary to be kept separate. But this has been, in many places, absurdly copied to an extent that gives more actual confinement than any visible fence whatever. At Streatham, the view towards the south consists of a small field, bounded by the narrow belt, and beyond it is the common of Streatham, which is, in parts, adorned by groups of trees, and in others disfigured by a redundance of obtrusive houses … Yet if the whole view in front were open to the common, it might render the house and ground near to it too public; and, for this reason, I suppose, some shrubs have been placed near the windows; but I consider that the defect may be more effectually remedied, by such a mass of planting as would direct the eye to the richest part of the common only; then, by raising a bank to hide the paling in such opening, the grass of the common and of the lawn would appear united … seen point blank from the principal windows …[18]

After the death of Lady Coventry in 1840, Coventry Hall was sold to a Mr. John Gray. It changed hands several times during the latter part of the century and by around 1900 it was in use as a convent and a red brick church had been built in the garden. Earlier in the 20th century, it succumbed to a ruthless conversion to council flats, its fine gardens and grounds lost beneath the tide of spreading suburbia.[19]

By the time he came into his inheritance, the 7th Earl was 51 years old. In 1808, he had succeeded his father as Lord Lieutenant and Custos Rotulorum of Worcestershire, and, when he inherited the earldom the following year, he also served as Recorder of Worcester and High Steward of Tewkesbury. As it was now just over a century since the earldom had been conferred upon the 5th Baron Coventry, the 7th Earl's son-in-law, the redoubtable Sir Willoughby Cotton, decided the time was ripe to secure the title of Marquess of Malvern for his father-in-law. It was a fine gesture, typical of Cotton's enthusiasm for pomp and ceremony, and it took some time for Lord Liverpool to restrain his enthusiasm. As far as the 7th Earl was concerned, he was simply content to claim his birthright. He had been excluded from Croome Court and Coventry House virtually since childhood and detached from the social and official responsibilities of his family for years. Croome, the focus of his father's ambition, harboured particularly bitter memories and it was ironic that once this visual feast became accessible to him he was blind.

89   General Sir Willoughby Cotton by Count Alfred D'Orsay, *c*.1840.

Impetuous as ever, he sought to establish his authority at once. If the mass felling of trees in 1810 had caused a shudder of dismay through the parishes of Croome and Pirton, this was nothing compared with the alarm raised when the 7th Earl doubled the rents. Not until 1820 did his tenants dare to raise an objection and petition Lord Coventry for a rent reduction. A new survey was commissioned from Thomas Hopcraft in 1810, the Panorama Tower was completed between 1810-12, and Pirton Court was repaired and altered in 1815 to provide a comfortable home for the 7th Earl's son, the Rev. Thomas Coventry, who had been recently installed as rector of Croome and Pirton. But then the 7th Earl's interest in his new role began to ebb away. There followed a period of calm and consolidation at Croome as the parkland matured to its full magnificence. A few repairs were carried out to the hot houses, the Rotunda, and, in 1830, to the balustrading on the north front of the house. Elsewhere on the estate a few hedges were laid, and one or two roadways were improved. That was all.[20]

Only very occasionally did events threaten to disrupt the steady rhythm of seasonal activity. For example, in 1826, Croome became so over run with rats that Thomas Player, a rat-catcher from Tewkesbury, was taken on on a permanent basis for 15 guineas per annum to rid the house of rodents.[21] Aside from such minor upsets, the herd of Holderness and Alderney cattle continued to graze the pastureland (in 1823 there were 93 altogether) and, under the expert management of William Dean, the planting was nurtured to its full potential. Dean had been taken on as head gardener, or 'Botanical Gardener' as he preferred to call himself, in 1799, and he remained at Croome till his death in 1831. His *An Historical and Descriptive Account of Croome D'Abitot* was published in 1824, and included the remarkable *Hortus Croomensis,* a complete list of all the plants growing at Croome at that time, and four illustrations, drawn by J. Pitman and engraved by C. Turner, of the Mansion, the Church, the Temple Greenhouse and the Rotunda. The book provides an excellent record of Croome in its prime, and the descriptions of the two alternative circuits, the three-mile walk and the 10-mile ride, evoke all the beauty and grandeur of Brown's landscape. The fine prospect from the Rotunda provoked a typically eulogistic response:

> Here, from its windows, and from its high grounds, before the spectator is spread-as if on a vast canvas-a view, which, in all that constitutes a landscape, rich, diversified, extensive, and well-combined, is rarely exceeded. Immediately before, and around, the eye wanders, delighted, over the gently varied surface, the winding waters, and the scattered or clustered woods, of the park. Nothing can surpass the grandeur of the trees, rising in majestic loftiness, or throwing their deepening shades, in wide expanse, on every side. In various directions, pleasing distances are caught, and agreeable objects discovered. The deer, grazing in groups, or bounding after each other in long irregular lines, give variety and animation to the scene. The large mass of plantations, bending, with a noble sweep, round the whole, strike with great effect; and, soaring above them, bursting finely on the sight, appear the more distant hills-forming a bold circuit-of which, on one side, are the *Malvern* and *May Hills*, and the *Breedon* and *Broadway,* on the other.[22]

To inhabit this earthly paradise with sightless eyes would seem a cruel twist of fate, but the benefits were not just visual. The guest list at Croome remained impressive during this period and included such celebrated figures as Arthur Wellesley, 1st Duke of

Wellington. Wellington had become acquainted with the Coventry family through Willoughby Cotton, who had served with him in the Copenhagen expedition of 1807. During the winter of 1814, just months before Waterloo, Lord Coventry conferred the freedom of the city of Worcester upon Wellington, who wrote to Lord Coventry from Paris to express his thanks. Gradually they became better acquainted, as witnessed by his letters to Lord Coventry from Stratfield Saye near Reading over the next few years, which refer to their previous conversations at Coventry House and to future invitations to Croome.[23]

The Prince of Wales, who acquired the title of Prince Regent in 1811, was a good friend of Lord Deerhurst's and was also invited to Croome on a number of occasions. However, in 1815 he appears to have declined an invitation to attend the sumptuous entertainment at Croome, attended by the Mayor and Corporation of Worcester, to mark his 53rd birthday.[24] Such was his unpopularity by this time, he should have been pleased that he still had sufficient friends left to honour the event. That year, he had decided to seek a divorce from his wife, Caroline of Brunswick, who was suspected of adultery and had been banned from Court. The letter from the Lord Chancellor requesting Lord Coventry's attendance at the second reading of the Bill to dissolve the marriage some years later on 17 August 1820 remains in the Croome archive.[25] Despite the Prince Regent's absence, the county gentry and nobility thoroughly enjoyed the party. After light refreshments at noon, they were free 'to amuse themselves on the water and about the very beautiful park, plantations and pleasure gardens' till five o'clock when a delicious dinner

90 The staircase at Coventry House, Piccadilly, London.

was served. The intended purpose of the event was, one suspects, quite incidental to the enjoyment of the occasion.

At Coventry House, the 7th Earl entertained his guests on an equally grand scale and could boast one of the finest cellars in the capital.[26] The modest kitchens that had proved quite adequate during the time of the 6th Earl were deemed insufficient and were refitted, and a new dairy was constructed in the rear yard. The entire house was also altered and redecorated under the supervision of the architect Thomas Cundy (1765-1825), surveyor of the Grosvenor estates.[27] It is unlikely that the house was in dire need of refurbishment, but the 7th Earl wished probably to erase as much evidence of his father's occupation as was practicable—and the walls were rather bare now that the paintings were gone. An elegant wrought-iron balcony was added across the façade at first-floor level and, within, the stair hall was fitted with new scagliola columns, and the fine, iron balustrade probably dates from this time. Some new doorcases and two new chimneypieces were also installed, almost certainly to replace those that were removed to Coventry Hall.

In 1812, the 7th Earl asked Samuel Pepys Cockerell for his advice on a scheme to build houses on land adjacent to Coventry House in Piccadilly.[28] Nothing came of this and, in the same year, a sale of building materials took place on the site, which raised £447 5s. 6d. Possibly these were intended for the proposed houses and Lord Coventry was obliged to sell them when his plans fell through. Alternatively they may have been surplus materials from the work undertaken on Coventry House.

These were the last alterations to be undertaken at Coventry House under the ownership of the Coventry family. After the 7th Earl's death, an attempt was made to dispose of the house to the Earl of Surrey. Then, in 1848, the 9th Earl assigned the remainder of his lease to Julius Lesouef, who turned the building into the Coventry House Club, a notorious gambling establishment. By 1854, it had reverted to a private house once more, and was occupied by the Comte de Flahault de la Bellarderie, a Bonapartist and one of Napoleon I's *aides de camp* who had been appointed Napoleon III's ambassador to Britain. He remained there till 1868, when the house became a club once more, the St James's Club, founded by the Marques D'Azeglio to provide a meeting place for secretaries and attachés after Court balls and parties. It remained the premises of the St James's Club for almost a century, and during this period it was extended by E.R. Robson (1836-1917), best known as first architect of the London School Board (1870-89) and the Education Department (1889-1904). Robson rebuilt the rear offices, somewhat unsympathetic and ungainly blocks of stock brick, but he did install some fine stained-glass windows, which overlook the rear court.[29] The building now houses a language school for foreign students and has been renamed International House. It has retained much of its outstanding work by Robert Adam, and its fine façade has survived virtually unaltered. Together with Burlington House, Egremont House and Apsley House, it is among the most important survivors of the palatial private houses of the nobility that once lined Piccadilly.

The 7th Earl of Coventry and his second wife, Peggy Pitches, had ten children, five sons and five daughters, but one son died an infant. The first child, the eldest son and heir, George William, Viscount Deerhurst, was born on 16 October 1784. It was perhaps inevitable that his father was anxious to establish a close and affectionate relationship with his eldest son, and the family correspondence and other relevant papers suggest that he succeeded, although this may have helped to alienate Deerhurst from his brothers and sisters. A rare and memorable double portrait in watercolour was painted around 1820 by Richard Dighton of the 7th Earl and Lord Deerhurst, who are parading arm in arm, perhaps along the streets of Bath or Cheltenham, clearly enjoying all the attention their wealth and status could muster.

The eldest daughter, Augusta Margaretta, was born on 11 September 1785. In May 1806, she married the virtuous and valiant Willoughby Cotton (1783-1860), whose distinguished military career ensured his steady advance to the rank of general and a knighthood.[30] Although Cotton was frequently abroad, in India, Jamaica or wherever his services were required, his sterling qualities and utter respectability proved a tower of strength to the Coventry family as they became dogged by personal and financial difficulties during the first half of the 19th century. Cotton became particularly close to the 8th Earl towards the end of his life, referring to him as his 'dearest old friend'. Lady Augusta was a loyal and patient wife, and endured admirably his long absences abroad at their London home in Lowndes Square. After Cotton's late retirement, they spent the summer in Cheltenham, where Cotton spent his evenings at the *Queen's Hotel* improving his embroidery skills, oblivious to the amusement of his fellow guests. He and Augusta had two children. The eldest child, Corbet, became a distinguished soldier like his father and also rose to the rank of general. The younger child, Augusta Mary, married Colonel Henry Vaughan Brooke (1805-58) of the 32nd Light Infantry, and she presented the east window in the chancel of Severn Stoke church in memory of her husband. Augusta outlived her husband by five years, and died aged 80 in 1865.

Georgiana Catherine, almost exactly a year younger than Augusta, was born on 13 September 1786. On 24 February 1804, Lord Deerhurst wrote to tell his father that Georgiana, by then 18, had eloped with a Mr. M.W. Barnes, a soldier and son of a lawyer from Reigate in Surrey. Mindful of the circumstances behind his first marriage, Deerhurst had no wish to make an issue of the elopement. However, William Barnes, Georgiana's father-in-law, was less easily placated. He was determined that the marriage settlement would reflect Georgiana's ample fortune, while only promising to settle his son's estate on her, valued at a mere £400 p.a.[31] Legal complications ensued which lasted until around 1812, during which time William Barnes continually applied to Lord Coventry for money to buy his son a house and pay the servants' wages. When William Barnes died, the Reigate estate was sold, and Georgiana and her husband moved into a cottage near Crawley. Although comfortably provided for, they continued to demand financial assistance, notably towards the education of their son, Walter. In 1819, they leased a house in Ostend, in the hope that the sea air would improve the health of their daughter, Julia. There Barnes attempted to apply for the position of Consulate of Ostend, but when nothing came of this application, they returned to England and went to live in Weymouth, where they continued to rely upon the support of Georgiana's family. Barnes would seem to have been a perpetual scrounger, who regarded his marriage as a meal ticket for life.[32]

After Georgiana came a sequence of boys. John Coventry was born on 30 June 1789. Indolent and indulgent, he remained undecided about a choice of career. He haunted dubious establishments in Worcester, and when life at Croome failed to enchant, he embarked upon a reckless affair with his sister-in-law Lady Mary Beauclerk, second wife of Lord Deerhurst, from which her husband never recovered. In an effort to secure an appointment for John as far from Croome as possible, the 7th Earl wrote to the Prince Regent at Brighton in March 1816 to see if he would find him a position with Princess Charlotte and her husband Prince Leopold of Saxe-Coburg. He received a

prompt but unhelpful reply, and the
following November he attempted to gain
support for John as candidate for the
county seat in parliament, which had
recently become available as a result of the
death of Lord Beauchamp. Colonel Henry
Lygon planned to succeed his brother,
and as Lord Beauchamp's daughter Emma
had for a brief period become the first
wife of Lord Deerhurst, he wrote to Lord
Coventry, advising him to abandon the
idea, which would result in 'a painful contest
with his family'. In 1821, the 7th Earl
purchased a cornetcy (a commission as a
cavalry officer) in the 10th Hussars for

91 A group portrait of six of the children of the 7th
Earl and Countess of Coventry. English School, pencil
drawing.

John, and by 1826 he held a similar commission in the 10th Light Dragoons for a
few years.[33] But by the 1830s, John had begun to drift back into gambling and eventually
he was declared a bankrupt. He died in 1852.[34]

The third son of the 7th Earl was born in 1791 and christened Thomas Henry,
but he died an infant and when another boy was born the following year, on
18 September 1792, he was called Thomas Henry in memory of his elder brother.
Thomas Henry obtained his degree at Christ Church, Oxford, in 1815 and the following
year was ordained a chaplain to Lord Coventry and appointed to the living of Pirton
and Croome. This position was not secured easily, as the Bishop of Worcester was
aware that Thomas regularly accompanied his brother John on his escapades in
Worcester and participated in the entertainment with considerable enthusiasm.[35] Thomas
became a Freeman of Tewkesbury in 1816, and two years later he moved into Pirton
Court. There followed a brief spell of diligent service and study, so that in 1826 he
was given the additional parish of Hill Croome, and in 1827 he was awarded an
MA degree at Oxford. In 1833 he succeeded the Rev. J.S.S.F. St John, a relative of
the 6th Earl's second wife, Barbara St John, as Rector of Severn Stoke. The St John
family objected strongly as, by this time, Thomas's relaxed attitude to his responsibilities
was a source of local gossip. His sermons are said to have been delivered in a cold,
inanimate and spiritless manner and were invariably rushed to allow sufficient time for
more pressing engagements, notably hunting and sampling the contents of his ample
cellar. Thomas never married, but was much attached to his young ward, Henrietta
Louise, who was alleged to be his illegitimate daughter. Towards the end of his life,
he left an increasing amount of his church duties to his curates and spent most of
his time at his London home, 13 Wilton Crescent, where he died on 20 August 1869.
Henrietta married a Parisian, called Dunand, and moved to France, but in 1874 she
returned to Severn Stoke to attend the dedication of the T.H. Coventry memorial
window in the chancel of the church.[36]

92 The 7th Earl of Coventry and Viscount Deerhurst, by Richard Dighton.

On 3 June 1794, a third daughter, Jane Emily, was born to Lord and Lady Deerhurst, later 7th Earl and Countess of Coventry. Described as 'delicious' by the popular press, she was as dutiful and responsible as her elder sister Augusta, and was especially close to her mother with whom she corresponded regularly. She married James Goding in 1828, but they had no children. Lady Jane survived her husband and lived till she was 85, the classic Victorian aunt, and an asset to the local community.

Another son, William James, was born on New Year's Day in 1797. Thirteen years younger than his eldest brother, he also had an affair with his sister-in-law, Lady Mary Beauclerk, the second Viscountess Deerhurst, in 1814. Eventually Deerhurst forgave William, whose youth and inexperience made him easy prey to Lady Deerhurst's machinations. Like his brother Thomas, he was made a Freeman of Tewkesbury in 1816, and later he served in the Worcestershire Yeomanry. On 26 July 1821, he married Mary Laing, the daughter of a Jamaican merchant. They appear to have eloped, and her father, James Laing, wrote an apologetic letter to Lord Coventry the following November with details of his reduced financial circumstances and a promise of a £500 annuity.[37] William and Mary moved into Levant Lodge in Earls Croome, but Mary found the house cold and draughty so they went to live at Moat Farm nearby, a new house rebuilt from materials reclaimed from the old manor house. In 1827, following the birth of their first son, William tried to persuade his mother to acquire Welles Peace, or Welles House, in Earls Croome, on his behalf. This house, now known as Earls Croome Court, was the 'new' manor house built by the Jeffery family in the 16th century. They did not move in till around 1845, during the minority of the 9th Earl, when they altered and extended the house to provide additional service accommodation. William represented his family during the minority of the 9th Earl, and when the 9th Earl came of age, he let William and Mary live at Earls Croome Court, rent free, for the rest of their lives. Earls Croome Court is now the home of the present Earl and Countess of Coventry.[38]

William developed a passion for farming. Mary sent excited letters to Lady Coventry describing their successes and failures, the variety of new crops they were experimenting with, the amount of butter they made each week, and the number of new lambs born each spring. She helped in the fields and was a keen gardener. In a letter to his mother of June 1830, William wrote proudly of his wife's geranium collection, which included 56 varieties in total, 'which have been given to her, & are quite Beautiful'.[39] Their commendable enthusiasm failed to compensate for their lack of experience, and Lady Coventry sent regular baskets of provisions to help them out when the harvest failed and their supplies ran low.[40]

It cannot have been easy for William and Mary to provide for their growing family of five sons and four daughters. The eldest child was born on 5 September 1826, 'a very nice little creature', and Lord Deerhurst decided he should be called Gilbert after the 4th Earl.[41] William and Mary had other ideas, and christened him William George (1826-70) instead, although they did decide to call their fourth child Gilbert. William George married Frances Norbury in 1865 and his eldest son was christened Gilbert William. The south window in the chancel of Severn Stoke church is dedicated to the memory of William George and his wife.

William and Mary's second son, Henry William, was born on 24 December 1829. He became Rector of Severn Stoke after the death of his Uncle Thomas, and he also served as Rural Dean and Hon. Canon of Worcester. On 21 April 1868, he married Leila Louise (d.1899), second daughter of G.C. Colquitt-Craven of Brockhampton Park, Gloucestershire, and they had three daughters, Blanche Katharine Adine, Sybil Augusta and Winifred Leila, and a son, Fulwar Cecil Ashton, OBE, a Superintendent of Road Transport on the Great Western Railway. Henry was ordained in 1853, and the 9th Earl gave him the living of Woolstone and Oxenton, near Cheltenham, where he remained for 15 years before he moved to Severn Stoke in 1870. He had proved himself a fine athlete at Oxford and had also travelled extensively, notably to Russia and to Poland, where he witnessed the Warsaw uprising of 1848. Perhaps his broad experience of life helped to make him such an excellent and popular rector. He revived parochial life, and helped bind the community together with his enthusiasm for local festivals and for the elaborate decoration of the church. In 1872, he embarked upon a major restoration plan for the church, with funds contributed largely by members of the Coventry family.[42] He held the incumbency for fifty years until his death on 10 April 1920.

William and Mary's younger children were John Willoughby (1837-1905), Gilbert George (1842-1906), George Walter Thomas (1843-1927), Eleanora Julia (d.1897), Frederica Mary (d.1898), Barbara Frederica Beaujolais (d.1903) and Mary Theresa Burdett (d.1910). John Willoughby became a captain in the 17th Foot (later the Leicestershire Regiment), George became a solicitor, while Gilbert was ordained in 1867 and was curate of Hill Croome from 1868-9. He became Rector of Woolstone and Vicar of Oxenton in 1870, when his brother Henry moved to Severn Stoke.[43]

William died on 11 March 1877 and his wife, Mary, died 15 years later, on 29 December 1892. He had two younger sisters. Barbara was born on 15 July 1799. When she was 15 she was given an Italian tutor, a Signor Guazzaroni, who remained a close friend and often sent her presents, including a gift of cats.[44] Barbara eloped in 1818 with the dashing and impetuous Lt.-Col. Alexander Crawford (d.1838), later Colonel Crawford. They travelled to Paris, but there Lady Barbara was confined to bed with a severe attack of gout and forced to submit to the daily application of leeches. Her husband was obliged to seek amusement elsewhere, and, by unfortunate coincidence, he happened to run into his wife's sister, Lady Augusta, and Willoughby Cotton. Crawford insulted Lady Augusta, and the outraged Cotton challenged him to a duel in the Bois de Boulogne. Lord Deerhurst was to be Cotton's second, but at the last moment the duel was called off thanks to the intervention of mutual friends. Meanwhile, Lady Barbara's father-in-law, James Crawford, was doing everything in his power 'to mitigate the calamity' brought upon both families by the elopement which filled the newspaper columns.[45] Such was the scandal, the Prince Regent himself offered to intervene on Lord Coventry's behalf. Lord Coventry never forgave his daughter completely, and when Crawford learnt that she had been excluded from her share in her father's estate, he was 'incensed to the last degree', and only after prolonged and bitter legal wrangling was the matter finally settled. In February 1838, Crawford contracted a severe throat infection. This spread to his lungs and by May he was dead. Barbara, already in ailing health, never recovered from his death and she died the following September.

Not long after Barbara's elopement, the 7th Earl's youngest daughter, Sophia Catherine, decided to stage her own romantic drama. She was born in 1802, 18 years after her eldest brother. At the age of 17 she fell in love with Sir Roger Gresley, son of Sir Nigel Bowyer Gresley, 7th Baronet of Drakelow Park, near Burton-on-Trent. After his father's death in 1808, Sir Roger had become a ward of Lord Beauchamp, probably through the local connections of his mother. He met Lady Sophia when he was 19 and at Oxford, and, always a serious-minded young man, an elopement was out of the question, so he wrote to Lord Coventry to ask for Sophia's hand.[46] Throughout 1819, he continued to seek Lord Coventry's consent, as did his solicitor, who assured Lord Coventry that Gresley was descended from William the Conqueror's cousin and standard bearer. Lord Coventry remained unimpressed until Gresley played his trump card and informed him that he was due for an annuity of £6,000 once he came of age, and that by Lord Beauchamp's will he would inherit property worth well over £30,000. His persistence was rewarded and he became freely admitted into the Coventry household, at which point his mother, who had previously taken little interest in his plight, threatened to charge the Coventry family with 'concert, design and conspiracy'. Lord Coventry advised Gresley to travel abroad for a while, and he was accompanied, rather ill-advisedly, by Sophia's dissolute brother, John. In Belgium they met Lady Georgiana and Barnes, primarily as Lord Coventry had asked John to look into Barnes's affairs. They then moved on to Paris, but cut short their stay when they received news that Lady Gresley was proceeding with her court case. Public interest in the case was intense, but fortunately the family was acquitted and, on 2 June 1821, Sir Roger and Lady Sophia were married. During the next few years, Gresley worked hard to justify Lord Coventry's faith in him. He bought a large house in

Mayfair, and he fought to obtain a Tory seat in parliament. His bid for the Lichfield seat in 1826 was unsuccessful, but he was returned for Durham in 1830, for New Romney in 1831, and for South Derbyshire in 1835. During this time, he also became an accomplished author, was honoured with an FSA, served as a captain of the Staffordshire yeomanry, and shortly before his death he became Groom of the Bedchamber to George IV. Sir Roger and Lady Sophia had a daughter, Editha, born in 1823, but she died an infant. Gresley died on 12 October 1837, and two years later, on 16 July 1839, Sophia married Sir Henry William Des Voeux. He died on 4 January 1868, and Sophia spent much of the last years of her life in the company of her sister Jane, till her own death on 29 March 1875.

One mystery in the life of the 7th Earl remains unresolved. Some time after his second marriage, he appears to have begun making payments to a woman called Mary Ann Kitching.[47] She was the servant of his physician, Dr. Battine, and may have been his mistress, perhaps one of many. Lady Coventry was well aware of her existence and occasionally corresponded with her. Around 1815, Mary Ann Kitching had a child, William. The 7th Earl was probably the father, although Battine was convinced he was the son of his groom, Cornelius Walker. Whatever the case, the 7th Earl was persuaded to pay Mary Ann one guinea per week towards the maintenance of the child for a period of eight years. In 1826, Lord Coventry received a letter from a John Howard, who claimed to be the husband of Mary Ann, informing him of her death and demanding quarterly payments towards the maintenance of his stepson, William, and an account was set up at Coutts under the name of George Capron. In 1830, Lord Deerhurst was consulted about William's indenture papers, and he appears to have been in touch with a Henry Boyce, who claimed to be William Kitching's half-brother and who purchased wine and other goods abroad on Lord Coventry's behalf. On 6 July 1838, it was Boyce who wrote to the 8th Earl to inform him that William, their half-brother, was dead.[48]

From around 1820, the 7th Earl's health began to fail. Compensation for the painful gout and other discomforts he suffered was the prospect of a trip to Bath, often accompanied by Lord Deerhurst. An enthusiastic writer of verse, in 1815 he had he penned an amusing and colourful account of his favourite spa to one of his friends.[49] The poem begins:

I have hobbl'd to Bath—and all the world knows
That from these warm streams no-one can write Prose ...
Tis long I've sought Health and exemption from pain
In patience and flannl and hops; but in vain—
Have slighted gay Bacchus, and sneerd at his Vine
Spurnd Venus herself, and her children divine—
The former your Lordship well knows—and, if just
Lady Coventry'll swear to the latter I trust!
I've only two maidens, and that's not too much
One to give me my stick and the other my crutch,

Then I rise from my Sopha to take my Sedan
Tho'not from the Baths or the Pump Room a span
As if I should go to the Rooms, rather bolder,
Just to throw a red Roccalo over my shoulder
Having now to mount high no ambition at all
Content if in future I only can crawl,
These beautiful Hills clad with Houses and Streets,
I've postpon'd to Bath's lower and snugger retreats,
And opposite lodge to the Abbey Church door
With a fat fine old Widow whose name's Mrs Moore ...

It later develops a more bitter and sombre tone:

> In the Senate no firm Opposition is seen,
> To Jobs and Oppression should Ministers lean
> No man, as of old of dignified Worth
> As Pitt, Fox and Sheridan, Burke, Furlow, North
> While Courts are corrupted by Friction and Flaw,
> And Justice is kick'd out by trick of the Law.
> Boys and Girls, Wives and Husbands pursue a wrong'd vent
> And a man has Estates without payment of Rent.
> Relations I've none to detain me at home,
> Or frustrate the wishes I've long had to Roam
> Two sisters-alas one by ? misled-
> -T'other barrd my access from my Father's deathbed ...

This implies that it was his sister, the hypochondriac Anne Margaret, who kept him apart from his father at the end of the latter's life.

The 7th Earl had reason to feel bitter, but at least he could rely upon the unfailing loyalty of the Countess of Coventry, who provided invaluable support, particularly towards the end of his life. During the 1820s, as his health deteriorated, she took over the responsibility of running the estates, and he also gave her control of his bank account so he must have been aware that he would soon lose control of his mental faculties. Regular reports were sent to the Countess in London from the agents and bailiffs at Croome, many of which make interesting reading.[50] For example, on 20 May 1827, John Mitton informed her:[51]

> The Stock is all very well at this time and the two olde Turkeys at the Dairy are very near atchin but the young one is lost for it layed a stray and I believe the Fox took it of the nest when it was layin in the Church Shrubbery ... The crops of grass and corn are very promisin ... at present whe have had a very fine rain this last Wick and very fine growing Weather at this time but the Cows pastors are short owing to it being over stocked but it will much mend now it is thined. Whe have not brought any horses in yet but will as soon as whe can have sum that will sute our purpose four whe must have and then whe shant want any Oxen and three of them to be Grays to make up a good Gray team to come up to the house with the Cole ...

Lord Deerhurst undoubtedly helped his mother during this difficult period, but readily criticised her decisions. For example, when the steps at Croome needed repairing in 1830, she ignored his advice on the most economic means of tackling the task so that he quite lost his patience, writing to her: 'I have at times hardly supposed you would give me the chance I wish'd to exert of saving your pockett ...'. There were also reports from Edward Brasher, the steward at Streatham. In one letter, he informed her of the shortage of coal at Coventry Hall, that the black and white cow and the young heifer had calved, and that hefty supplies of pork, bacon, chickens, eggs, fruit and butter had recently been despatched to Coventry House.[52]

Lord Deerhurst had reason to feel anxious about the estate. It is clear from the accounts for this period that it had begun to feel the effects of increased taxation and agricultural change. Mitton mentions that 'there is not so much to do as there was' and that the 'Dairy people' are restless and short of work. The number of livestock on the estate dropped significantly during the 1820s, and there was no surplus income to provide for necessary repairs and investment on the estate.

By 1830, the letters between Lord Deerhurst and his mother imply that the 7th Earl's mental and physical health had reached a critical level. He was confined to his bedroom at Coventry House, visited by a stream of anxious doctors and relatives, each offering a different diagnosis and possible treatment. Lady Coventry seems to have been too distressed to reach a decision, much to the irritation of Lord Deerhurst. Exasperated, he disappeared to the Isle of Wight to stay with his friend, the architect John Nash, in his magnificent castle at East Cowes, and from there he pleaded with his mother to listen to professional advice.

On 26 March 1831, the 7th Earl died. The news of his death nearly killed Lady Sophia, who had always been his favourite daughter and to whom he had left his splendid and treasured collection of Worcester porcelain.[53] His funeral was a more subdued affair than the celebratory atmosphere that had attended that of his father. Memories of the rift between father and son lingered in the minds of all present, of the father's stubborn pride that had broken his son's spirit more readily that the physical blindness which he had overcome with great courage.

The Countess Dowager lived for a further nine years, but for much of this time she suffered from a lingering illness. She died at Streatham on 15 January 1840, aged eighty-one.

George William, 8th Earl of Coventry (1784-1842)

The 8th Earl of Coventry was a complex and tormented individual. At times he relished his role as responsible family figurehead, dealing out wise words to his relatives. Then without warning he would abandon the moral high ground and disappear for weeks to Brighton or Cowes with the Prince Regent and his circle to add to his collection of mistresses and indulge his passion for sailing. He was notoriously thrifty, which did little to benefit the estate, but he could waste a small fortune when the mood seized him. His dual personality is reflected in his correspondence. His letters to his family and friends could be witty and affectionate, or cold and distant, depending upon his fluctuating moods rather than their content, and he could scold his mother for her incompetence and indecision while begging her advice in the following sentence. Little wonder that his family grew increasingly wary of his sheer unpredictability.

With hindsight, it is easy to attribute the 8th Earl's behaviour to his father's overwhelming need to secure his affections to compensate for his callous rejection by his own father. A sensitive and intelligent man, this would have placed a huge moral and emotional burden upon him, and it cannot have helped that two of his younger brothers had affairs with his wife. The tragic events that led up to his death confirmed his worst fears and insecurities, and finally his sanity deserted him altogether.

The 8th Earl of Coventry was born on 16 October 1784, the eldest child of the 7th Earl's second marriage to Peggy Pitches. Much of his childhood was spent in the company of his mother's family and friends in Streatham. In 1792, aged eight years old, he wrote in neat and flowing handwriting to a Mr. Welch, a family friend, about a wedding in Streatham he was soon to attend with his parents:

> Georgiana reminds me that I have owed you a letter since last year. We hope you are well and wish
> you was here to go with us to the rejoicings in honour of Mr Piozzi's Wedding as we are to dine in
> a tent, and the lamps (like Joseph's Coat of many colours according to Mr Trimmer) begin already to
> embrace the trees ...[54]

He obtained his degree at Christ Church, Oxford, in 1802, and spent the next few years developing his interests in shooting, sailing, drinking and generally enjoying himself on a comfortable annuity of £1,600. His father turned a literal and metaphoric blind eye to his activities. On June 1808, he married Emma Susannah Lygon, second daughter of Lord Beauchamp of Madresfield Court, Worcestershire, a most promising alliance between two such distinguished Worcestershire families. Lady Emma's condition may have demanded some degree of urgency with the ceremony, for a son, George William, was born on 25 October 1808. The dynasty was secure, and the old 6th Earl was still alive to rejoice in the birth of his great-grandson.

Just two years later Lady Emma died, and it was then that Viscount Deerhurst made his first serious mistake. In June 1811, he eloped to Scotland with the beautiful and wealthy Lady Mary Beauclerk (1791-1845), following in the footsteps of Lady Georgiana and Mr Barnes. Lady Mary was the only daughter of Aubrey Beauclerk, the 6th Duke of St Albans, descendant of the son of Charles II and Nell Gwyn. Deerhurst and his new wife were remarried on 6 November 1811 on their return to England, and their marriage settlement is of interest, partly because it confirms the contemporary value of the Croome estate at between £30,-40,000 p.a., with timber worth £10,000.[55] The circumstances that surrounded it also implied that much of Lady Mary's appeal to Lord Deerhurst may have rested in her wealth. The Duke agreed to settle £10,000 p.a. on Lady Mary and Lord Deerhurst, a sum 'likely to be increased considerably', and he also left much of his property to his daughter. This was generous, but not as much as Deerhurst had hoped for, a fact he attributed to the Duke's recent investment on his estate, but he conceded in a letter to his father that his income 'will now be excellent & I shall only have to return you my thanks for all your latter kindness to one whilst on short allowance, and in future to be able to live in conformity to my rank and station in life, which will make me most happy ...'.[56] This attitude may have had much to do with Lady Mary's subsequent behaviour.

Two children were born, the elder, Mary Augusta, in 1812, and Henry Amelius Beauclerk in 1815. Mary Augusta married the 4th and last Lord Holland, but no children were born of this union. Mary Augusta appears to have been a favourite of Queen Victoria's and, when she died on 23 September 1889, the Queen sent a wreath to her funeral with the special message 'a mark of regard from Victoria'. Unusual at this time, Mary had been a devout Catholic, and she had built a church at St Anne's Hill, near Chertsey in Surrey, which became her mausoleum. Henry Amelius Beauclerk became an officer in the army. He married Caroline Stirling Dundas in 1837 and they had six children. The boys were all called Henry and the daughters were all called Mary and, to confuse matters further, the eldest daughter's full name was Mary Frederick Dundas. Their eldest son, also called Henry Amelius Beauclerk, became a captain in the Grenadier Guards and he married Lady Evelyn Mary Craven, sister of Blanche, Countess of Coventry, and widow of George Brudenell-Bruce.[57]

Not long after her marriage to Lord Deerhurst, Lady Mary had an affair with two of her husband's younger brothers. Deerhurst was so shocked that he suffered a severe mental breakdown and, in one of his letters to his mother, he refers to the 'subject that has nearly brought me to my grave with distress, & involved me perhaps in everlasting misery for the future'.[58] But as he continued to wallow in self-pity, Lady Coventry grew impatient with him. She warned him repeatedly that 'unless you can rally & absolutely obliterate the late subject of misery in our family & immediately adopt your usual course thus giving the lie to what the Town ... would be delighted to Publish—inevitable ruin must ensue to every Branch ...'.[59] This harrowing period was not over yet. Lady Mary had embarked upon a brief affair with a Colonel Sanders of Lee Bridge, Kent, not long after her marriage, and now he decided to blackmail Lord Deerhurst. Mrs. Sanders even joined in, eager to reap some benefit from her husband's philanderings.[60] Then, in March 1818, Lady Deerhurst gave birth to an illegitimate child. The baby was smuggled out of Coventry House in a parcel by her maid, Mrs. Loran, closely watched by two of Lord Deerhurst's servants, and was taken to a nearby house. There, it was reported to Lord Deerhurst with a chilling formality, '... it was disposed of in such a way to render the identity of the Infant almost impossible'. The whole sordid business made a legal separation between Lord and Lady Deerhurst a matter of the utmost urgency, and Lady Deerhurst left for Rome, taking their daughter, Mary Augusta, with her. There she remained, living in some style for the following thirty years, but not entirely forgotten by the British press. In 1836 it was reported that an armed villain, Rocco Ottaviani, a former *fachino* or house porter at the Palazzo Barberini, had entered her bedchamber and attacked her. She had attempted to escape but a struggle ensued during which she had fought valiantly and hid in an adjacent room. Trapped in a corner, a further more violent struggle occurred, reported to last an astonishing twenty minutes, during which time she was stabbed several times and half strangled. Her assailant left her for dead and escaped down the back stairs with all her jewellery. Such incidents were not uncommon in Rome at this time, where rich tourists supported a thriving population of thieves and bandits, but Lady Deerhurst's bravery was exceptional. Lord Deerhurst, by then 8th Earl of Coventry, was unlikely to have been sympathetic. In 1841, when it was reported to him that his estranged wife was suffering from a 'sudden and serious indisposition', he expressed himself in a way 'to lead to the belief that he entertained the most cheering hopes for the future!' As it happened, his estranged wife outlived him. She died in Naples on 11 September 1845, from consumption.

It has already been suggested that Lord Deerhurst may have appreciated her wealth rather more than she found flattering. In 1825, he insisted that his father reduce his annuity by one hundred pounds to £1,500, hardly a sacrifice, but probably intended to set an example to other members of his family. Now that the Coventry family had exposed a weaker and more vulnerable flank to the popular press, rumours of the 8th Earl's thrift grew well beyond the bounds of credibility. All his clothes, it was purported, were purchased from second-hand shops, and it was said that he dined with his tenants six days out of seven. If this was true, perhaps it revealed a compassionate desire to break down the barriers of privilege between himself and his tenants. One newspaper was not so easily convinced: 'How noble is it', it reported with glee, 'to find a Peer of the realm, possessing his thirty thousands a year, dining off a rasher of bacon, and preferring that rasher at another's expense!'. Any minor act of generosity by the 8th Earl was seized upon as an opportunity to ridicule him:

> This is certainly the age of wonders. It is said that the leopard cannot change his spots, but we must now believe the contrary. A dinner was lately held at Tewkesbury among the new corporation, and we are told that 'the Earl of Coventry kindly presented the venison'. Are we to believe that he presented the venison free gratis and all for nothing? Is it likely, we ask, that this man, the meanest of the meanest among the aristocracy … would give away a haunch of venison, when he will not allow any one of his own brothers, relatives or acquaintances—for friends he cannot have—to take away a single head of game from the ground on which it is shot? … The presenting of venison by Lord Coventry is about as liberal and gratifying as the presenting of a bill by one determined to sue you, if it be not paid.

As a young man, the 8th Earl's failed political career had prompted further unwelcome publicity. He had been asked to put himself forward for the county elections in 1806. As the two county seats were traditionally held by a member of the Lygon, Foley and Ward families, Viscount Deerhurst declined the invitation as he had no wish to challenge their position, especially as the question of the Lord Lieutenancy would shortly arise on the death of his grandfather. His tact was rewarded when he became Lord Beauchamp's son-in-law two years later. Worcester was the more obvious choice. It had a large electorate and, as bribery was regarded as an essential electioneering tool, adequate funding rather than popular principles could achieve the desired result. A high proportion of Worcester freemen lived in London, and the more money available to pay their expenses to Worcester the better. However, in the election of October 1812, Lord Deerhurst found to his cost that he would need more than a title and ample cash to sway public opinion. Undaunted, he launched a full-scale attack on his opponent, Colonel Davies, in 1816. Davies was 'a quiet gentlemanly man with little to say for himself', but who had just been left £120,000 by his father and was determined to buy his way into parliament. Although a stranger to the county, he was aware that he had an excellent chance of success now that the reputation of the Coventry family was being ripped to shreds by the newspapers. Handbills were printed that declared Davies a 'Champion of Liberty', and an Enemy to the Corn Bill, and less convincingly that 'Slaves of Tyranny in Foreign Climes have fled before him'. The reference to the Corn Bill, the unpopular Corn Law of 1815 that ensured an artificially high price for British grain, was a well-aimed attack on large landowners such as the Coventry family. Lord Deerhurst's response was comparatively subtle (see illustration 93), but probably he protested a little more than was wise. In the wake of the Napoleonic Wars, his noble birth could no longer convince

93 One of Lord Deerhurst's posters for his political campaign of 1816.

Stand at Ease!

Brother Freemen,

By the Death of your lamented Representative, Mr. Robarts, you are called upon to exercise your Privileges of returning to the House of Commons a proper Person to succeed him in the Representation.

Some Hand-bills have appeared which would fain persuade you, that no Person connected with the Peerage, or, in plain terms, descended from the *House of Croome*, is eligible. The House of Croome, like the Thistle in the Ass's Throat, is bitter to the taste of this Hobbling Party, who are professed Levellers, and want no distinction of Persons. *Be not deceived.* " *Evil Communications corrupt good Manners.*" Do not listen to the Oratory of those who quit the " *Coblers Stall*" to harangue you with the Palace Yard Jargon, or suffer yourselves to be led away by a repetition of fallacious assertions, made by false Friends of Liberty, and Disciples of *Cobbett, Hunt, Burdett and Co.* These would be *Jacks' in Office, and who alone are able to work a radical Reform* ; but rally round the Standard of DEERHURST, in whom is blended every requisite and every qualification for a *Member of the British House of* COMMONS.

A FRIEND to his COUNTRY.

November 28, 1816.

an electorate who sought a commercial candidate for a flourishing industrial city. When he pointed proudly to the portrait of his grandfather on the walls of the Guildhall, his naivety was easily misinterpreted as arrogance. A vicious duet was published anonymously in the local newspaper, which guaranteed his public humiliation:

Electors: Time was the mighty Cock of Croome   Lord of the dunghill! 'tis thy lot
           Could wave on high its brilliant plume   To be so fixed upon one spot,
           In either calm or gale;   That 'dunghill' thou hast struck;
           But now so fallen, shorn, undone,   Yet cock-like, should'st thou chance to crow,
           The many are reduced to one   We still defy thee, CROOME, to shew
           WHITE FEATHER in its tail!   One particle of pluck!

Deerhurst: Enlightened men! You know I vowed   Though of my plume one only quill
            That of your love I was so proud,   Is all, you say, now left me—still
            I game would ever die;   I ought not to complain;
            And when I find both far and near,   And though no 'pluck' myself, yet you're
            The *game* I've made of you, it's clear   Too apt to pluck us all, I'm sure,
            I have not told a lie.   To let it long remain.

Vilified by the press and betrayed by his wife and brothers, Lord Deerhurst, sought solace in a string of dubious liaisons.[61] It is not necessary to dwell upon these indiscretions at length, but the sample below illustrates well the daunting complexity of his private life. One of his earlier acquaintances, who was 'slipshod and without stockings' when he knew her, later married Lord Berwick, and she was described by Deerhurst as 'a vile witch' in a letter to his father of 20 August 1820. Another, known as Eliza, lived in a fine new house in Bath Road, Worcester, for which he paid the rent of 5s. per week, and between 1831-9 he also provided a home not far from Coventry House for Annie Edwards and their child. Annie's sister, Amelia, was very protective, and she demanded payments that rose from £50 per quarter to a substantial £100 per month towards the child's upkeep. Deerhurst claimed that Annie's only fault was her temper, which had 'unhinged his mind', and he told her sister that he continued to 'love her still as I do my eyesight', a revealing analogy suggestive of the paranoia which gradually overwhelmed him. There was another child in Stratford-upon-Avon, born to a baker's wife, and repeated requests for money to put the child in a good school. Little wonder that, in 1830, Deerhurst invested in a 'Confidential Letter Case', invented by a W. Hancock of the Butter Market at Bury St Edmunds, to keep his growing collection of embarrassing correspondence.

Just two of his mistresses were accepted within the Coventry household. The more important was Elizabeth Williams. She was a local girl from Severn Stoke, born Elizabeth White or Whyte, and she was installed at Severn Bank House from around 1820 onwards.[62] She and the 8th Earl had three children, George, Elizabeth and James, and she appears to have changed her name to Williams on the birth of her eldest son so that he might share a similar name as his father. In his will, the 8th Earl left Elizabeth Williams his Sandford and South Littleton estates, which later passed to their children, and he also provided £18,000 towards their maintenance and education. The daughter, Elizabeth, married a solicitor from Ledbury in 1842 and it was while staying with her daughter in Ledbury that Elizabeth Williams died in 1845, aged forty-three. The eldest son, George, died in Boulogne aged forty-one. His remains were brought back to Severn Stoke, where an imposing tombstone was erected in his memory.

Jane Barker seems to have become a favourite companion around 1841. She was married to an opera singer, George Barker, and sometimes her husband accompanied her on her outings with Lord Coventry to the theatre or on his summer sailing holidays on the Isle of Wight. On such occasions he was inclined to refer to her as his 'god-daughter'. She was in her late twenties, well-educated and an affectionate woman, and the 8th Earl drew strength from her vitality and cheerful disposition. Possibly the Barkers exploited the 8th Earl's position and vulnerability to their own advantage, although no evidence of this can be gleaned from the fifty or so letters from Jane Barker among the family archive.

Sailing offered a less troublesome means of escape. The 8th Earl's interest in sailing had begun at Severn Bank, from where he had watched the incessant train of trows and barges glide past on the river below. In 1815, he bought a 75-ton schooner, named *Mary*, possibly after his wife, which he sailed off Cowes, by then as fashionable a resort as Brighton. He became a founder member of the Yacht Club at Cowes, later the Royal

Yacht Squadron, and he kept his schooner there for 12 years, before trading it in for a 71-ton cutter, the *Ariel* (sometimes referred to as the *Auriel*), which he kept until his death in 1842. Sailing was an expensive hobby. In January 1834, he was advised that the *Ariel* would cost at least £300 to repair and, horrified at the cost, the following July he instructed his captain, Mr. R. Stephens, to try to sell her in St Ives in Cornwall. Stephens failed to find a suitable buyer prepared to pay more than 'a tolerable fair sum' so, in May 1841, the *Ariel* was repaired and refitted at Cowes.[63] The re-fitting was lavish, and included a new suite of mahogany furniture in each of its nine cabins, four looking-glasses, a well-equipped galley and a new mahogany water closet.[64]

More traditional pursuits filled the winter season. The 8th Earl preferred shooting to hunting, but his pleasure became marred by the contemporary objection to the sport on the grounds of cruelty as implied by a long poem that he wrote in defence of true sportsmanship:

> Hail! Happy sports, which yellow autumn cheer,
> And crown the ripened honours of the year:
> The muse to you her willing tribute pays
> In artless numbers and incondite lays;
> Would paint the pleasures which to you belong,
> And bid the partridge tale adorn her song.
> … All who tremendous howl the forest's pride,
> Or range in harmless flocks the mountain's side;
> Each fish that cuts with fins, yon wat'ry way,
> Each bird that flits through realms of liquid day,
> Instructed man his line of duty knows,
> Nor hesitates to do what God allows.
> Now to capacious barns the happy swain,
> On loaded teams bears home the golden grain;
> Or forms in well compacted heaps its store,
> While frequent sheaves adorn the fields no more.
> Now oft the choral harvest home we hear,
> To none more grateful than the sportsman's ear;
> These sounds, which pleasure to his breast convey,
> Announce destruction to the feather'd prey.
> … Fond of the licensed joys September yields,
> With early step, I tread the spangled fields;
>
> With buskin'd foot I brush the morning dew,
> The flying game with ardour to pursue.
> … The random shot I scorn, and doubtful aim,
> Nor wish by chance a hapless bird to maim;
> But from the rest I single one alone,
> Nor fail to bring the fated victim down.
> … Fond youths, unskilled their ardour to contain,
> While the warm blood impetuous swells each vein,
> Too hot to think, too eager to debate,
> Too rash the proper moment to await;
> At rising coveys with impatience stare,
> And fire their useless guns at vacant air;

Let care and quickness mark your better sport,
Your judgement sound, deliberation short;
So shall the baffled shot bring rare disgrace,
And your swelled bag bring home the frequent brace.
Let the fierce huntsman, with his circling crew,
Through many a maze the timorous hare pursue;
Let others draw with care the enclosing net,
And catch whole coveys at a single set.
Yours be the joys which partridge shooting yields,
Be mine with dog and gun to range the fields;
And ever scornful of the insidious snare,
Wage with the flying game more open war.[65]

Such an apology would have appeared quite absurd to his grandfather. However, his father's predicament was a constant reminder of the risks involved with field sports, and in 1831 the 8th Earl, then Viscount Deerhurst, had suffered a narrow escape when out shooting with his brother-in-law, Colonel Crawford. Three years later a more serious incident occurred, when the 8th Earl's eldest son and heir was blinded in a shooting accident in a horrific repetition of the 7th Earl's fate. This realised one of the 8th Earl's greatest fears and added to his increasing paranoia about his own eyesight.[66]

The 8th Earl's eldest son, George William, Viscount Deerhurst (1808-38), was the precocious infant who had planted an oak tree at Croome in memory of his great-grandfather when only 14 months old. The only child of the 8th Earl's first marriage to Emma Lygon, he had grown up among his numerous aunts and uncles at a time when friction within the family was at its height. Nicknamed 'the simpleton Deerhurst'

94   Croome House and estate by E.F. and T.F. Burney, c.1784, one of a number of illustrations intended for Nash's county history. Pen and Wash.

by the press, he became a lieutenant in the 2nd Life Guards, and his life had established a predictable pattern until one fateful day in 1834 when he was twenty-six. On 1 September, he was out shooting with two friends and Sir Charles Cockerell's gamekeeper at Donnington, just a few miles from Sir Charles's splendid new Indian palace at Sezincote in Gloucestershire, designed for him by his brother, Samuel Pepys Cockerell. Deerhurst was wandering around about 120 yards from his companions on low ground that lay between the dogs and the birds on the wing, steadily moving closer to the birds and out of view of his friends. Suddenly, he turned round and was hit by a shower of shot in the side and face. The shot barely passed through his clothes and only caused slight flesh wounds, but one pellet hit him directly in the right eye. He was rushed back to Sezincote, from where Sir Charles sent daily bulletins to his father in London on the state of his health. According to one of his medical advisers, Dr. Wingfield, the shot had entered his eye behind the cornea but he was unsure where it had lodged and there was a fear that it would work its way into the brain. Although Deerhurst remained at Sezincote for several weeks, his father never actually visited him. Miraculously, he suffered no pain or fever, and is said to have remained remarkably cheerful. An operation to remove the bullet was considered far too risky, but as he could soon tell light from dark there was hope of a full recovery. However, his eye remained misshapen and inflamed, and only after the application of leeches did it return to its proper state, although the vision remained unimproved. Lady Barbara'a tutor, Senor Guazzaroni, recommended the use of electricity to stimulate the nerves, but this idea was rejected as too dangerous and Deerhurst resigned himself to his fate with the same courage his grandfather had done. He did, however, have reason for optimism. At Sezincote, he found an attentive nurse in the form of Sir Charles's eldest daughter, Harriet Anne Cockerell (1812-42). They became inseparable, and their decision to marry delighted their respective families.

Harriet was a distant relative of Samuel Pepys, indirectly descended through John Jackson, son of Pepys' sister Paulina. The friendship that had existed between Pepys and Sir William Coventry had ensured that the Coventry and Cockerell families had always remained on good terms and, like her distant ancestor, Harriet was a keen observer and an enthusiastic diarist. Among the Coventry archive is a charming account of a European tour she made with her family in 1828 when she was 16 years old. She travelled from Boulogne via Abbeville to Dieppe, then inland to Paris, Dijon, Lyons and onto Switzerland, returning home via Germany. Unfortunately the second volume of her journal is missing, but the first volume provides many fascinating and evocative descriptions of the sights she encountered on her travels.

July 22 Tuesday (Dieppe)

Walked to the pier, the sea <u>very, very</u> rough & saw the Castle, before Breakfast. Bought some little ivory things, very nicely carved, for which Dieppe is famous. Started after breakfast at ½ after 9 o'clock, had a most beautiful view of Dieppe & the sea at a distance as we ascended the hill. Passed a great many manufactories. The apple trees were in rows on each side of the road and horrid straight rows of poplars, very straight and tall and extremely thin-regularly starved; ropes were stretched across from tree to tree & lamps were suspended in the centre. We arrived at Rouen at ¼ before 4 o'clock, which was noisy

(Hotel de France, I mean was noisy) but good. Walked out after dinner to the Boulevard; the streets were very dirty. Met a very civil young woman who showed us the statue of Jean d'Arc who was burned for sorcery and another market place in the middle of which was the Guillotine where a man was killed two days before for poisoning his wife and a deserter was shot about a week before.

August 3rd Sunday (Paris)

Went to Pere la Chaise which we all liked very much & there we enjoyed a beautiful view from it of Paris, in short it was quite a Panorama. We went into one of the vaults (which held 32 bodies) there were 8 in it. I touched one that was full, it felt very damp. Mama called for Dada's snuff directly we came out of it. We went to see the Great Elephant in Plaster of Paris coming home. It is an immense thing, it is 50 ft high & there is to be a Room in the stomach, a staircase in one of the front legs & a tower at the top. It is intended for a fountain and mounted will be 80 ft high. They have been 12 years about it & will be four years more before it is completed in bronze.

August 18 Monday (Geneva)

Went … to Fernay the residence of Voltaire; of course saw the room in which he lived & the tomb in his bedroom, where his heart was, but which is now removed to Paris. The gardener's son…told us an amusing story of Voltaire and Gibbon, the latter wished very much to see the former, & therefore went to Fernay & staid there 2 or 3 days, but after sending messages to him and not being able to see him he went away, but soon returned & knowing that he had a favourite mare, he told the Coachman to take it to Voltaire's bureau in the garden. Voltaire (being at the window) was in a great rage & came into the garden to see what they were doing with his mare & Gibbon, being hid behind some trees, by that means saw Voltaire but his servant said 'I beg your pardon but my master (Voltaire) desires me to ask you "Pour 10 sous pour avoir vu la bete" ' so Gibbon said in return 'Je te donnerai vingt sous si je veux la voir encore une fois?' Voltaire being pleased with his answer invited him to dinner next day & sent his carriage for him and they were the greatest friends possible.

Lord Deerhurst and Harriet Cockerell were married on 15 March 1836. A large and splendid wedding was organised at Sezincote, and the couple spent their honeymoon at Buckhurst, near Windsor, before moving into Severn Bank. It was a happy outcome of a potentially tragic incident, and the newspapers were respectfully guarded in their comments, although it was reported that the tailor's bills were all paid by Sir Charles, so that 'the simpleton Deerhurst would be rendered decent to appear at the altar'.

A daughter, Maria Emma Catherine, and a son, George William, were born in quick succession, but there was little time for celebration. In August 1838, Lord Deerhurst caught a severe cold on his return from a party held by the young Queen Victoria at Buckingham Palace. Powdered squills, ginger grains, potash and orange peel proved ineffective, consumption set in, and by 5 November he was dead.[67] Although never an attentive father, the 8th Earl was deeply shocked. Two years later, the 8th Earl's elderly mother also died and this sent him into a steeper decline. Then, in January 1842, Harriet, already seriously ill with consumption, died at Pau in France on her way to Lourdes to seek a cure. She was 29 and had been in delicate health since the death of her husband.

These last few years of the 8th Earl's life proved the toughest test of all. There were spells of lucidity and calm when he tried to reassert his control over his family and the management of his estates, but any effort to restore public confidence in his abilities became futile. For example, in 1840, at a Conservative dinner in Worcester, he received an abusive anonymous letter from an employee of Dents the glove manufacturers that called him an outcast from society and a disgrace to his coronet. He was laughed at in Parliament and relentlessly lampooned by the press, but still he refused to withdraw from political life. Just weeks before his death, he attended a heated debate on the Corn Law question, but he was clearly unwell and was 'judged to be labouring from a disordered state of the intellects'. He died on 15 May 1843 at Coventry House of an 'unsound mind', aged fifty-nine.

His funeral was a surprisingly grand and elaborate affair attended by hordes of people and the police were called in to keep the peace. The coffin, draped with crimson velvet with gold trimmings, was flanked by golden Egyptian columns and was almost lost among the mass of plumed horses, robed officials, uniformed guards and milling crowds. The cost of this lavish funeral gave the *Worcester Journal* a splendid opportunity for a final twist of the knife:

> Here's Deerhurst at last, with all pomp and parade,
> To 'the tomb of the Coventry's' sadly conveyed;
> And knew he his burial would five pounds exceed,
> He would certainly think he was *dear hearsed* indeed

Colonel Crawford had died just a day after Lord Coventry and was buried beside him, which prompted the newspaper to add a second verse to this disrespectful tribute;

> Here lies Mr Crawford to moulder and rot,
> Who married Lord Coventry's daughter,
> And always was known by the name of *Teapot*
> From being so much '*in hot water*'.

Three codicils had been added to the 8th Earl's will made in 1835; the first of 1836 he tore to pieces, the second of August 1840 appeared to have been made solely for the benefit of his housekeeper, Sarah Andrews and its validity was doubtful. The third of November 1840 bequeathed an annuity to a mysterious Fanny Maria Brunton. Nothing in the life of the 8th Earl seemed simple. Indeed his life was so fraught with conflict, public insult and personal tragedy that it is difficult to ascertain the true nature of the man. In a letter to his brother William, written some years previously in 1830, he had said of his former friend, the late King, George IV: 'in my conscience I believe his heart was always in the right place—however others may differ who judge only from circumstances over which Kings even have no control and condemn without time, sense and judgement'.[68] Possibly he considered the same was true of himself.

The reputation of the Coventry family had suffered severely during his lifetime. Quite where the inspiration and leadership would come from to effect a reconstruction nobody dared assume. The 8th Earl's son and heir was dead, and the title was devolved upon his young grandson, the second child of Viscount Deerhurst and his wife, Harriet Cockerell. George William, now 9th Earl of Coventry, was just five years old and happily unaware of his fate. He was destined to hold the title for an astonishing 86 years.

IX

The True Country Gentleman

George William, 9th Earl of Coventry (1838-1930)

> It was a lovely evening in autumn, towards the end of October, and the setting sun was gilding with its dying rays a fine old house in Midlandshire—the rooks were leisurely [flying towards] their nesting place, the starlings were wheeling round the blackthorns in the fox covert near the house, and a heron, flapping lazily along, was just visible through the mist which was rising fast from a river close by. But these were the only signs of life to be seen; for the blinds were all down in the house, and no noise proceeded over from the stables. The name of the place was Allenby Hall; it was well known in the County of Midlandshire as the property of Lord Cannington, whose family had possessed for more than three hundred years the large estate and fine old Elizabethan house … but on the evening of which we visit all was still far and near … for Lord Cannington had died suddenly that morning, in the prime of life, in the midst of all his happiness the hand of death had borne him from the wife he worshipped, and the fine old property he had had such good reason to be proud of—and there was great mourning for him throughout the county for he was liked and respected by all who knew him—he had been in life the true type of a country gentleman …

The 9th Earl had inherited his mother's enthusiasm for keeping diaries and journals. One winter's evening, with little to report on the day's activities, he began a novel. From the opening paragraph above, it is evident that he intended it to be partly autobiographical. Over the next couple of weeks the story grew, but then his interest began to wane, and it deteriorated into a series of dislocated jottings about the new Lord Cannington's social life and hunting exploits. The 9th Earl was only 27 at the time and, in real life, fact proved more promising than fiction, for he played his part as aristocrat, patron and country gentleman with far greater conviction than he could have imagined. Jovial and rather vague, and known to his close friends and family as 'Covey', he posed proudly for photographers alongside his wife, his prize bull or his racehorse, his clothes always a little awry, and a benign and a rather bemused smile playing across his face. No county function was complete without his presence, no hunting party nor race meeting seemed so successful in his absence. His popularity among his tenants was unprecedented, and he seemed to be regarded with genuine affection wherever he went. He enjoyed life to the full, and was truly aggrieved to witness the slow disintegration of rural society in the wake of the agricultural depression.

Born the same year as his father died, in 1838, the 9th Earl came into his inheritance just a week after his fifth birthday. The title had become tarnished, and the estate was in decline, but his tender age proved a positive advantage. Above all, it bought time.

It provided a valuable pause between the old and the new rule, a prudent interval after the misfortunes and scandal that had dogged his predecessor, when old loyalties could be re-established and the estate brought under control in order to confront a new era of progress and reform. The young Victoria was now on the throne, the industrialisation of Britain was in full stride, the First Reform Act, the first major landmark of electoral reform, was in place, the population was expanding rapidly, and there was an increasingly vocal and ambitious middle class to contend with. The Coventry family were among many of their rank who were obliged to re-evaluate their role and adjust to the changing social and agricultural patterns of the industrial age.

The family archive reflects this new change of pace and direction. Gone are the reams of intimate correspondence, the complex legal papers, and the scathing newspaper reports. Instead there are collections of autograph letters, the 9th Earl's diaries, glowing accounts of the family's achievements gleaned from the sporting press and social journals, and numerous photograph albums to bring the story to life. Some of the best of these cuttings and photographs are included in the Coventry albums, a series of nine huge scrapbooks that were created by Blanche, Countess of Coventry, in tribute to the family's history and achievements. The scarcity of personal correspondence is significant. Probably much of the archive was collated with a strict eye for propriety and public image, most probably by Blanche and later by her grandson, Colonel Osbert S. Smith, who is known to have attacked some of the 9th Earl's diaries with a censorious pair of scissors. The need to shape the views of future historians was an important consideration.[1]

The 9th Earl and his elder sister, Maria Emma Catherine, were brought up at Sezincote after their parents' death, but they visited Croome regularly. There is a charming painting by William and Henry Barraud of the two children posing outside an embattled house, no doubt intended to resemble Severn Bank. Maria is seated upon a white pony, while George William adopts a self-conscious, cross-legged pose clearly transplanted from the studio to the riverbank (colour plate XXIII). The 9th Earl was passionate about horses from an early age, and one of his letters of this period, written to one of his numerous uncles in cross-cross style, describes his recent hunting exploits on his favourite pony 'Spicy':

> ... the hounds looked like large rough terriers with shaggy hair ... we at last broke cover and ran about five fields when we doubled back again into the woods and stayed there all the rest of the day (without a killing and with only about two couple of hounds together).[2]

In 1851, just before he went to Eton, James Williams, his former headteacher, sent him a long letter in which he referred to the 9th Earl's recent visit to watch the cricket at Lords, and gave him the following advice: '... continue in the same honest and honourable career that you have followed here ... [for] ... altho' life may not be all pleasure, your own conscience will be an ample reward ...'.[3] Among his other, more famous, admirers of this period was the Duke of Wellington, who is said to have walked with him on Sundays from Halkin Street to Apsley House, no doubt offering him the benefit of his valuable advice.

From Eton, the 9th Earl progressed to Christ Church, Oxford, and between 1856 and his coming of age on 9 May 1858, he spent much time at Croome, where he took an increasing interest in his inheritance that boded well for the future. During his minority, his great-uncle William took responsibility for the estate, with assistance from his guardians and trustees, Richard Temple of The Nash, Kempsey, Worcestershire, a family friend and distant relative of the Temple family of Stowe, Buckinghamshire, and his grandfather, Sir Charles Cockerell. As the 8th Earl and his mother had barely kept abreast of the necessary repairs and maintenance, the general management of the estate had grown slack. The agents and bailiffs, who had been employed during the time of the 7th Earl, had either left or died, and no new agent was appointed until John Hill took over in 1868. The rental income had risen steadily to keep in line with rising costs and taxation, while many of the farms and cottages were suffering from neglect. Following the death of the 8th Earl, an order in Chancery obliged the trustees to conduct a thorough survey of property and rentals and take appropriate action. The survey was commissioned in July 1844, and a staggered programme of repair and restructuring took place over the next few years.[4]

It was then estimated that the estate covered around 16,000 acres in Worcestershire and Gloucestershire, 9,500 of which lay within the parishes of Croome, Pirton, Severn Stoke, Hill Croome, Earls Croome, Ripple, Defford and Allesborough. Work was carried out to the mansion house, offices and all the park buildings at Croome, together with Brown's buildings at High Green, the inn, cottages, smithy and workshops, and most of the farmhouses and cottages in the outlying parishes. The only work that was postponed till the 9th Earl took over was the rebuilding of the forcing houses in the kitchen garden and of the bridge at Knights Hill Pool, which had collapsed beneath the feet of the 8th Earl some years earlier. The sum of £200 was contributed to the repairs to the church, and a number of new cottages were built and others purchased from the Poor Law Commissioners in Pirton, Severn Stoke and elsewhere. New almshouses were also built at Severn Stoke, Birch Farm was refurbished on behalf of Lady Augusta Cotton, and around £800 was allocated to complete the additions to Severn Bank House, begun in the 1820s by the 8th Earl, which was subsequently let at £300 per annum to the Dent family. William Coventry moved into Earls Croome Court, and Moat Farm, where he had lived previously, was altered and let. This programme of work cost many thousands of pounds, but the benefits more than justified the expenditure. A pattern of efficient management and capital investment was established which was continued over the following decades, confidence was restored among the tenantry, and the family could again meet the public gaze with pride.

On 7 February 1858, the 9th Earl's sister Maria married the Hon. Gerald Henry Brabazon Ponsonby (d.1908).[5] Then in May of the following year, the 9th Earl came of age. The day was treated as a local holiday, and the response was most gratifying. The *Illustrated London News* devoted a couple of pages to the event.[6]

The high esteem in which the family is held in Worcestershire … was shown by such a demonstration as was probably never known before in the County … The village of Severn Stoke adjoins the ancestral seat, Croome House and also Severn Bank, the residence of the late Viscount Deerhurst, father of the present Earl. It was therefore the centre of attraction, and was thronged with visitors. At three o' clock a.m. bell-ringing and salvoes of cannon commenced, and were continued throughout the day. The houses were decorated with evergreens, flowers, flags, and elaborate devices; while the roads were spanned by triumphal arches … At ten o' clock congratulatory addresses were presented at Severn Bank—one from the tenants, and another from the inhabitants of Pershore to which his Lordship replied in a feeling and appropriate manner. At eleven o'clock Divine Service was performed at Severn Stoke church, which was crowded. His Lordship attended thither by Viscount Elmley, Lord H Lennox, the Hon. W Coventry, and other distinguished friends … A procession was afterwards formed, headed by Pershore brass band and banners, to Cubsmoor, an elevated site near Croome House, where an immense tent had been erected. Here meat of every kind, to the extent of about a ton, nine cwt, of plum pudding, twenty-three bushels of bread, three hogsheads of ale, and two hogsheads of cider, were distributed amongst the labouring families, as were also the plates, manufactured at Worcester for the occasion. Dinner being concluded, his Lordship visited the tent, and was received with loud cheering and waving of handkerchiefs. Dancing and rustic sports, with a magnificent display of fireworks, concluded these rejoicings.

There was a banquet at Worcester Guildhall, games and celebrations at Upton upon Severn, dinner and dancing at Baughton, Hill Croome and Earls Croome, a dinner and dance at Pinvin, and 'an abundant feast' at Powick. Next day a massive celebration took place in Pershore for anyone unable to attend the events of the previous day. The streets were hung with garlands and festoons and the town was inundated with visitors. A procession through the town continued to Wick House, where games and sports took place attended by the Earl, who presented the prizes. From this day on, he was established as one of the popular men in the county.

95 The celebrations at Wick House, Pershore, to mark the coming of age of the 9th Earl of Coventry, from the *Illustrated London News*, 28 May 1859.

96 The Entrance Hall at Croome Court, late 19th-century.

97 The Saloon at Croome Court, late 19th-century.

98 The Gallery at Croome Court, late 19th-century.

One of the 9th Earl's first duties when he came of age was to rescue his great-uncle William from his debts in return for the work he had undertaken on the estate. These were not substantial, a little over £2,000, but he also let him live at Earls Croome Court for the remainder of his life at a nominal rent of £1 p.a., with the additional benefit of an annual allowance of £500.[7] Behind this gesture of gratitude, he nurtured suspicions about William's honesty. In his diary he refers to the 'pilfering of pictures' and other items that had occurred during his minority, but he was too much of a gentleman to confront his great-uncle. Next he sought to secure a suitable countess. On 22 November 1864, his diary entry reads: 'Proposed to Lady Blanche, I was accepted by her.' He had dinner with her the following evening, and on 24 November he bought her a ring for £45 and a locket for £50. His habit of recording the cost of almost everything in his diary bordered upon obsessional, and it would seem that his accustomed air of vague geniality concealed an adept accountant and born administrator. After a useful week's work in London, he set off for Sezincote for a weekend's hunting, and the next reference to his fiancée occurs on Wednesday, 25 January 1865, when he jotted down the following: 'Was married at St George's'. He listed the bridesmaids and then added: 'Bought a small casket (£35) for Blanche at Lambert & Rawlings, but did not pay for it'. That was it.

Lady Blanche Craven (1842-1930) was the third daughter of William Craven, 2nd Earl of Craven, of Combe Abbey, Warwickshire. Her distant ancestor had been the wife of the 2nd Baron Coventry, and she and her two sisters, Lady Cadogan and Lady Wilton, were known in society as the Three Graces. The marriage took place at St George's in Hanover Square, where the 6th Earl and Maria Gunning had married just over a century previously, and the wedding reception was held at the Craven's London home at 16 Charles Street, Berkeley Square, and was noted for its horticultural display. The rooms were filled with exotic plants of every description and at the head of the dining table were hung six bunches of black grapes from Combe Abbey. Boasting a total weight of 36 pounds, these had been shown the previous Saturday at Kew where they had won first prize. The cake was more extraordinary still. Several feet high, it was smothered with a heady mix of acanthus, honeysuckle, orange and jasmine blossoms, and the hexagonal lower tier supported six flower pots holding more orange blossom and jasmine. Above this rose three further tiers and on the top was perched three

99 A chalk drawing of Lady Blanche Craven by E. Eddis.

dolphins whose tails met to support a vase of lilies. The ceremony complete, the Earl scribbled in his diary: 'Came to Croome by special from Oxford—£17.10.0'. Did he really need to remember the price of the train ticket ? He had bought Blanche an exquisite toilet service of embossed gold and numerous pieces of jewellery as additional wedding presents, including a magnificent butterfly pendant, with diamond wings and rubies for eyes alighting on a crystal globe, yet he still thought the fare extortionate. It can't have helped that the train was running late and, when Lord and Lady Coventry arrived at Pershore station, the postilions in charge of their carriage had disappeared for a quick trot round to keep the horses warm. The Earl and his new wife were obliged to sit in the waiting room for ten minutes till their carriage returned.

The local festivities to mark the occasion were on a similar scale to those that had celebrated Lord Coventry's coming of age. A triumphal arch was erected at High Green, and there were dinners and parties galore. The *Worcester Journal* described the union of the Coventry and Craven families as 'most auspicious', adding: 'Now that he has taken home a wife to grace the hospitalities of Croome, and to share the honours of his house, an additional lustre will be added to his Lordship's doings.'

Lord Coventry described Blanche as 'the best wife a man ever had … of whom whatever I said would fall short of the truth'. They had nine children, six boys and three girls. George William, Viscount Deerhurst, was born in 1865, Charles John in 1867, Henry Thomas in 1868 and Reginald William in 1869. There followed three daughters: Barbara Elizabeth in 1870, Dorothy in 1872 and Anne Blanche Alice in 1874. William Francis was born in 1875, and then a decade passed before Thomas George was born, twenty years after his eldest brother.

Serene and dignified, only rarely did Blanche allow glimpses of her private self to stray into the public domain. She appears every inch the proud and prim Victorian matriarch but, beneath the bland façade, she was a most enterprising woman who shared her husband's enthusiasm for life. For example, she took up horse riding after her marriage and was soon acknowledged as an expert horsewoman, and she was a keen cyclist and regularly rode around the park on her tricycle. She thought nothing of accompanying her husband on an uncomfortable and tedious fishing expedition to Norway when pregnant with her first child. Among the numerous gushing articles in the society journals, one from *Madame* by a Mrs. Darling-Barker was notably more perceptive in its description of Lady Coventry. After a brief account of the family's new London home, 1 Balfour Place, 'a most delightful house with a great deal of frontage' and with open landings fitted as sitting-rooms to form 'pleasant retreats where the young people chat', Mrs. Darling-Barker then presumes to list her hostess's finer qualities:

> She is what is so aptly termed a 'womanly woman' which is the most winsome attraction a woman can possess. No terms are too favourable to describe her kindliness and sympathy to everyone … She has all the subtle gentleness that wins confidence, and the sterling good sense that keeps her from letting her good nature abuse her judgement … to know Lady Coventry is to love her.

Blanche enjoyed collecting autographs. One Christmas at Croome, she even made all the assembled family sign their names on a sheet of notepaper. It helped to keep a register as the family began to multiply and disappear abroad. She trawled through the archive to make a selection of her favourite autograph letters from royalty, political and artistic figures such as the Prince Regent, Newcastle, Chatham, Adam, Wellington, and Sir Joshua Reynolds.[8] This was a task enjoyed by many aristocratic ladies of the period, almost an extension of their housekeeping skills, but to Blanche it seems to have acquired particular significance as a matter of propriety and presentation in order to set the record straight, quite literally.

Croome assumed fresh importance under the ownership of the 9th Earl as the hub of a large and close-knit community. This was an essential part of the plan. In reply to a toast to his health at his coming-of-age celebrations, Lord Coventry had remarked that: 'he was

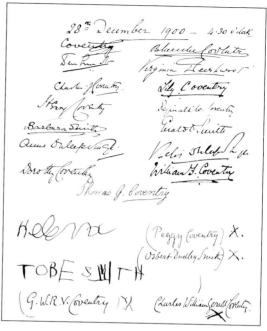

100 Family autographs.

ardently attached to the country, and he should be pleased to spend his days in the midst of an affectionate tenantry, and in the domain of his ancestors'. He took immense pride in his country seat and, in September 1865, not long after his marriage, he commissioned a series of remarkable photographs of Croome from F.C. Earl, a Worcester photographer, which today provide an invaluable record of the house and park in the mid-19th century. During his lifetime, the house reasserted it importance as the focus of the locality, and the hordes of residential and casual staff, the gardeners, the estate workers and all the tenants made up a small, thriving, self-sufficient society, seemingly immune to the outside world. By the turn of the century, Croome could boast a water-softening plant, two fire engines, and a private gas works. The last was an invaluable improvement, as the 9th Earl noted in his diary on 9 December 1873 that the mansion house alone had consumed an awesome 290 tons of coal in 1871. Comfort had always been a consideration in the design of the house, but during the second half of the 19th century any hint of formality gave way to a heap of homely clutter. The house became crammed full with furniture transferred there from Coventry House and Snitterfield, a new collection of paintings to replace those sold in 1810, and endless trophies, souvenirs and other paraphernalia linked with the family's favourite sports and pastimes. A cutting from the 'Home Chat with Celebrities' column, clipped from one society journal for inclusion in the family albums, described a typical scene at Croome as follows:

A picture of beautiful and refined home life, light and sunshine filtering through carefully lace-shaded oriel windows, five in number, antique couches tapestry covered, bestrewn with cushions huge in size, soft and inviting, delicate satinwood corner cupboards enshrining many treasures of ceramic art, Empire tables, littered with costly knick-knacks, and amongst it all the beautiful mistress of this English home, seated busy at her embroidery frame, while she talks to her pretty daughter, who has just come in from the Park, and is still in her riding habit. Such is the picture, as pretty a one as anybody could wish to see.

The formal entrance hall was transformed, its Bath flagstones covered with oriental rugs and numerous oak chairs and chests brought from Snitterfield. Over the fireplace hung, not a vast and intimidating ancestral portrait, but a new painting by Sir Frederick Grant, a gift from the North Cotswold Hunt in 1873. Opposite were paintings of his favourite horses and below a record of victories achieved at the Essex Agricultural Show by his prize bull 'Fisherman' and his progeny. Behind the elegant columned screen loomed the head of a giant boar, killed by the Comte de Paris, a friend and regular guest. In Lord Coventry's study, Canalettos, Gainsboroughs and Hogarths jostled for space among the boot-pulls, seed catalogues, farm account books, cigar boxes and fruit manuals, and in one corner lay the crumpled remnants of the Lord Keeper's robes. The 9th

Earl liked to use the gallery as a dining room, with the table set in the bay window so that he could look out at the herons nesting on the river and had Tom Coventry's rocking horse, 'Bumper', looking over his shoulder. Lord Coventry and his sons made themselves a smoking room in the basement, which they lined with old college prints and photographs, favourite items of furniture and stacks of parliamentary journals. The place was no longer just a showpiece, it was a much-loved home.

Blanche's talents as a society hostess were celebrated. Queen Victoria only ever visited Croome as a girl, when she is said to have planted an acorn, but the Prince of Wales, the future Edward VII, and the Duke and Duchess of York, later George V and Queen Mary, knew Lord and Lady Coventry well. Prince and Princess Christian of Schleswig Holstein were also frequent guests, as Princess Christian, a daughter of Queen Victoria, was Lady Dorothy's godmother. Other family friends included the Duke and Duchess of Teck, the Duc d'Aumale, the Comte de Paris, and also the Duc d'Orléans and his

101 The Duke of York's visit to Croome in 1898. Blanche is seated centre left, in the middle row, with the 9th Earl standing directly behind her and the Duke of York standing to the Earl's left.

102   Croome Court from the south, *c*.1902.

family, who lived nearby at Woodnorton, near Evesham. The Duke and Duchess of York stayed at Croome for a couple of nights at the beginning of April 1894, when they visited Worcestershire to lay the foundation stone at the Victoria Institute in Worcester. Lady Dorothy recorded the following details of the visit in her diary:[9]

Pershore station and the town were nicely decorated, and a crowd of people witnessed HRH's arrival. There was very little cheering which made it somewhat awkward, it is such an unusual event to have such a visit, that the people hardly knew how to take it ... The boys stood on the steps to receive HRH and Tom made many a bow, we and Beauchamp and the Hindlips, who had arrived, were in the saloon. We then had tea, and after a good deal of conversation, Mother asked the Duke to plant a tree ... Then we children and Beauchamp and papa of course, accompanied HRH to the Shrubberies, first going through the stables, none of them knew a horse from a cow except Lord Hindlip, so that was not much of a success. The tree was all ready to be planted and Child [the head gardener] stood near with the spade. HRH did his part in a workmanlike way, laughing and chatting the whole time. The gentlemen then continued their walk round the lake etc and we went in to help mother receive Lord and Lady Cobham and Lady Elcho. We dined at 8.30 ... The dining room looked beautiful, decorated with papa's beautiful plate ... Dinner did not take very long, it was beautifully done. The Mayor had his servant waiting at table, arrayed

in the most gorgeous of liveries, then we had two extra waiters from Gunters, great fine men, with beautiful manners. The three drawing rooms were thrown open and we all sat mostly in the tapestry room. The gentlemen came out very soon after us, and the Duke was so nice going round the room talking to the guests. But this thoughtful act was nipped in the bud by Lady Hindlip who went straight up to HRH and asked him to play Bezique with her ...

She goes on to describe the events in Worcester the following day: the dust rising in clouds from the horses' hooves and powdering her clothes and hair, and the crowds of people that lined the streets, though the best fun of all was 'hearing the people about criticise the Duke'. That evening, the poor Duke was cornered once more by Lady Hindlip, and he left Croome promptly the next morning.

Stanley Baldwin, Conservative politician and three times prime minister, often attended the house parties at Croome, which was located just a few miles from his Worcestershire home, as did the actress, Ellen Terry, who described the surroundings and company at Croome as 'Manna in the wilderness'.[10] She often called in on her way to Droitwich, where she went to recuperate from her demanding schedule. Like G.F. Watts, Edward Godwin and George Bernard Shaw, Lord Coventry found her charms irresistible. In

August 1900, he sent a magnolia from the gardens at Croome to her room in the *Raven Hotel* in Droitwich. She was delighted with the gift, writing to him with thanks: 'It fills my room with a wonderful perfume and with shut eyes I can imagine myself in—almost any place than salt Droitwich!' Gustave Hamel, the aviator, caused great excitement when he attempted to land his plane on the lawn in front of the house. Lady Coventry had been to watch him give a flying demonstration and was so enthralled by his performance she immediately invited him to stay. He wrote back from the Royal Aeronautical Club in Piccadilly on 4 November 1913 to explain that he could not accept the invitation as he was about to compete in the Hendon to Brighton race. Early the following year, Hamel gave a flying exhibition at Pershore racecourse, and this time he was determined to keep his promise to Lady Coventry. A large, white cross was laid out on the lawn in front of the Court and one Sunday evening, just as the rector had begun his sermon, Hamel flew low across the park to announce his arrival. Everyone rushed outside to see the plane, but Hamel overshot the landing area and struck a tree. Humbly apologetic and deeply humiliated, Hamel lodged at Croome for the next few days, while his plane was transported to Defford station for repairs. The experience must have shattered his confidence for on his journey home he vanished without trace, never to be seen again.

Lord and Lady Coventry took great pride in the pleasure gardens and the parkland. New hothouses were built in the kitchen garden, which attained new heights of productivity under the direction of the gardener, William Child. Both Lord and Lady Coventry loved cut flowers and insisted on fresh flowers in the house every day. Lady Coventry was particularly partial to lilies of the valley, and Lord Coventry always had a fresh carnation in his lapel buttonhole. In 1887, *Gardening World* described the kitchen and pleasure gardens at length, and was especially impressed by the various melon, cucumber, fig, peach and mushroom houses and the innumerable rare and magnificent trees, the purple beeches, stone pine, tulip tree, and the variegated oaks and elms.[11] Croome was also featured in an early edition of *Country Life*:

> a delightful prospect is disclosed of landscape beauty, with green expanses and umbrageous depths picturesquely disposed. On the right flows a river of artificial origin ... finally expanding into a large lake ... Spanning the water is a Chinese bridge, also the work of [William Halfpenny] Brown, and from the ascent beyond, where stand some noble trees, there is a broad outlook towards the mansion, with the tower of the church rising among the trees to the left. The pleasure grounds are near the house, and have been famous ever since they were formed for their splendid specimens of exotic plants and trees. In the home shrubbery the variegated hollies, evergreen oaks, yews, laurels, and other plants and trees are exceedingly beautiful. The dairy and hothouses are nearby, and are always attractive, the one for its delicious coolness, the others for the richness and rarity of their contents ... Much is there to be seen of choice evergreen and deciduous trees and shrubs in the various shrubberies and wildernesses, in the groves, the arboretum, and the park, cedars also, and grand oaks and planes and many more. The flower garden is a radiant realm of unfailing sweetness, and there are orangeries and conservatories full of beautiful things; statues also of druids and nymphs, an artificial ruin and the circular Doric building with a dome, designed by Wyatt to command a prospect of the lovely surrounding landscape ...[12]

A stunning set of photographs accompanied the article.

During the earlier part of the 9th Earl's ownership only modest sums of a few hundred pounds annually were spent on new planting. The park still supported 400 fallow deer in 1867, and 300 in 1892, and apart from the work to the kitchen garden, it was more a question of maintenance. The Chinese bridge had disappeared during the first half of the century, but it was not until the close of the century that any other significant changes were implemented to meet rising costs. The Flower Garden and Nursery, north-east of the park, were turned into orchards, the Greenhouse Shrubbery and Menagerie Wood were reduced in size, the dog kennels to the east of the park were demolished, and the Roundabout Plantation also disappeared around this time. Not that this deterred *Country Life* from exhorting the beauties of Croome in yet another article of 1915. Buildings and landscape still appear to have been kept in excellent condition at this time, and, interestingly, the article refers to around twenty heron's nests on the lake and to the abundance of owls in the park, which gave the Park Seat its nickname of the 'Owl's Nest.'[13]

The fifth and final phase of drainage was carried out during the late 1840s, following a report by William Branston of 1847, but the problem was never totally solved. Between 1883 to 1905 the estate accounts refer to annual expenditure on drainage often costing over £1,000. Elsewhere in the park, another attempt was made to exploit the salt springs at Defford. Following the example of the 6th Earl, Lord Coventry had the springs analysed, but the results only confirmed the previous findings that the saline properties were not of sufficient concentration for commercial purposes. Instead, he decided to build a small bathhouse for his private use. This had a glazed roof and was lined with white tiles, and the saltwater was pumped into large supply tanks nearby and heated with copper furnaces. There was even an adjoining bathing pool for his horses. Between 1870 and 1880, Lord Coventry regularly took baths there, but eventually he found its distance from Croome inconvenient. A Mr. Archer of Malvern tried to persuade him to build a hotel and turn Defford into a health resort, but he disliked the idea of such a development on the fringes of the park.[14] The furnaces and pumps for the bathhouse were sold off in the 1950s, and now only the brick shell remains.

The appointment of John Hill as the new agent was an important landmark in the history of the estate. Hill held the post for 53 years, from 1868 to 1921, and formed a highly successful partnership with his employer. Hill came from Penkridge in Staffordshire, and lived at Church House in Severn Stoke rather than in the former agent's house at Croome. This enabled the 9th Earl to accommodate his head groom in the agent's house, a modest but elegant house by Brown located immediately to the east of the stable block. Hill was liked and respected by the tenants, and his patience, practical knowledge and sound management helped to lessen the impact of the agricultural depression, increased taxation and the shock of the First World War. When he arrived in Croome in 1868, Worcestershire was still a predominantly agricultural county and wheat was the principal crop. The county had benefited from a sequence of good harvests, and there were excellent profits arising from the demand for food from the expanding towns. There followed a period of cold wet summers and poor harvests which, combined with the import of cheap grain from America and elsewhere, brought about a decline

103   John Hill.

in the price of corn, and consequent unemployment and a migration to the towns. The introduction of new machinery on farms had also increased the number of unemployed labourers, even if it had brought relief from the more arduous and repetitive tasks. Government policy on corn imports, and other regulations and taxes that affected the social and economic life of the countryside, infuriated Lord Coventry. He spoke out frequently on the subject and wrote innumerable articles and letters to the newspapers and the agricultural journals to argue his case. For example, on 25 December 1879, he wrote to the assistant commissioner of the Royal Commission on Agriculture, listing the current problems suffered by Worcestershire landowners, and objected strongly to the way the railways conveyed foreign meat and grain at much lower rates than British produce. He also expressed particular concern about the increase in the Highway Rate. Farmers, Lord Coventry argued, preferred the old turnpike system founded on the principle that those who used the roads should pay for them. This, he believed, was also a deterrent to thieves, as a horse of his had been driven fifty miles the previous year before it was identified.

As the difficulties increased, Lord Coventry and his agent became determined to prove that sound and efficient management and investment could withstand the forces of change. Around a hundred new cottages were built on the estate during the lifetime of the 9th Earl, several new farms and new stables. The repairs and alterations begun during his minority were rigorously sustained, and he jotted down his thoughts on possible improvements and repairs regularly in his diary as they occurred to him. Typical entries occur in 1905, when the need to put a new roof on a shed at Cubsmoor is noted alongside the income from his gold mining investments. Although the 9th Earl is said to have claimed that successful farming depended upon 'white-faced cattle, black-faced sheep, farmyard manure, and early planting', this was clearly role-playing as in practice he was far more enterprising than this. The author, A. Rider Haggard, believed that the progressive agricultural methods practised on the Croome estate established an exemplary standard. In his book, *Rural England*, of 1902, he described the famous herd of Hereford cattle, the new cottages let at low rents of 1s.-1s. 6d. per week, and the 321 allotments, and was impressed by the new dipping tank and sheep tank at Severn

Stoke. He included an interview with Lord Coventry, who took the opportunity to attack government policy. 'I think the Chancellor of the Exchequer should impose a shilling duty upon wheat', he remarked, 'so that England should be placed on even terms with foreigners.' Haggard expressed particular interest in the range of alternative crops grown on the estate to help withstand the problem of cheap imports, notably the plum and apple orchards with their innumerable varieties of fruit, the hop plantations protected by screens of spruce, and the vast acreage of peas. The reference to the extensive orchards is important, as by the late 19th century fruit production had become one of the principal new sources of revenue in the region, due to the surge in market gardening around the vale of Evesham. This had taken advantage of the improving rail network and, by 1906, over 2,000 tons of fruit and vegetables were dispatched every week to the towns and cities from the area. In 1890, Lord Coventry established a jam and pickle factory in a former industrial building near Pershore station. This enabled his tenants to sell their produce to the factory at fair market prices thereby saving the cost of railway carriage and risk of sending large consignments of perishable goods on long journeys. According to his diary, the factory cost just under £700 to build, and it processed fruit from over 30,000 strawberry plants, a similar number of raspberry canes and currant bushes at Croome, as well as much of the fruit from the orchards. The tenants welcomed the idea, but the profits proved disappointing, and in 1901 its management was transferred to Beach and Sons of Toddington, Gloucestershire, who ran a similar and much larger enterprise in Toddington on behalf of Lord Sudeley.

Another of the 9th Earl's pet projects of this period was the idea of agricultural credit banking. This had originated in Germany, and he believed it would give the numerous smallholders in the area a better chance of independence and prosperity. He was also an enthusiastic supporter of agricultural co-operative societies to help farmers market their produce. Other enterprises to help his tenants included a plan to build a light railway to run between Worcester and Upton, and a new road bridge at Pixham, near Kempsey, proposed in 1896 to replace the ferry and thereby cut three miles off the journey west towards Malvern and Herefordshire. Both the latter projects were abandoned later as they were not financially viable.

There is every reason to believe that this paternalistic attitude towards his tenantry was entirely genuine. For Lord Coventry made himself very accessible and, as an informed and enthusiastic landlord, he was very sympathetic to their needs, preferring to discuss problems 'on site' where he could get a true grasp of the problem rather than from behind a desk in his study or in Hill's office. Every year on Christmas Eve, he and Lady Coventry gave out gifts of beef and bread to their tenants and their children. This tradition went back well over one hundred years to the time of the 6th Earl, but under the 9th Earl it had become not simply a charitable handout but an informal and enjoyable occasion which marked the start of the Christmas festivities. The event took place in the barn, east of the stables at Croome, and in 1915, for example, 270 large loaves and 100 small loaves and two 'fat beasts' were distributed among 167 families on the estate, 637 people in all.[15]

104   Lord and Lady Coventry distributing beef and bread to the Croome tenants on Christmas Eve.

105   Lord Coventry and one of his prize bulls in the park at Croome.

For Lord Coventry to donate two of his prize cattle was a truly noble gesture, for he took immense pride in his herd of pedigree Herefords. His aim was to breed a true competitor to the popular Shorthorn, and this he achieved with remarkable speed and skill. He began the herd in 1875, when he acquired the nucleus of his stock from William Tudge of Adforton in Herefordshire. Between 1878 and 1925, when he sold the herd, he showed his cattle at every Royal Show and won over three hundred prizes, notably with bulls such as 'Good Boy' and 'Rare Sovereign'. When he sold the herd in 1925, he had 28 breeding cows, 24 bull and heifer calves and four bulls. As a result of his efforts, he was welcomed on the Council of the Smithfield Club, the sup-reme society for cattle, and he also became President of the Worcestershire and the Bath and West Agricultural Societies and President of the Royal Agricultural Society, having served on its council for around sixteen years. He even attempted to establish a South African herd of Herefords, and sent out two of his bulls to his son, Charles, who was then an officer of the Bechuanaland Mounted Police. Remarkably, they survived the sea trip, and managed the three-week hike to their destination. One died some time later, but the other flourished long enough to establish a large herd, although this was wiped out eventually by *rinderpest*.

Although the 9th Earl was extremely proud of his Hereford herd, horses remained his chief passion and he bred them with similar success. After he came of age, his horse 'Wanderer' won a race at Harpenden, and this encouraged him to acquire several excellent stallions, including 'Tim Whiffler' and 'Umpire', and various brood mares, notably 'Virago', to breed a stable of winners. A gallop was constructed in the old park at Pirton to train his racehorses, which cost just over £352, but it proved worth the expense. His racing colours of brown body and blue cap were first published in 1858 and, by 1859, he had been elected a member of the Jockey Club; he was elected steward of the Club in the following year.[16] The first of his new stock of racehorses, 'Elcho', won the Goodwood Stakes. Other victories followed close behind, the most memorable being his two successive wins at the Grand National in 1864 and 1865 with his two mares, 'Emblem' and her sister 'Emblematic', ridden by the celebrated cross-country jockey George Stephens. Neither of these horses had been bred at Croome, but he had spotted their potential and had them trained by Edwin Weaver of Bourton-on-the-Hill. There were further successes with, for example, 'Chimney Sweep' and 'Steamboat', but after 1870 Lord Coventry's horses appeared less frequently in the racing columns, possibly because he is alleged to have entered them under the assumed name of 'Mr. Morton'. His sons, Charles and Henry, took over the running of his racing stables by the late 19th century, but Lord Coventry continued to attend race meetings at Worcester, Cheltenham, Epsom and elsewhere. Pages from his diary torn from their binding suggest that he bet frequently and not always successfully. It is doubtful whether Blanche approved. He contributed much to the development of the racecourse at Worcester, where he instituted the Coventry stakes, a race for two-year-old horses, and he became accepted as an authority on horse breeding in the pages of the racing press.

Whenever possible, he preferred to be in the saddle himself, and following his hounds, in particular. Some claimed he lived to hunt. A founder and member of the National Hunt Committee, he remained a leading spirit in the sport for over fifty years. Like

106 'Emblem', Lord Coventry's first racehorse to win the Grand National.

many of his ancestors, he gave vent to his enthusiasms in an outpouring of verse. The following lines are taken from a lengthy poem on the pleasures of the Epwell Hunt:

> As Epwell's wide heath, t'other day I pass'd over,
> The hounds I perceiv'd, were then trying the cover;
> Enraptured I heard them, and mounting my horse,
> Soon discover'd the pack which had found in the gorse,
> Two hundred crack sportsmen enliven'd the scene,
> All determin'd to ride and professedly keen;
> Though the morning was cold, and the frost over night,
> Made the country around in a terrible plight,
> Yet Reynard broke cover disdaining to stay,
> And in view of the Field, went most bravely away …

At first he rode with the Worcestershire Hunt but, in 1868, when the Cotswold Hunt split, he was invited to be the first Master of the new North Cotswold Hunt. The distance from Croome to Broadway proved no obstacle to so keen and energetic a man. He rose early, rode the 18 miles to the meet, hunted all day, and rode home refreshed from the day's activities. It was while out hunting with the North Cotswold that he suffered an unfortunate accident, which he described many years later as 'the most dramatic incident of my life'. He and Lady Coventry were galloping at full stretch up a slope towards a hedge, little knowing that this concealed a disused quarry. It was too late to stop when they realised their error, and both of them plunged nearly thirty feet to the quarry bottom. Miraculously, Lord Coventry and his horse survived the incident unhurt, if a little shaken. Lady Coventry was not quite so fortunate. Her horse broke its back and she was knocked unconscious, although she suffered no permanent damage. In view of the misfortunes of his ancestors, Lord Coventry had a remarkable escape. He cheated death a second time when the grandstand collapsed at Cheltenham. As his seat disappeared beneath him, he managed to grab hold of a pillar from which he hung twenty feet from the ground till help arrived. In 1873, he gave up hunting with the North Cotswold, as the distance proved too time-consuming and the opportunity arose to establish his own pack at Croome.[17] The Marquess of Queensberry had retired as master of the Worcestershire Hunt in 1872, and a division of the county was negotiated whereby the earl established a new pack known as 'the Earl of Coventry's Hunt', based at the new kennels in the former Menagerie at Croome. His pack was already widely admired by this time and his stallion hound 'Rambler' soon established a national reputation for his ability 'to jump his fences like a steeplechaser'. Between 1886-92 and 1895-1900, Lord Coventry was honoured with the Mastership of the Queen's Buckhounds, and this prompted him to sell his hounds to Mr. Lort Phillips, and the hunt was re-named 'the Croome'. However, the family's close association with the Croome continued for, in 1899, his son Henry and son-in-law, Gerald Dudley Smith, became joint Masters till 1901, when Dudley Smith continued in the Mastership alone until 1910. The 10th Earl acted as Master from 1932-40, the Countess, his widow, continuing the tradition as Joint Master from 1942-6 and 1948-9, and their daughter, Lady Maria, taking over the hunt's Joint-Mastership in 1976.

Fishing was another of Lord Coventry's favourite pastimes. In 1880, he decided to rent a six-bedroomed fishing lodge, Wardens House, in Leintwardine, Herefordshire. The house had an adjoining cottage for the staff and a large garden with access to idyllic stretches of the River Lugg. He joined the Leintwardine Fishing Club, and he and the boys spent many happy hours either fishing or visiting the cattle fair in Ludlow. Blanche and the girls went for long walks, and were occasionally invited to Downton Castle for the day. They kept a diary of their holidays there and liked the area so much that, in 1891, Lord Coventry decided to buy the house and cottage.[18] It remained a popular retreat for the Coventry family until 1920, when the 9th Earl's rheumatism made fishing impossible.

In the summer of 1865, when Blanche was four and a half months pregnant with their first child, Lord and Lady Coventry set off on a fishing expedition to Norway. They embarked on 10 June and, after a rough crossing, arrived in Norway three days later. Lord Coventry spent most of the next few weeks fishing, apart from one day when he decided to hunt for reindeer with the resident guide. They had little success, but the guide impressed him enormously. That night he noted in his diary that Norwegians are 'naturally wonderfully active specimens of humanity'. Elsewhere he is less enthusiastic about his hosts, and considers them 'avaricious' and 'bad fishermen', and that the 'chief reason for their not fishing lies in their fear of the necessary outlay required for rod, tackle etc'. Neither did he or Blanche like their accommodation. He described the rooms as 'full of sombre and heavy furniture, nothing gay or fanciful'. However, the fishing was excellent, and by 28 July he had caught 109 fish in all, with a total weight of 1,364 lbs. On 30 July they set off for Copenhagen by phaeton and steamer. It was a hazardous journey, 'the reckless manner of driving nearly brought us to grief in turning in at a gateway … for we charged it gallantly and the result was the closest shave we ever saw'. The inns were uncomfortable and 'literally swarming with flies', but fuelled with an ample breakfast of bacon, eggs, smoked salmon, 'capital cream and delicious strawberries', they made good progress. On 6 August they arrived in Copenhagen, where they stayed at the *Hotel Royal*. The next day was spent shopping, apparently for biscuit casts of Mercury, Hebe, Venus and various other deities, and the Earl sketched a few buildings. They then caught the night train to Hamburg, and from there they travelled on to Cologne, before returning to London by train and Channel steamer.

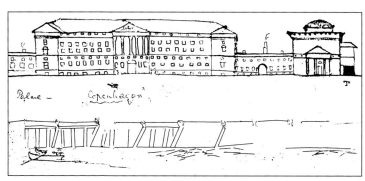

107 A drawing by Lord Coventry in Copenhagen during his fishing trip to Scandinavia.

Somehow, Lord Coventry also found time for cricket. During his minority, he had supported the amateur Worcestershire team known as the Gentlemen of Worcestershire, and in 1859 he was elected president of the Marylebone Cricket Club (MCC). Although he never showed much aptitude for the sport, he had his own eleven which played on the Severn Stoke ground at Cubsmoor, and a brief moment of glory occurred in 1860 when he took 10 wickets in a match against Tewkesbury. His support of the flourishing new county team made a valuable contribution to its development. In March 1865, he chaired the meeting at the *Star Hotel* in Worcester to establish a suitable county ground, now famous for its picturesque riverside setting. His sons showed greater promise. Henry was in the Eton eleven and played for the county, while Charles played for England out in Cape Town.

Despite the 9th Earl's attachment to his estate and his love of country pursuits, he still found time for his official duties. As a staunch Tory, he once remarked in a newspaper interview that he felt that his administrative talents had been overlooked and should have fitted him for many high offices of state. His chance came in 1877, when he became a Privy Councillor, and from 1877-80 he was Captain and Gold Stick of the Corps of Gentlemen-at-Arms, but he never took full advantage of these opportunities. He seemed content to express his views to the press and maintain a heated correspondence with the opposition, while keeping a relatively low profile in parliament. Only once did he take the House by surprise, when, in 1909, infuriated by Lloyd George's attempts to undermine the House of Lords, he made a heartfelt attack on the Budget and other policies of the Liberal government. It was at county level that he made his most significant contribution. From 1891 onwards, he was Lord Lieutenant and Custos Rotulorum of the county, and between 1880-8 he was chairman of the County Quarter Sessions. He also served on the county council and, with Mr. Willis Bund, chairman of the council and local historian, he fought for the retention of the northern areas of the county that were absorbed into Birmingham. He became a High Steward of Tewkesbury in 1901, and was presented with the Freedom of both Tewkesbury and Worcester, and he contributed much to the administration and morale of the local militia, notably as Hon. Colonel of the 3rd and 4th Battalions of the Worcestershire Regiment. His son, Charles, became a lieutenant in the same regiment in 1885. Although his ancestors had held similar appointments, the 9th Earl felt a far greater need to justify public confidence in his abilities, and never neglected his duties. (Colour plates XXIV and XXV.)

The golden wedding of Lord and Lady Coventry, in January 1915, had a special significance. The celebrations were on a similar scale to those of their wedding day, 50 years previously, but a mellow sentimentality stole across the entire occasion. It was an excuse for a party, a time to forget the war and defiantly reinforce bonds of loyalty and re-enact old traditions as if nothing had changed. The bells rang out from Tewkesbury Abbey and beef, beer and bread were distributed among the poor. John Hill and the other heads of department presented Lord and Lady Coventry with a set of gold penholders, the household staff at Croome gave them a golden loving cup, and the tenants from Croome each donated a small sum towards a glittering candelabra. A dinner and dance took place in every parish on the estate and, at the dinner at the *Boar's Head* in Severn Stoke, Lord Coventry was reported to remark:

> We have indeed been a united Clan, and I gratefully recall the many occasions on which you have evinced your attachment to Lady Coventry and myself, and the other members of my family, and which will always live in our remembrance.[19]

His use of the past tense may have been intentional. Cracks had appeared beneath the façade and, although the philanthropy and hospitality, the handouts and the house parties, continued, by 1915 the estate was struggling for survival. The 9th Earl was well aware of the serious nature of the problem—he had been wrestling with it for almost forty years—and by the time he had reached his 54th birthday the weight of his responsibilities had begun to show. A newspaper remarked rather insensitively: 'Lord Coventry does not bear his age with much buoyancy. He has in the last five years become very grey, and his face has been freely lined by the artist Care, who does not spare the peer any more than the peasant …'. It was not just the future of the estate that weighed heavily upon the 9th Earl; there were other anxieties, not least Viscount Deerhurst. Since the age of four, the implications of his birthright had been impressed upon him, when he was forced solemnly to present the prizes at the church fête. His parents set such a daunting example that when the chance arose he escaped overseas, where his bad habits would be less subject to scrutiny.

George William, Viscount Deerhurst was born on 15 November 1865 and went to Eton. After he failed to get into Sandhurst, he went instead to Trinity College, Cambridge. There, he sought relief from the tedium of his studies in gambling and rifle-shooting, and he was the youngest marksman ever to be awarded the bronze medal of the National Rifle Association. From Cambridge he went to Dresden to study German, and there he was offered the appointment of Aide-de-Camp to Sir Henry Loch, Governor of Victoria, Australia. It was a brilliant opportunity brought to an abrupt end after an altercation with a notorious bookmaker, and Deerhurst seized the chance to join the gold rush in Queensland. This was the type of adventure he craved, and once he is reported to have struck a vein of quartz six inches thick which contained around 50 oz gold to the ton. He would have remained in Australia indefinitely, but an attack of fever drove him home in 1888. At his father's recommendation, he became a stockbroker on the London Exchange, but he showed little aptitude for the profession and, when he was offered a vacancy in the police force in Cape Town, he accepted it readily. On his arrival, he was told that no vacancies existed, but the matter was soon forgotten as his lust for gold-digging and big game hunting lured him inland. With a rifle in one hand and a shovel in the other, he was in his element. Haggard may have been inspired by his example, but his father was less than impressed, and soon he was summoned home. Bored and back in London, Deerhurst relapsed into his former bad habits, and his dissolute and extravagant lifestyle resulted in his being declared a bankrupt in 1890. His insolvency was attributed primarily to his losses in betting and gambling, and he owed as much as £17,000 to a moneylender with whom he had shared a mutual interest in horseracing. Reluctantly, his father came to his rescue, but four years later, Deerhurst's prospects improved considerably when on 10 March 1894 he married a rich and pretty heiress, Virginia Lee Bonynge. She was the daughter of William and Rodie Daniel of Farmington, USA, and the adopted step-daughter of a Californian millionaire, Charles William Bonynge, a former gardener who had made his fortune from the silver mines in Nevada and settled in London in 1888.[20] Deerhurst and Virginia were married at All Saints, Ennismore Gardens and moved into Pirton Court. Viscountess Deerhurst soon proved herself a true asset to the local community and a favourite of Queen Victoria's daughter, Princess Christian, but not before the press had delved deep into her background to embarrass the family. Stories appeared about American millionaires who put their feet on dinner tables and picked their teeth with bowie knives. Worse still, it emerged that her natural father had shot himself when he learnt that his former wife had married Bonynge. All this did little for the image of flawless respectability that Lord and Lady Coventry had recreated so painstakingly and effectively.

The difficult relationship between Viscount Deerhurst and his father at this time was exacerbated by the sale of the magnificent tapestries at Croome. During the 1880s, the 9th Earl sold the tapestries and matching chairs and sofas from the Tapestry Room to a French collector for £50,000 to raise necessary funds. The walls of the Tapestry Room were recovered with a sombre, green damask and the room was used as a place to play cards after dinner. The money that remained was invested in Lord Coventry's own name, but, in theory, the contents of the Tapestry Room were family heirlooms, which he had no right to sell.[21] It emerged that, in 1887, he had commissioned a new inventory of the contents of Croome, based on an earlier one of 1831, in which the contents of the Tapestry Room were omitted quite deliberately, presumably as he had decided to sell them. Deerhurst was outraged at what he believed was a deliberate and underhand means of depriving him of his birthright. Only after long and acrimonious debate was it agreed that the tapestries should be legally classed as 'fixtures', and that Deerhurst should be paid £5,000 from the sale, together with any monies left after expenses had been subtracted, to be invested in securities. But it was not until the 1920s that the whole business was finally resolved. The new Trustees of the Croome Estate took ownership of the investments purchased by Lord Coventry, and Lord Deerhurst agreed to give back his £5,000. It was a great pity that one of the family's most prized possessions became a cause of such deep resentment between father and son.

Less upsetting personally, but equally unwelcome, was the business of the Baccarat Scandal, the famous libel case of 1891, which occurred just after Deerhurst's bankruptcy. Cheating at cards was hardly unusual, but the incident gripped the public imagination, partly because of the high stakes involved, but primarily because the Prince of Wales, the future Edward VII, was included among the assembled company. The incident occurred on 8 September 1890 at a house party at Tranby Croft, near Hull, the home of a local shipowner, Sir Arthur Wilson, at which Lord and Lady Coventry happened to be present. Every evening, at around 11 o'clock, Wilson and his guests settled down to a game of baccarat and, on this particular occasion, Wilson claimed that he had detected one of his guests, Sir William Gordon-Cumming, cheating. They were using noiseless counters made of Russian leather,

and Gordon-Cumming was alleged to have dropped additional counters onto the table
when he knew he was winning. Wilson mentioned his suspicions to some of his friends,
and it was agreed that the following evening a chalk line would be drawn on the table
behind which all stakes were to be placed to avoid any confusion. Despite such precautions,
this time Gordon-Cumming's behaviour aroused the suspicions of all five other players
at his table. It was agreed that the matter be placed in the hands of General Owen Williams
and Lord Coventry, both of whom were old friends of Gordon-Cumming and could
be relied upon to deal with the matter in the most tactful and appropriate manner. To
cause minimum offence, they decided that the accused should sign a secret memorandum
swearing that he would never play cards again. The Prince approved of the scheme and
Gordon-Cumming reluctantly signed the memorandum, although he claimed he was
innocent. That might have been the end of the matter, but the story leaked out, largely
due to the Prince's involvement, and Gordon-Cumming was dismissed from the army.
He decided to sue the five witnesses for libel, and the case was brought before the High
Court where both the Prince of Wales and Lord Coventry were obliged to give evidence.
The 9th Earl wrote in his diary on 4 February 1891: 'Our [his and Williams'] just desire
throughout the sad business has been to keep the name of the Prince out of it, but the
lawsuit which is threatening would appear to defeat our object'.

Then, in January 1896, Lord and Lady Coventry received news that their second
son Charles had been killed in the famous Jameson Raid. The raid into the Transvaal
from Mafeking had taken place on 29 December 1895 in an attempt to overthrow the
president, Paul Kruger, and had ended unsuccessfully just a few miles from Johannesburg.
Led by Leander Starr Jameson, a doctor in the diamond-mining camp at Kimberley
and a friend of Cecil Rhodes, it had made a significant contribution to the outbreak
of the Boer War. Charles shared his elder brother's thirst for adventure but channelled
his ardour along a more acceptable path. A popular soldier, renowned for his courage,
and a favourite of his father, he had been in Africa for eight years prior to the raid.
He joined the Bechuanaland Border Police in 1889 and had obtained a company in
the 3rd Battalion Worcestershire Regiment in 1892, when he had served with distinction
during the Matabele campaign and was recommended for a DSO. News of his daring
deeds were printed in the Worcestershire papers, including extracts from his letters to
his parents. One such account describes the attack by the Matabeles on their waggons:

> They came after us, but directly the Maxim guns opened fire on them they retreated and we pursued
> them to some Kopjes or hills ... Then came some fun. We all dismounted and fired at then as they
> bobbed up and down behind the rocks. I had seven or eight shots at them, but I do not know if I
> killed one or not.[22]

Such sentiments would certainly not merit publication today, but at the time Charles was
a local hero. The news of his death arrived on 6 January, just two days after Lord
and Lady Coventry had been informed that he was only slightly injured in the raid.
His obituary was published in the papers, then, just hours before a memorial service
was due to be held at Croome, a telegram arrived with the news that he was still alive.

The shot, which had appeared fatal, had bounced off his gun and narrowly missed his spine causing only flesh wounds. The sheer uncertainty of it all was most traumatic, but arrangements were quickly made to hold a service of thanksgiving instead. Telegrams of sympathy and congratulation arrived together, including those from the Queen at Osborne House, and the Prince of Wales from Lowther Castle. Only later did it emerge that, after Charles had been wounded, he had been captured by the Boers, tried and sentenced to five months' imprisonment.

Charles married Lily Whitehouse on 16 January 1900, and they had two sons, Charles and Francis, both as brave as their father, who later distinguished themselves in the Second World War. The eldest son, Charles William Gerald, was 14 when the First World War broke out and a naval cadet. The zeppelins had evidently captured his imagination, as witnessed by his poem 'The Truth about the Kaiser', which was published in the *Osborne Chronicle*:

> There was a noble Kaiser once, who wished to walk in France
> But though he always won the day, he never could advance
> For when he rode towards the coast, in mud and slush and rain
> There came a hated British shell which drove him back again.
>
> There was a mighty Zeppelin a flying overhead
> A hated British shell arrived and packed it off to bed.
> The engineer he cried 'Alas!' no iron crosses I'll win,
> For now that hated British shell has spoilt my Zeppelin.
>
> There is a red hot oven, full many a league below,
> Where wicked men like War lords and Prussian bullies go,
> And what avail will be his pride, his crown, his Zeppelin,
> When once a hated British shell has come and popped him in.

Sadly, his boyish excitement soon evaporated when news reached him of his father's predicament. Undeterred by his experiences in Africa, Charles had again embarked on active service during the First World War, and again only narrowly escaped death. He was captured in the Suez Canal on 23 April 1916 and sent to Yozgad, where he contracted typhus fever so severely that he lay unconscious for four weeks and suffered a stroke which left him deaf, partially blind and temporarily paralysed in his right leg. He was sent to Turkey to recover, and wrote to his father from Psamatia on 20 August 1916 complaining of the terrible conditions in which he was held and begging him to use his influence to get him sent home:

> It is impossible to believe that a supposed to be civilised country could treat any other human beings in the way we have been treated and if the British govt. does not step in and take our parts I shall … think that they are just as uncivilised as the Turks.

Charles never recovered his health or confidence. On his return home, he went to live at Earls Croome Court, and he died in 1929, outlived by both his parents.

There was also underlying anxiety about their youngest son, Tom. In 1905 at the age of 20, he disappeared to Canada to become a farmer. Around 1910, he returned

108 Tom Coventry and his family.

briefly to England when he married Alice Ward from Suffolk, but when war broke out he became a private in a Canadian regiment. When his regiment sailed for Europe, his parents hoped he would visit them in England, but he was sent off to Siberia and returned to his estate in Canada at the end of the war.

Fortunately, their remaining six children were less adventurous. Their fourth son, Reginald, or 'Reggie', quite exceeded their expectations when he established himself as an eminent lawyer with commendable speed and was elected Recorder of Stoke-on-Trent. He married Gwenllian Pascoe Morgan, widow of St John Browne Killery, in 1911 and in 1926 was married for the second time to Frances Constance Jeffreys. Later, he was knighted for his services, a true throwback to the 17th-century origins of the family. Henry married Edith McCreary, the daughter of a New York colonel, but William never married. Barbara became a JP; she married Gerald Dudley Smith, a lawyer and also a JP, and they lived at Levant Lodge in Earls Croome. Dorothy married Sir Keith Alexander Fraser, while Anne married Prince Victor Albert Jay Duleep Singh of Lahore, a Captain of the Royal Dragoons. She was a courageous and unusual woman, who was later awarded the *Médaille de la Reconnaissance français* and the *Médaille de la France Liberée* for her outstanding services during the War.

At the start, the First World War had seemed sufficently unreal to be played out like some elaborate and patriotic game. The Territorial Army was camped in the park at Croome, and the concerts and high spirits were cosily remote from the imminent horrors of trench warfare. As events unfurled, the new responsibilities for Lord Coventry as Lord Lieutenant of the county provided little time for reflection. At a recruiting meeting in Dudley in 1915, he spoke of the calamity of the War, the murder of Edith Cavell and how 'almost every house and cottage in Worcestershire had suffered a loss'. He embarked upon a gruelling round of fund-raising speeches to raise money for the prisoners-of-war belonging to Worcestershire fighting units, not least the 2nd Battalion under Colonel Hankey, which had saved the British line at Gheluvelt during the Battle of Ypres. There were other concerns too, of special interest to Lord Coventry, such as the meat shortage, which he believed was due entirely to the short-sighted agricultural policies introduced in recent years. Some vindication for his criticism emerged when meat prices rose sharply after the War, and farmers hurried their immature cattle to market, which simply prolonged the shortage. When the War Cabinet forbade further horse racing in 1917, he objected strongly to what he regarded as 'this disrespectful treatment' of the Jockey Club and he argued, a little lamely perhaps, that racing served a valuable purpose in improving the speed and endurance of thoroughbred horses for military purposes. More to the point, he thought it senseless to 'cast aside with a supreme indifference' work which over three centuries had made British bloodstock the best in the world.

His diaries during this period make little reference to the War, and are still filled with scribbled notes and accounts concerning estate business, so that the entry for 7 July 1917 comes rather as a shock:

> I was about to leave Paddington station at 10.30 when a guard, coming to the carriage windows, informed me that he had orders to detain the train, as a large force of enemy airplanes were on [the] way … to bombard the station. Thank God our guns kept them off, and after a wait of half an hour we proceeded.

One suspects the sheer inconvenience of it all outweighed any concern for his personal safety.

Lady Coventry and her daughters became absorbed with fund-raising schemes, and in 1915 they organised a concert at Croome in aid of the Red Cross, at which Lord Coventry gave a memorable performance when he read a short extract from his favourite novel, the *Pickwick Papers*. However, their principal contribution to the war effort concerned the need to organise employment for women within the county. Lady Barbara was involved with the schemes for the collection and distribution of fruit and vegetables at Upton, where she converted a building into a shed for drying herbs for medicinal purposes and as a supply depot, but it was probably Lady Deerhurst who most excelled in her new responsibilities. She worked for the Queen's Work for Women Fund, was Chairman of the Women's Unemployment Committee and the Women's War Agricultural Committee, and she founded the Worcestershire Fruit and Vegetable County Society, copied by the Board of Agriculture for other counties. When Lady Coventry wrote a letter to the *Worcestershire Advertiser* in May 1917, in praise of the special contribution made by the women of the county to the war effort, she could be justly proud of the role played by her own family.[23]

The euphoria that accompanied the peace celebrations engendered a fleeting aura of confidence and optimism. That August there was a massive party in the Temple Greenhouse, but the grim repercussions of the War soon smothered such sentiments. At a Welcome Home lunch at the Guildhall in Worcester for the prisoners-of-war, Charles referred in harrowing detail to his experiences in Turkey, the floggings, hunger and privations. It was a powerful and compassionate speech, for his physical suffering was apparent and he could inspire much sympathy among his audience. His black humour injected a little levity into the occasion, in particular a story about a sentry post at the prison at Afion-Kra-Hissar. Apparently, one day a sentry forgot to hand his ammunition over when he was going off duty. The new sentry went to report the problem, but discovered that all his superior officers were drunk, so he went to the prisoners and begged them not to escape as he would be unable to shoot them. The sheer absurdity of it all was vital to ease the tension.

Immediate decisions had to be made concerning the future of the estate. The simplest solution would have been to sell part of it to raise funds and reduce the tax burden, but this idea was rejected by Lord Coventry, who explained in a newspaper interview:

> I could not bear the idea of severing my connection with those who have for so long been associated with me in good and bad times, and from whom I have received so many demonstrations of friendship through many long and happy years.

So in 1921 the estate was placed in the hands of the Croome Estate Trust. On 9 May 1921, Lord Coventry wrote to his tenants to thank them for their support over the years:[24]

> More than 62 years have passed since I succeeded to the possession of Croome, and during all this long period of time I have been very proud of the friendship, and—may I say—the confidence of the tenants on the Estate. We have indeed been a united Clan, and I gratefully recall the many occasions on which you have evinced your attachment to Lady Coventry and myself, and the other members of my family, and which will always live in our remembrance.

Once a decision had been reached about the estate, other issues of immediate personal concern fell neatly into place. That September, George William Reginald Victor, the eldest son of Viscount Deerhurst, married Nesta Donne Philipps, the eldest daughter of the shipping magnate and MP for Carmarthenshire, Owen Philipps, the 1st and last Baron Kylsant. The wedding took place a week after his 21st birthday and the accompanying celebrations helped to obscure the bleak reality of the aftermath of war. The following year, George William's sister, Helena Blanche, married the 6th Earl of Harrowby, and then, in 1925, their sister, Viscount Deerhurst's youngest daughter, Peggy Virginia, married Eustace Benyon Hoare. Lord and Lady Coventry also celebrated their diamond wedding that year, a particularly happy occasion as their youngest son, Tom, now 37, came home, thanks to his new appointment with the British Columbian government in London. This was all a major boost to morale. Even Viscount Deerhurst was a reformed character.

Since his bankruptcy, Lord Deerhurst had directed his energies towards county affairs with remarkable vigour. During the War, he had commanded two battalions of national reservists and later served in France, and on his return he worked hard with his family for the former prisoners-of-war in the county. He served as a county magistrate for forty years, was elected a member of the county council in 1914, and served on numerous committees and took a particular interest in the housing situation. During January 1926, he even worked as a bricklayer in New York and claimed to have laid 1,000 bricks a day with his bare hands to prove his theory that the housing shortage in Britain was largely due to the restrictive working practices.[25] However, his political ambition began to get the better of him. In 1922, after he failed to win a local Tory seat in the election, he began to devote such large sums of money to his political interests that by 1927 it was a matter of weeks before he was declared bankrupt for the second time.[26] He knew that he was due to inherit money from the estate of his mother's sister, the Countess of Wilton, but only following the death of a certain Mr. Pryor. The possibility of a second bankruptcy, and such a vast and useful inheritance just beyond his reach, began to take a toll on his health. In July, he was taken ill at his club. In a London nursing home, news reached him of Mr. Pryor's death, but just two weeks later, on 8 August 1927, he died.

Lord Deerhurst was buried at Croome, and a memorial service was held in Worcester Cathedral to commemorate his work for the county. For the second time in 84 years, the direct heir to the earldom had died before he had inherited the title and his eldest son, George William, became the new Viscount Deerhurst, but not for long.

His grandfather, the 9th Earl of Coventry, died on 13 March 1930, following an illness that lasted 12 days. He was nearly ninety-two. Three days later, Blanche, Countess of Coventry, was also dead. She was 87 and, within an hour of her husband's death, she is said to have retired to bed, not ill, but simply as she had no desire to go on living.[27] A joint funeral was arranged, a simple affair at the 9th Earl's request, and their coffins were draped with wreaths of woven orchids from the estate. Memorial services were held in London at St Martin-in-the-Fields and at Worcester Cathedral, where the Dean is recorded to have remarked that 'their deaths together seemed less of a tragedy than the death of one alone'. They had been married for 65 years.

The 9th Earl had led an extraordinary life. He was the longest holder of any peerage in the history of the House of Lords. He had lived through the Victorian and Edwardian periods and one World War, and he had known both Wellington and Stanley Baldwin. Throughout this time, he never wavered from his course. He was determined to excel in his role as landlord, agriculturalist, sportsman and patron, to be a true country gentleman, and he succeeded. Towards the end of his life, he confided to a journalist:

> If I were to advise young people how to live happily, I think I should tell them to live in the country, to live an outdoor life, to get as much exercise as they can ... You cannot do better than that if you want good health, and then happiness usually follows.

A trifle trite perhaps, and afterwards Lord Coventry may have regretted such a thoughtless remark as he was all too aware of the devastating effects of rural unemployment on the countryside. Throughout his life, his enthusiasm and commitment to his role had been constantly curbed by change. He had tried to adapt, revealing admirable enterprise and resilience, but it was too much to expect him to abandon the old values, the old way of life that he seemed to epitomise, and that drew people to him. His un-worldliness was part of his appeal. By the time he died he had become a local and national institution.

109   Lord and Lady Coventry on the steps at Croome.

X

Resurgam

Tom Oliver, Project Manager, Croome Park, The National Trust

Continuity of purpose and radical change are paradoxical bedfellows. Yet their peculiar union is synonymous with the history of Croome. As this text has shown, the resolve and leadership of the Coventry family over 350 years has been the greatest influence on this place, its communities and landscape. And yet the revolutionary changes wrought by the 6th Earl between 1747 and 1809 turned Croome into the crucible from which poured the single greatest English contribution to western art. Ambitious this claim may be, but nowhere else in this country can lay a greater claim to the origin of the Englishness of the natural landscape style: a style of landscape design which swept the world and which addressed every aspect of the sense of place.

True to the Croome paradox, it was the stability of the next one 150 years that ensured the design of Brown and the 6th Earl should survive, free from the blurring of confusion of subsequent design. England is a treasure house of layered landscapes, where the taste and energy of succeeding generations has been laid down, one style overlying another. Far, far rarer are those places where a single vision is still clear. Croome is one of these, a happy result of continuity following radical change.

Recent history has dealt the same fate to Croome again. The role of the National Trust is to work with the same peculiar combination of change and continuity, to retain the significance and singularity of Croome. Overall, the objective must be to end the uncertainty over the future of the landscape through comprehensive, rigorous restoration and the solid assurance of inalienability. This is the principle whereby land and buildings are held by the National Trust for the nation for ever, a bond only dissoluble through Act of Parliament.

The National Trust is very much a newcomer, owner of the park for only a few of the last four hundred years. In order to understand its task at Croome, it is wise for the Trust to contemplate the great forces that have been at work since 1948. In that year, the close link between the Coventry family and the landscape of Brown was broken with the sale of the Court. At times, the whole design must have seemed destined to become irretrievably fragmented. It is fortunate that the combination of circumstances and the work of many different people has led to the securing of the future of Croome.

When Barbara Jones published her history of follies in the 1950s, the prospects for designed landscapes were at their most gloomy. Great houses were being demolished at the rate of two a week. The bleak savagery of the post-war attitude to tradition and inheritance bit deeply into the integrity of such places, their significance ridiculed or ignored. Jones described her regular encounters with ornamental buildings smashed or stunted to the point of collapse. The paintings of Felix Kelly record the grim sense of the condemned, in garden after garden, park after park.

At Croome, the assault had begun during the Second World War with the construction of a new RAF airfield on the eastern part of the south park. What had been an apparently limitless expanse of open downland, ancient trees and common land, was suddenly marred by an accumulation of runways, new roads and rapidly-constructed buildings. The tide of destruction lapped against the edge of the main design; the hospital compound for the base was set within the 18th-century orchard, only yards from the Wilderness and the sweep of the inner park.

No sooner had the airfield been closed in 1957, than a new menace loomed. The new M5 motorway snaked like a perverse mockery of Hogarth's serpentine line of beauty through the western park. The tranquillity and the drainage of the park were damaged. The links from east to west through the design, already disrupted by the RAF to the east, were mutilated to the west by the loss of the Worcester Drive.

For some time, the void left by the departure of the family from the Court allowed the fabric of the Coventry legacy to decline just as in countless other designed landscapes. In 1968, Pevsner, writing about Croome, described some of the ornamental buildings as being in 'a desperate state of neglect'. The Shrubberies, possibly the single greatest element of revolutionary design at Croome, were replanted as efficient grids of commercial forestry. All the while, agricultural intensification escalated throughout the country, leaving its mark at Croome in an ever-increasing expanse of arable land where once parkland had been. The natural processes of decay, laced with the attrition of petty vandalism and theft, played their part too. Dutch elm disease, destructive everywhere, was a particular calamity at Croome, which had large numbers of fine trees.

But in the true spirit of the Croome paradox, the landscape was yet being protected against the day when the wider forces at work would turn decisively in favour of appreciation and restoration. The achievements of those who held the line through the barren years of garden history and conservation should be properly recognised.

Despite coming perilously close, the RAF did not violate the core of the designed landscape. A Wellington bomber belly-landing on the south lawn came nearest to threatening the destruction of a key element of the work of Brown. The orderly regime of the RAF deliberately set out to protect the buildings and their landscape from the attentions of thieves and vandals.

The new motorway, initially of four lanes, was built through the undulating landscape of the western park with immense skill, keeping visual intrusion to a minimum. This was done at a time when the design of large new roads was in its infancy and the priority of historic landscapes was very low indeed.

Commercial forestry in Brown's Shrubberies acted as an insurance against their complete conversion to agriculture and preserved the critical detail of subtle earthworks,

110   A panoramic view of Croome Park.

paths and boundaries, all of these more precious than inevitably-declining 18th-century trees.

Working with the Historic Building Council, the Croome Estate Trust undertook a substantial programme of restoration. In 1981 part of the park was sold to Royal & Sun Alliance, who continued the work. Without a doubt, had repair and restoration not been undertaken, the buildings described by Pevsner would not have survived to be counted in the appraisal of the park undertaken by the National Trust during 1995.

For much of the time since the Second World War, the Court itself and the church were also fortunate. In 1948 the Court was bought by the Roman Catholic Archdiocese of Birmingham and became a school. After 1979, the Society for Krishna Consciousness took on the Court and continued the regime of benign management. It was only when the Court became the subject of property speculation, after 1986, that the fabric began to suffer.

Although the church was made redundant in 1975, it has since been under the sensitive and effective care of the Churches Conservation Trust. Without their management, the future of one of the finest elements of the design would have been in doubt. The church has remained open to the public, lovingly protected by Mr. and Mrs. Gerrard, who can remember the 9th Earl. A service is held in the church each July, on the nearest Sunday to the patronal festival of St Mary Magdalene.

While Croome held on, the status of historic landscapes slowly changed for the better. A profound change in attitude to garden history and conservation was taking place. Dorothy Stroud's biography of Capability Brown of 1950, reprinted in 1975, rehabilitated his reputation after years of indifference, which kindled a new interest in scholarship concerned with the designer of Croome and his contemporaries.

Since the early 1980s, the discipline of historical research, analysis and restoration of gardens, buildings and landscapes has advanced dramatically. More recently, this expanding subject has broken through from the relatively closed world of professional garden history and become an increasingly popular field of study and general interest. This is equally applicable to the conservation of landscapes.

First, the interest and appreciation of the subject has grown. Later, the response of government has been to provide more protection and support for those buildings and places which are thought to be worthy of conservation. Meanwhile, the knowledge, methods and philosophy behind the appraisal of great buildings and landscapes have become more sophisticated and more credible. Resolve has strengthened to use such new legislation and guidance for effective intervention when buildings and landscapes are threatened. A relatively recent development, but one of enormous significance in the case of Croome, was the founding of the Heritage Lottery Fund in 1994. This is the context in which the National Trust became involved with Croome a year later. In July 1995, James Lees-Milne, the architectural historian who made a crucial contribution to the work of the National Trust and who had close connections with Worcestershire, was asked to comment on the importance of Croome. His response was emphatic: 'I have always considered Croome one of the great Midlands country houses and it can be called No.1 of Worcestershire's ancestral seats.' (Colour plate XXVI.)

The National Trust responded to a direct threat to the park and the surroundings of the Court. A longstanding planning permission for the use of the Court as a hotel was expanded dramatically to include considerable new building and a 27-hole golf course on 350 acres of the inner park. Research and lobbying by the Hereford and Worcester Gardens Trust led to a serious appraisal of Croome by the Tewkesbury office of the National Trust. Meticulous financial planning and the strong support of garden and landscape experts drawn from as wide a field as possible allowed a persuasive case to be put to the Heritage Lottery Fund for a very substantial grant. In particular, the support of Jeremy Benson, Gilly Drummond, Richard Haslam, and Hal Moggridge helped to ensure the success of the Trust's approach. In April 1996, the HLF gave £4.9 million to buy and restore the park. The vendors, Royal & Sun Alliance, also made a large donation of £300,000. Together with National Trust resources of another £2.5 million, the acquisition and endowment of the park was secured.

Throughout the negotiations which led to the rescue of the park, the importance of the Court itself was not ignored. Although strenuous efforts were made to include the main buildings in the restoration plan, circumstances conspired to prevent this happening. The scale of the work necessary on many of the buildings and indeed the magnificent scale of the buildings themselves proved too great for the various plans proposed. The National Trust has since placed great importance on building good relations with the owners of the Court in order to achieve successful restoration of Brown's central design as a seamless whole.

The importance of the archive, so carefully conserved by the Croome Estate Trustees, became apparent in the first phase of the restoration process. A comprehensive research project, commissioned by the National Trust, was undertaken by Camilla Beresford. Thanks to the opportunity to use the archive granted by the Croome Estate Trustees, it rapidly became clear that the estate records would be the principal source informing a thoroughly rigorous and authentic restoration. Best of all was the collection of spectacularly accurate and detailed estate plans, which showed with great clarity how the design had developed between 1750 and 1810. Other vital material included William Dean's guidebook of 1824, the associated *Hortus Croomensis*, which listed the entire collection of plants then growing at Croome, and a collection of watercolours at Worcester Record Office which showed the first flourishing of the design during the 1780s.

So important is Croome in the history of landscape design in general and of Brown in particular, and so impressive the existing site and records, that the purpose of the National Trust is clear. Nothing less than a return to the land use, planting, materials and, where possible, management and maintenance methods which first made Croome what it is, will do. Where modern intrusion, such as that of the airfield or the motorway prevent this objective, carefully designed responses are needed which learn from the techniques and inspiration of Brown. The restoration process is a master class, attended at a remove of 250 years, but taught by a figure whose ability is now unchallenged.

The restoration of Croome is set out in the Conservation Plan for Croome Park written in 1998 and the Restoration and Management Plan completed in 1999. The first of these documents analyses the design and its content, and sets out the policies for the future. The second contains detailed plans and schedules the work to take place from 1999 to 2007. A maintenance guide will follow, ensuring that the texture of the design is maintained correctly, whether in the management of plants, paths, trees, watercourses or boundaries.

The whole endeavour is benefiting immensely from the explosion of interest and expertise in garden history and the development of better procedures and techniques. All these are helping to make the process of investigation and understanding of the design more accurate, less suffused with the taste of the present and less influenced by unjustified assumptions of the past. After all, nothing could be less respectful of a great design than a complacent and inaccurate recreation of the original.

Almost as much as the remarkable original enterprise, the restoration is a big idea. Its successful implementation will require the wisdom and contribution of a very wide circle of people and organisations, experts, professionals and volunteers, all of whom in their different ways can see the vision for themselves and are included in the process of restoration. The National Trust's own expert staff, the advisers appointed by the Heritage Lottery Fund, and the Croome Forum, consisting of a wide range of disciplines and interests, already make a vital contribution.

This history of the Coventry family tells how it has come about that Croome represents so many things that make up the post-Reformation history of England. The greatest of these is now the responsibility of the National Trust, in whose care Croome is held for ever, for everyone. No finer compliment can be paid to those whose vision and ability created it in the first place.

Epilogue

The history of the Earls of Coventry follows a course familiar to many of the landed aristocracy. A rapid ascent under the Stuart monarchy, accompanied by the acquisition and growth of their country estate, and royal recognition for their services to the Crown during this period of civil strife. But it is also a history of uncommon achievement not least because, as the family developed and improved their country estate, it became not just a chief source of their wealth and influence and an emblem of their success but a bold, ambitious and seminal work of art. The popularity and influence of the family during the Victorian era was also quite exceptional, for they excelled in their role as patrons, benefactors and society hosts. Each peak of achievement within the family history relied heavily upon the special talents of particular individuals. If the 1st Baron had been a man of less integrity, the 6th Earl less ambitious, and the 9th Earl less idealistic, the story would lose much of its rhythm and pace.

The agricultural depression, taxation and, ultimately, the impact of the First World War, destroyed the equilibrium. Slowly and insidiously, the lifeblood was drained out of Croome and its dependent communities. But Croome was more fortunate than many similar estates. The mansion house survived intact surrounded by its parkland when many country houses fell victim to brutal conversion, decay or wanton demolition. Estate cottages and farmsteads throughout the outlying countryside still mark the extent of the family's former domain. The Coventry name recurs among the inscriptions in the parish churches and churchyards, the inn signs, and the plaques on schools and almshouses throughout the locality. This is all somehow reassuring, but it is not only the physical evidence that is important. Among the many people who continue to live and work on the estate the sense of identity remains, some of whom still recall the time when the Earls of Coventry lived at Croome. The sense of loyalty and security, the simple certainty of a clearly-defined role within a close-knit community has proved hard to replace.

Public enthusiasm for historic landscapes and buildings and concern for their protection has escalated in recent years. Now that the survival of the designed landscape at the heart of the estate is assured, future generations will visit Croome to marvel at its audacity and ambition, at the inimitable genius of its designer. The sheer indulgence, extravagance and imagination behind it are irrepressibly seductive: a perfect and fantastic landscape wrought from the foetid Worcestershire marshlands, lovingly tended and virtually unchanged for generations, now re-emerging almost unscathed from the undergrowth.

Croome was a collective achievement of far-reaching historic and aesthetic significance, its rescue an outstanding collective effort and a salutary lesson. But let us not allow our sense of collective pride to obscure our gratitude to the family for whom it was created. Croome will remain the most important legacy of the Earls of Coventry. Now, as the history of this celebrated family and their estate enters a new phase, is a particularly auspicious moment to commemorate the tercentenary of the earldom.

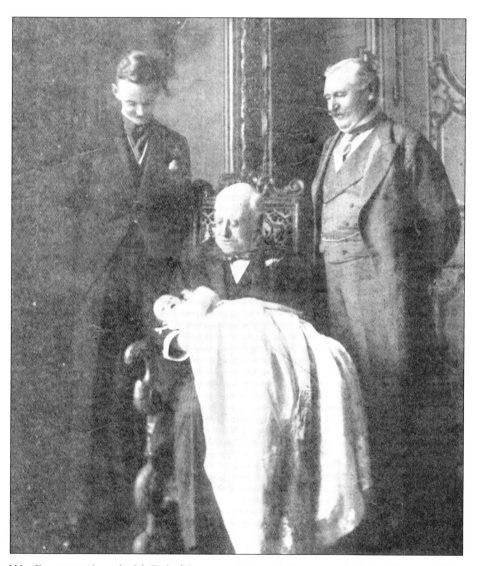

111 Four generations: the 9th Earl of Coventry with his eldest great-grandchild on his knee. Behind him stands, to the left, his grandson, George William, later 10th Earl of Coventry, and on the right, his eldest son, George William, Viscount Deerhurst.

Notes and References

Abbreviations

AA: Antony Archive
BA: Beaufort Archive
BL: British Library
CEA: Croome Estate Archive
DNB: *Dictionary of National Biography*
VCH: *Victoria County History*
WRO: Worcestershire Record Office

Chapter I: Introduction

1. W. Dean, *An Historical and Descriptive Account of Croome D'Abitot* (Worcester, 1824), p.11.
2. AA:CVZ/Y/34.

Chapter II: Origins

1. The Mayor of London has been referred to as Lord Mayor since medieval times even though the designation rests on prescriptive use and not on any specific grant. The Lord Mayor has presided over the London Court of Aldermen since the early 13th century. (Rev. A.B. Beaven, *The Aldermen of the City of London*, 2 vols., London 1908 and 1913).
2. CEA: F65-68.
3. Beaven, I, p.10.
4. CEA: Box 20. F74/5.
5. Oxfordshire Archives: For example, a Coventry family is recorded to have owned half a hide (around fifty acres) of land in Great Tew manor at this time.
6. Rev. H.E. Salter, *Liber Albus Civitatis Oxoniensis* (Oxford 1909), and *Munimenti Civitatis Oxonie* LXXI (Oxford Historical Society, 1917), p.179, 185, 200, 204.
7. *VCH* (Oxon), 9, p.183.
8. *VCH* (Oxon), 5, p.66.
9. *VCH* (Oxon), 12, p.41.
10. *VCH* (Oxon), 12, p.46.
11. *VCH* (Oxon), 5, p.253.
12. Oxfordshire Archives. MS Wills Oxon 11/3/41.
13. Oxfordshire Archives. MS Wills Oxon 195, fol.9v.
14. *VCH* 12, p.41.
15. CEA: Box 55. Lincolnshire Papers.
16. CEA: F41/2.
17. CEA: Box 55.
18. LA: Langhorne Burton papers. LB 3/1/3.
19. CEA: Box 15 F65-F68.
20. An old English coin stamped with the figure of an angel.
21. I would like to thank Mr. D.V. White, Rouge Croix Pursuivant, for this information.
22. Dr. T.R. Nash, *Collections for the History of Worcestershire*, 2 vols. (Worcester 1781-2), 1, p.267.
23. *VCH* (Worcs.), 3, p.317.
24. *VCH* (Worcs.), 3. p.314.
25. T. Habington, *A Survey of Worcestershire* (begun 1586, published by the Worcestershire Historical Society, Oxford, 1895-9).
26. *Ibid.*
27. *VCH* (Worcs.), 3, p.314.

28. The 17th-century pedigree in the Croome archive states that Sir Thomas's three sons were called, John, Thomas and George, and that John became a draper in London. It claims also that it was George's sons, Thomas and William, who settled at Redmarley d'Abitot. There is no mention of Walter Coventry at all. This error (if indeed it was an error) was rectified in the 18th-century pedigree as by then the earldom had reverted to Walter's descendants.
29. Redmarley D'Abitot was part of Worcestershire until the county boundary changed in 1930 when it became part of Gloucestershire.
30. I am most grateful to Angela Chapman, a descendant of the 9th Earl of Coventry, for this information.
31. Nash, *History of Worcestershire*, vol. 1, p.373.

Chapter III: A Judicious Ascent
1. Clarendon, *History of the Great Rebellion*, 4 vols. (Oxford 1704), I, p.37.
2. BL: Sloane 3075, f.2v Also CEA: F65.
3. According to Pepys, Lord Keeper Coventry's son, Sir William Coventry, owned a portrait of his father by Syman Stone, a professional copyist. This was probably a copy of the famous portrait by Cornelius Jonson (Cornelius van Ceulen Janssen), for whom the Lord Keeper sat on several occasions (Pepys, 7, 27 June 1666, p.183). Clarendon owned a portrait of Lord Keeper Coventry by Jonson, and there are also five engraved portraits known to exist by Droeshout, Elstracke, Houbraken, Martin and Vandergucht.
4. Clarendon, p.37.
5. CEA: F74/75.
6. The date of Lord Keeper Coventry's death is sometimes given as 1639. This confusion occurs as the date has been left in the Old Style or Julian calendar and has not been translated into the Gregorian calendar, which came into force after 1752.
7. See biography of Lord Keeper Coventry, *History of Parliament* (unpublished draft, 1996), History of Parliament Trust.
8. CEA: F40.
9. CEA: Box 30 A.J.P. Hess, *St Oswald's Church in the Parish of Backford*, 1998.
10. There may have been an illegitimate son in this or a later 17th-century generation. An undated document in the family archive refers to a Thomas Fox of Edwinstow in Nottinghamshire who was appointed guardian to a Thomas Coventry, an infant kept at Rudford Abbey, Notts. CEA: F40.
11. CEA: F74/75.
12. Spedding, *Life of Bacon*, 6, p.97.
13. *History of Parliament*.
14. G. Goodman (ed.), *The Court of James I*, 1, p.318.
15. Quoted in *History of Parliament*.
16. Clarendon, p.37.
17. S. Friar and J. Ferguson, *Basic Heraldry* (London, 1993), p.20, 48.
18. Spedding, 7, pp.534-5.
19. CEA: F76.
20. CEA: F56. Including pardons, releases, alienations etc.
21. See unpublished notes on the Lord Keeper's Papers by C.J.R. Russell at Birmingham archives.
22. This tradition is believed to have begun with Sir Nicholas Bacon in the reign of Mary I.
23. In his will he also a left a gilt basin and ewer that had been given to him by James I to his eldest son. This has never been traced. Jill Tovey has suggested that a casket on a carved stand made for the 6th Earl by Vile and Cobb may have been designed to hold an heirloom or other item of great value such as the basin and ewer.
24. See A.B. Wyon, *The Great Seals of England* (London 1987). Also details supplied by the V & A and compiled by A. Fearn (1993).
25. See *VCH*, 2, p.256 ff.
26. Hampshire Record Office: 1M53/1711-16, 1718-21, 1726-33.
27. See Survey of Severn Stoke, Clifton and Black Naunton by Mark Pierce of 1635. CEA: Box 10.
28. CEA: Box 55.
29. CEA: F58.
30. AA: CVVZ/Y/34.
31. CEA: Croome Accounts 1617-36 CP 14/5. The similarity in the shillings and pence could be due to an error or sheer coincidence.
32. CEA: Box 1 E56. Estate letters 1632-1716.
33. CEA: Box 1 E56. Estate letters 1632-1716.

34. R. Latham and W. Matthews (eds.), *The Diary of Samuel Pepys* (London 1983), vol. 7, 26 August 1666, p.261.

35. W. Dean, *An Historical and Descriptive Account of Croome D'Abitot* (Worcester 1824), p.18.

36. Clarendon, p.104.

Chapter IV: The Children of the Lord Keeper

1. CEA: F74, F75.
2. CEA: *The Story of Clifton Campville*, published privately by the Pye family (1895).
3. R. Latham and W. Matthews (eds.), *The Diary of Samuel Pepys* (London 1983), vol. 8, 17 February 1667, p.70.
4. See Longleat Coventry Papers, vols. XCII, CIV, CV and CVI. Family and personal correspondence of Henry Coventry and Sir William Coventry. BL: Add.MS.25115025 and MSS 32094-5.
5. See Wood, *Fasti Oxoniensis*, 1, p.275.
6. Burnet, *History of My Own Time* (Oxford 1823), 1, p.531.
7. *Country Life*, 37 (1915), pp.482-9.
8. A 'letterbook' that relates to this trip to Breda is in the private possession of the Duke of Northumberland.
9. In 1660 it was called the *Naseby*, but had since been refitted and renamed.
10. Pepys, vol. 8, 27 July 1667.
11. Pepys, vol. 8, 12 October 1667.
12. Pepys, vol. 8, 16 November 1667.
13. *DNB*.
14. See his will CEA: F41/A/16.
15. *VCH* 3, p.88.
16. See Berrow's *Worcester Journal* (1 April 1876).
17. Burnet, 1, pp.237-372.
18. See BL. Papers relating to the Navy 1644-99. 18986 f.406.
19. Pepys, vol. 3, 8 July 1662.
20. Pepys, vol. 3, 14 September 1662.
21. Pepys, vol. 9, 9 March 1660.
22. Pepys, vol. 3, 7 June 1662.
23. BL: 12,097. Autographs of statesmen and nobles.
24. Pepys, vol. 9, 4 July 1668.
25. Pepys, vol. 9, 7 December 1668.
26. *DNB*.

Chapter V: The Estate and the Earldom

1. BA: Fm T/A 4/4/5, 9.
2. CEA: Estate Box 1 ES6.
3. See H. Colvin, *A Biographical Dictionary of British Architects 1600-1840* (2nd. edition, London 1978), pp.554-61, 870-4.
4. AA: CVZ/Y/34.
5. Colvin, *Biographical Dictionary*, pp.655-8, 786-7.
6. See J. Summerson, *Architecture in Britain 1530-1830* (London 1953, paperback edition 1970), pp.162-5; and pp.134-7 for a detailed analysis of architectural developments of this period.
7. I am grateful to Nicholas Kingsley for his advice with regard to these papers.
8. GRO: D 2700. QV 1/1.
9. The chimneys are divided into three separate groups in Beighton's drawing but form a single row in the *c*.1750 bird's-eye view.
10. Colvin, *Biographical Dictionary*, pp.646-8, 777-9.
11. CEA: F59.
12. CEA: F78.
13. Oak Apple Day remained a public holiday locally until the mid-19th century. See B. Gwilliam, *Worcestershire's Hidden Past* (Bromsgrove 1991), p.37.
14. AA: CVZ/Y/34.
15. AA: CVZ/Y/34.
16. CEA: Parish Box 17, and AA: CVZ/Y/34.
17. C.S. Tomes, *Life in Worcestershire at the end of the Seventeenth Century* (Evesham 1911).
18. See Survey of the park by John Troath, February 1708-9. CEA: Estate Box 1 ES6 and Parish Box 4 CP5.

19. See English translation of the epitaph of 4th Baron Coventry, BA: T/A 4/4/5,9.
20. AA: CVZ/Y/34.
21. CEA: Estate Box 1 ES6.
22. *VCH*, 2, p.413.
23. See Warwickshire RO. L3/701.
24. 'Contracts & Memoranda & C. in the concerns of Fran: Taylor'. Warwickshire RO, L3/699, p.69.
25. WRO: BA 3487. 970.5:73.
26. See family documents at Cornwall RO. Also C. Gaskell Brown, *Mount Edgcumbe* (Cornwall 1998).
27. AA: CVZ/Y/34.
28. Shakespeare Birthplace Trust: DR 38/1.
29. There is an early 19th-century watercolour of the house by Thomas Ward (SBT) and also a drawing of the house (referred to as Snitterfield Hall) of *c.*1820 among the Aylesford Collection at Birmingham Reference Libary.
30. See J. Harris, *The Artist and the Country House* (London 1979).
31. See J. Shelby, 'An Eighteenth Century Warwickshire Village—Snitterfield' (Warwickshire Local History Society. Occasional paper No. 6 1986).
32. The 1st Earl of Coventry was never appointed Lord Lieutenant as is often stated. This office was held by Charles Talbot, Earl of Shrewsbury. CEA: Box 20. F74, 75.
33. AA: CVC/Z/20.
34. AA: CVA/H3/4. For example, the accounts for 1691 show that 200 plants were purchased that year at one shilling each, as well as garden seed worth 3s. 4d.
35. AA: CVC/Y/1 Coventry letters 1684-1699.
36. BA: Fm T/A. 4/4/9.
37. Grimes was a corruption of the name Graham and it is probable that Elizabeth chose to call herself Graham as it implied a more distinguished ancestry.
38. Nash, *Collections for the History of Worcestershire* (Worcester 1781-2), vol. I, p.262.
39. See BL. MSS 6292. f.13. Also BA Fm.T/A. 4/4/8 and CEA: Box 15 and 20, F74 and 75.
40. CEA: F17. I am grateful to Geoffrey Beard for this attribution.
41. See Nash, *Collections for the History of Worcestershire* (1781-2), 1, p.388.
42. CEA: Box 15.
43. To further complicate matters, in the 17th-century family pedigree in the Croome archive, Anne Powell is said to have been formerly married to William Coventry, the son of Lord Keeper Coventry's alleged younger brother, George. Interestingly, this reference is crossed out, perhaps at a later date and most probably after the 1st Earl's funeral.
44. See 'The Family of the First Countess of Coventry: and the Matrimonial Relations of Gregory King, Lancaster Herald', *The Herald and Genealogist*, 7 (1871).
45. *Ibid.*, p.15.
46. See Prattinton MSS relating to the Coventry pedigree at the Society of Antiquaries.

Chapter VI: Debts, Dowagers, Dormice and Divisions

1. BA: Fm T/A 4/3/19.
2. AA: CVZ/Z/22.
3. BA: Fm T/B 2/8.
4. BA: Fm T/B 1/3/140.
5. BA: Fm T/B 1/1/17.
6. BA: Fm T/B/3/71.
7. GRO: D 2700. QV 2/1.
8. This painting is among the private collection of His Grace the Duke of Beaufort at Badminton, south Gloucestershire. A garden pavilion still survives from this late 17th-century scheme, although it is now incorporated within a row of cottages.
9. S. Mitchell, *Dictionary of British Equestrian Artists* (London 1985), pp.469-71.
10. BA: Fm T/B 5/1.
11. AA: CVZ/Y/34.
12. AA: CVE/Z/11.
13. AA: CVA/H3/5-18. Rent Rolls and accounts.
14. AA: CVW/Y/17.
15. BA: Fm T/B/1/3/120.
16. AA: CVC/Y/3. Coventry letters 1711-36.
17. CEA: F76.

18. BA: Fm T/B1/1/8.
19. BA: Fm T/B1/1/8.
20. CEA: Box 20 F 74, 75. *Country News* (21 February 1763).
21. CEA: F32/19.
22. CEA: F32/2.
23. I am most grateful to Sir Richard Carew Pole for this information.
24. His passport, the details of his apprenticeship, and other papers that relate to the time he spent in Holland survive among the archive at Antony. AA: CVC/Z/19.
25. AA: CVC/Z/18. Letters to Gilbert in Holland 1683-91.
26. AA: CVA/H3/21.
27. AA: CVA/H3/4.
28. AA: CVC/Y/1.
29. AA: CVC/Z/20.
30. The baronetage became extinct in 1784.
31. Not to be confused with Hidcote Manor, renowned for its garden created by Laurence Johnston between 1907-30.
32. A south wing was demolished in the late 18th century. Norman Jewson altered and restored the house in 1924-30.
33. AA: CVZ/Y/40.
34. AA: CVC/Y/1.
35. AA: CVC/Z/20.
36. AA: CVC/Y/5.
37. AA: CVE/Z/2 and CVE/V(A)/3.
38. AA: CVA/AA/3, CVA/Y/34 and CVA/Y/21
39. In 1570, a well-known ancestor of Sir William Carew, Richard Carew (1555-1620), a scholar, antiquary and author of the pioneering *Survey of Cornwall*, published in 1602, had made plans to build a banqueting house on an island in the saltwater pool below Antony House for fishing feasts.
40. BA: Fm T/B1/3/71.
41. BA: Fm T/B1/3/120.
42. BA: Fm T/B1/3/71.
43. *Antony, Cornwall*, National Trust guidebook (1992).
44. BA: Fm T/B/3/71.
45. See letter from Agnes Keyte to the Countess Dowager dated 4 January 1714. BA: FMT/B1/3/71.
46. AA: CVA/AA/19.
47. AA: CE/E/22 and Colvin, *Biographical Dictionary*, p.671.
48. AA: CVC/Z/21-2 Letters from 1706-17 from the Countess Dowager to Lady Anne Carew.
49. The recipe book is kept at Antony but has no reference number.
50. CEA: F32/1.
51. AA: CVE/Z/10.
52. AA: CVW/Y/10.
53. Society of Antiquaries, Prattinton Collection.
54. AA: CVE/Z/10.
55. AA: CVE/Z/10.
56. AA: CVA/AA/3.
57. AA: CVA/Y/29.
58. CEA: Estate Box 1. ES23/2. John Taylor's Contract Book (1712-18). In 1750 Gold exchanged this land for fields elsewhere on the estate, which allowed the 6th Earl to expand the park further.
59. CEA: Parish Box 4 CP3.
60. AA: CVA/H3/22 and 27.
61. A catalogue of these pictures is among the Antony archive. AA: CVW/Y/19-21.
62. AA: CVA/AA/1.
63. AA: CVW/Y/21.
64. CEA: F76.
65. BA: Fm T/B1/3/71.
66. BL: Hardwicke Papers. DCCCVII 36175. 4055 f.99. It is possible that these letters may refer to the elder Countess Dowager, widow of the 2nd Earl, and an error may have been made in the cataloguing of the Papers. This hypothesis is based on the knowledge that the elder Countess is known to have been an enthusiastic collector and botanist and was a neighbour of Sloane in Chelsea.
67. Nash, *Collections for the History of Worcestershire*, 2 vols. (Worcester 1781-2), vol. 1, pp.260-4.

Chapter VII: The Grave Young Lord and his Grand Design

1. Nash, *Collections for the History of Worcestershire*, 1 (1781-2), p.261.
2. Some accounts state her father was Simon Holcombe of Devonshire.
3. See letter from G. Lambe to 6th Earl. CEA: F15/25.
4. *DNB*.
5. CEA: F41/10.
6. CEA: General Account 1719-1750.
7. CEA: Parish Box 4 CP4.
8. CEA: Parish Box 4 CP3.
9. CEA: Box 58.
10. CEA: Box 38 F27.
11. W.S. Lewis and R.S. Brown (eds.), *Horace Walpole's Correspondence*, vols. 1-48 (Yale 1937-83). Letter to Sir Horace Mann, 17, 23 November 1741.
12. The *London Evening Post* (26 to 29 May, 1744). CEA: Coventry Album, vol. 1, 1865-87, p.33.
13. L. Dickins and M. Stanton (eds.), *An Eighteenth Century Correspondence* (London 1910), pp.103-4.
14. CEA: F32/39.
15. *An Eighteenth Century Correspondence*, pp. 93-4.
16. CEA: F66/2.
17. Gilly Williams was among Walpole's closest circle of friends which also included George Selwyn and Sir Richard 'Dick' Edgcumbe.
18. See papers relating to the Somerset estates at Warwickshire RO, CR 3200 and to the Bulkeley estates in Hampshire, Oxfordshire and elsewhere at Hampshire RO, 1 M53, 8 M59 and 2122M87.
19. Patriot in this instance was a reference to the unlikely body of disaffected Whigs, Jacobites and Hanoverian Tories opposed to the pacific policies of Walpole and intent on seeking power and glory for Britain abroad through aggressive means rather than by diplomatic isolation.
20. CEA: F14/12 and F14/15.
21. CEA: F14/10.
22. WRO, BA 10110 970:5:73 and 8397777781 705:139.
23. Walpole. Letter from Lady Hervey, 31, 19 December 1765.
24. Walpole. Letter to George Selwyn, 30, 12 January 1766, p.210.
25. See CEA: F24 and F32.
26. CEA: F32/27A.
27. Walpole. Letter to Mann, 23, 18 January 1770, p.173.
28. CEA: F71.
29. B.L. Warren Hasting Papers. General Correspondence, vol. xlviii, 1803-4, MSS 29, 179 f.157.
30. B.L. Warren Hastings Papers. Supplement, vol. xxviii, Poetical Collections MSS 39898 f.14.
31. See P. Rogers, *Literature and Popular Culture in Eighteenth Century, England* (Sussex 1985).
32. 'History of the Tete-a-Tete', *Town and Country Magazine*, 7, Nos. 4, 5 (February 1775).
33. H. Bleackley, *The Story of a Beautiful Duchess* (London 1908), pp.11-12, 27-8.
34. Walpole. Letter to Horace Mann, 20, 27 February 1752, p.303 and 28 October 1752, p.339.
35. *Ibid.* 20, 27 February 1752, p.302.
36. Walpole, Letter to Horace Mann, 20, 27 July 1752, p.324.
37. *Ibid.* Letter to Mann, 20, 28 October 1752, p.338.
38. *Ibid.*
39. *Ibid.* Letter to Mann, 20, 27 March 1753, p.367.
40. *Ibid.* Letter to Montagu, 9, 6 November 1756, p.203.
41. *Ibid.* 20 April 1756, p.185. Bolingbroke's Jacobite connections underlined Walpole's concern.
42. *Ibid.* Letter to Mann, 20, 18 March 1756, p.539.
43. *Ibid.* Letter to Mann, 21, 1 November 1760, p.451.
44. BL MSS 6307 f.38.b.
45. CEA: F29/41.
46. In a letter to Miller of 3 February 1743, Sir Edward Turner remarks that Lady Coventry had produced a baby girl on the previous Wednesday evening. It may be presumed the child died shortly afterwards. *Eighteenth Century Correspondence*, p.219.
47. CEA: F81/1a.
48. CEA: F22.
49. Walpole. Letter from Selwyn to Holland of 9 September 1764. Quoted in 38, p.440.
50. CEA: F81/3.
51. CEA: Family Box 14. F58.

52. CEA: F66/3.
53. See J. Lane, 'The Furniture at Croome Court: The Patronage of George William 6th, Earl of Coventry', *Apollo*, vol. 145 (January 1997), pp.25-9.
54. An expression of particular relevance to Croome and first used by Lord Shaftesbury as early as 1709 and by Pope in his 'An Epistle to Lord Burlington' of 1731.
55. Letter from Miller to Lord Deerhurst, 3 August 1747. CEA: Family Box 5 F32/37.
56. CEA: F28:1/1.
57. CEA: Family Box 2 F15/2.
58. The bridge was illustrated in Halfpenny's *Improvements in Architecture and Carpentry* of 1754.
59. CEA: F32/33.
60. See Miller's Diary 1749-50 at Warwickshire RO.
61. *Ibid.*
62. *Eighteenth Century Correspondence*, p.214.
63. Warwickshire RO: CR 125 (153).
64. See CEA account books, Coventry's Childe's bank account (Royal Bank of Scotland archives), Brown's account at Drummond's 1753-83 (Royal Bank of Scotland archives) and Brown's own account book (Royal Horticultural Society archives).
65. CEA: Family Box 24 F64 and F68. Most of Adam's designs for Croome are either at Croome or at Sir John Soane's Museum. See Appendices III and IV.
66. Holland overcharged Lord Coventry by £40, which Brown later deducted from the bill.
67. See letter from Joseph Hurdman, agent to Lord Coventry. CEA: Parish Box 4 CP3.
68. D. Stroud, *Capability Brown* (London 1950, second edition 1957), pp.47-9.
69. See Bibliography, pp.221-2.
70. One of the mirrors was acquired by the V & A in 1991.
71. See drawings 11(35) and 11(36) at Sir John Soane's Museum.
72. David King notes that their design is unusual for Adam whose bookcases are usually made of painted wood and seldom glazed. D. King, *The Complete Works of Robert and James Adam* (Oxford 1991), p.228.
73. See E. Harris, 'Robert Adam and the Gobelins', *Apollo* (April 1962), vol. 76, pp.100-6 and W. Reider and others, *Period Rooms in the Metropolitan Museum of Art* (New York 1996), pp.158-67.
74. Possibly it served as the main staircase prior to the completion of the principal staircase. It was certainly more conveniently located near to Lord Coventry's bedroom.
75. CEA: F31/61.
76. See drawing 50(11) in Sir John Soane's Museum.
77. See Adam's bill, dated 6 May 1767, in the Croome archive and his design in Sir John Soane's Museum 6(177).
78. E. Harris, *The Furniture of Robert Adam* (London 1963), p.100 (134).
79. See A. Coleridge, 'English Furniture supplied for Croome Court; Robert Adam and the 6th Earl of Coventry', *Apollo* (February 2000), pp.8-19.
80. *Ibid.*, pp.17-19.
81. See drawing 21(111) in Sir John Soane's Museum.
82. *Trans. Worcestershire Archaeological Society*, 32 (1955), pp.17-18.
83. See drawing 50(13) at Sir John Soane's Museum.
84. This sketch is part of a private collection and efforts to trace the owner have proved unsuccessful. A plan of the proposed building survives within the family archive, and Dorothy Stroud has compared the design to the chapel at Compton Verney, Warwickshire, for which Brown supplied designs ten years later.
85. See drawing 50(17) at Sir John Soane's Museum. Faint sketches of garden buildings in landscapes appear on verso.
86. See D. King, *Complete Works*, pp.67-9.
87. See drawing by Adam in the Croome Estate Archive and two drawings at the V & A Museum.
88. CEA: Parish Box 4. CP1 and 4.
89. See drawings at Sir John Soane's Museum 29(136), 29(137), 9(122). There is also a drawing for a greenhouse, not the Temple Greenhouse which is referred to as the Conservatory 29(138). This was almost certainly intended for Croome (Croome is written on the drawing) but, if so, it is very early indeed as it is dated 14 June 1759.
90. CEA: Family Box 28. F62/35.
91. I am grateful to Stephen Astley at Sir John Soane's Museum for his views on the authorship of Dunstall Castle.
92. Catalogued as Seat in Pleasure grounds at Sir John Soane's Museum 19(142) and 19(143).
93. See drawings 19(145) and (146), and 44(104), (105) and (106) at Sir John Soane's Museum.

94. See Coade invoice July 1778. CEA: Family Box 27, F60/84.
95. P CEA: F28/1/2.
96. CEA: F81/6.
97. See Croome House Account 1772-87 Estate Box 21, where there is also a reference to ten ash chairs and the purchase of earthernware for the Menagerie.
98. See Robert Newman's bills for 1980-1 in the General Account.
99. The accounts of 1793 include payments for building a house and a fowl house at the Menagerie. The former could refer to the Adam building but is more likely to refer to an additional pen or aviary.
100. CEA: F16/10 and 12.
101. H. Repton, *Observations on The Theory and Practice of Landscape Gardening* (London 1803), pp.70-4.
102. WRO, BA 2432.x.899.192ff20a, 20b, 21a, 21b, 22b and 54a.
103. See J. Frew, 'Some Observations on James Wyatt's Gothic style 1790-1797', *Journal of the Society of Architectural Historians* (May 1982), 41, No. 2, pp.144-9.
104. See Dean and also A. Paton, 'The Botany of Croome Court', *Trans. Worcestershire Archaeological Society*, 6, 3rd series (1978), pp.71-3.
105. CEA: Parish Box 4 CP3.
106. CEA: Family Box 28. F62/67.
107. CEA: Parish Box 4, CP3.
108. See F. Grice, 'The Park Ornaments of Croome D'Abitot', *Trans. Worcestershire Archaeological Society*, 5, 3rd series (1976), pp.41-9.
109. See 'A History of 106 Piccadilly London Borough of Westminster'. CEA Box 9.
110. H. Colvin, *Biographical Dictionary*, pp.137-8.
111. CEA: F32/40.
112. CEA: F64/68.
113. CEA: ES9/2.
114. Warwick RO, CR 125 (153).
115. A.R. Ridley and C.F. Garfield, *The Story of the Lygon Arms* (Broadway 1992), pp.117-127.
116. CEA: F2/a1.

Chapter VIII: Blind Heirs and Disgraces

1. CEA: F41 A/10.
2. CEA: 1/C/3.
3. In the family archive (CEA: F6) is a collection of letters to the 7th Earl from an S. Coventry. She claims to be the widow of Thomas William the elder, and is described as a 'debauched and disgusting woman' by other family members. Apparently destitute and living in an attic, her demands for financial assistance became increasingly desperate and dramatic. Her identity has never been confirmed or disproved.
4. CEA: Estate Box 4 ES 17.
5. An unidentified portrait of a youth dressed in blue velvet among the collection of the Croome Estate Trust may be that of the 7th Earl.
6. CEA: F81/2.
7. *London Chronicle*, 19-21 October, p.384.
8. CEA: F144/6.
9. CEA: F73/15. I would like to thank Wendy Cook, Curator of the Museum of Worcester Porcelain, for confirming the details of this invoice.
10. CEA: F1.
11. CEA: F68/3/1-9.
12. CEA: F68/3/10.
13. CEA: F23a.
14. CEA: F68/3/3-4.
15. CEA: F68/3/7. Wyatt's bill is undated and may refer to the early stage of work from 1803 onwards or the completion of the project after 1811.
16. F. Arnold, *A History of Streatham* (1886).
17. CEA: F23/a/1.
18. H. Repton, *Fragments on the Theory and Practice of Landscape Gardening* (1816), pp.470-3.
19. CEA: F68/3.
20. CEA: F13, 25 and 31. Also see Bound Account 1827-9 and Labour Bills 1830.
21. CEA: ES 9/2.
22. W. Dean, *An Historical and Descriptive Account of Croome D'Abitot* (1824), p.63.
23. CEA: F32/9.

24. CEA: F76 and F18/13.
25. CEA: F24/37.
26. CEA: F3/8.
27. CEA: F68/2. Not to be confused with Thomas Cundy II (1790-1867), and Thomas Cundy III (1820-95), who succeeded to his practice and surveyorship of the Grosvenor estates.
28. CEA: F68/2/56a.
29. *Builder*, 20 (1889), p.294.
30. A contemporary salacious newspaper report suggests that they may have eloped. This is not corroborated by the family correspondence or elsewhere and seems unlikely in view of Cotton's character and response to the behaviour of Lady Augusta's younger sisters.
31. CEA: F4/2.
32. CEA: F4. Letters re: Georgiana's marriage 1807-26.
33. CEA: F5/2/4 and 6.
34. CEA: F5/2/1ff. Letters relating to John Coventry 1816-34. Also F41/A15 and will F41/A17.
35. CEA: F5/3/1ff.
36. See A.G.R. Cross, *Seven Stoke Parish Diary & Account 1867-1907*, Severn Stoke Study No. 5 (1997 unpublished).
37. CEA: F13/1.
38. CEA: F13/14.
39. CEA: F13/20.
40. CEA: F13/18-20.
41. CEA: F13/15.
42. I am most grateful to Bob Cross for this information. For further detail see his Severn Stoke Study No. 5.
43. See notes by 9th Earl. CEA: Box 20.F75/4.
44. CEA: F8.
45. CEA: F71/1-29.
46. CEA: See letters re: Sir Roger Gresley F9/1ff.
47. CEA: F20/21/26.
48. CEA: See Kitching letters F20.
49. CEA: F18/14.
50. In 1828, the Countess purchased a 15-acre messuage in Severn Stoke, the details of which remain unclear.
51. CEA: F31/42.
52. CEA: F21/22.
53. Lady Sophia bequeathed the 'Blind Earl' service to her great-niece, Lady Maria Ponsonby.
54. CEA: F2a.
55. CEA: F2/a2.
56. CEA: F20.
57. For further details and correspondence relating to Mary Augusta and the Holland/Coventry families see the Holland House Papers at the Dept. of Manuscripts, British Library.
58. CEA: F2a24.
59. CEA: F2a28.
60. See CEA: F2/a 4-36 for all correspondence relating to the marriage of Lord Deerhurst and Lady Mary Beauclerk.
61. See CEA: F10 and F25. Letters relating to the indiscretions of the 8th Earl.
62. Her mother Mary Whyte is buried at Severn Stoke. She died in 1840 aged 57.
63. CEA: F23/3.
64. CEA: F23/1.
65. CEA: F29/33.
66. See CEA: F11 for letters relating to Lord Deerhurst's shooting accident of 1834.
67. CEA: F75/1. Some accounts state he was buried on 14 November at Bourton House, near Moreton-in-Marsh, Glos. However, his remains now lie within the vault at Croome so presumably they were transferred to Croome at a later date.
68. CEA: F2b11.

Chapter IX: A True Country Gentleman

1. See CEA: Boxes 35, 36 and 37 and F73, 74, 75, 76 and 79. Much information within this chapter has also been gleaned from the nine Coventry albums, which were compiled by Blanche, Countess of Coventry, in strict chronological order. The date and source of information extracted from newspaper cuttings is given where known, but often this information was not included with the cutting.

2. CEA: F1/c/6.
3. CEA: F75.
4. CEA: ES12.
5. She lived quietly in London for the rest of her life, appearing dutifully at family functions and house parties, and she died on the same day as she was married in 1912.
6. *Illustrated London News* (28 May 1859), pp.521-2.
7. CEA: Box 20, F74/5.
8. CEA: F32A.
9. CEA: F66/4.
10. CEA: F32A.
11. *Gardening World* (26 February 1887), pp.409-10.
12. *Country Life* (25 April 1903), pp.536-42.
13. *Country Life* (10 April 1915), pp.482-9.
14. CEA: Box 20, F75/4.
15. *Worcester Journal* (2 January 1915).
16. CEA: Box 9, ES6/14.
17. *Country Life*, 'Legacy of the Coventrys', vol. 169, No. 4361 (19 March 1981), pp.706-8.
18. CEA: Box 20, F75/8.
19. *Worcester Journal* (23 January 1915).
20. Bonynge died at Pirton Court in 1917 and he is buried in Croome churchyard.
21. The tapestries and furnishings were acquired by the Samuel H. Kress Foundation shortly after the Second World War. The remaining furnishings remained at Croome until 1948, when the entire Tapestry Room, floor, ceiling, fireplace *et al*, was also acquired by the Kress foundation, who presented the complete room to the Metropolitan Museum of New York in 1958.
22. *Worcester Herald* (18 December 1894).
23. *Worcestershire Advertiser* (16 May 1917).
24. CEA: Box 20, F75/12.
25. *Worcester Herald* (13 August 1927).
26. CEA: F78.
27. *Worcestershire Advertiser* (no date, March 1930).

Appendix I

Principal Related Collections

Public

Bodleian Library, Department of Western Manuscripts, Oxford
Birmingham Central Library, Archives Division
British Library, Manuscript Collections
Gloucestershire County Record Office
Hampshire County Record Office
Royal Bank of Scotland Archive (Child & Co), London
Sir John Soane's Museum, London
Victoria and Albert Museum, London
Warwickshire County Record Office
Worcestershire County Record Office

Private

The Marquess of Bath at Longleat, Wilts.
The Duke of Beaufort, Badminton, Glos.
The Carew Pole family trust, Antony House, Cornwall
Croome Estate Trust

Appendix II

Estates held by the Earls of Coventry

This list is taken from the Rent Roll for the year 1808, just prior to the death of the 6th Earl when the estate was probably at its most extensive. I am most grateful to Jill Tovey for her help with compiling this information.

Worcestershire

Allesborough, Birlingham, Broadway, Broughton Hackett, Buckbury & Longdon, Croome D'Abitot, Defford, Feckenham, Grafton Flyford, Hill Croome, Earls Croome, South Littleton, Pirton, Powick, Severn Stoke (five tythings including Severn Stoke, Clifton, Kinnersley, Naunton and Kempsey), Upton Snodsbury.

Gloucestershire

Blockley, Brockhampton, Cockbury, Deerhurst, Hardwick Bryant, Mickleton, Mitton, Oxendon, Postlip, Redmarley D'Abitot, Tirley & The Haw, Woolstone.

Warwickshire

Snitterfield & Bearley.

The following estates were also held by the Earls of Coventry, or members of the family, at various times since the early 17th century, but by 1808 they had disappeared from the Rent Rolls:

Worcestershire

Eckington, Hanbury, Hampton Lovett.

Gloucestershire

Bisley, Corse, Eldersfield, Gotherington, Woodmancote.

Kent

Rotherhithe.

Lincolnshire

Twigmore, Stixwold. Probably others.

Middlesex

Edgware & Bois.

Oxfordshire
Bampton, Great Milton, Little Milton.

Staffordshire
Clifton Camvyle, Hampton.

Somerset
Rodney Stoke, Wiveliscombe (sold 1813).

Warwickshire
Griffe & Chilvers Coton, Woolvey.

There are also documents in the archive that suggest the family had connections with Messingham in Humberside and Manton in Leicestershire. The family also held various houses in London, one of which was demolished to enable the construction of Westminster Bridge in 1758.

Appendix III

Drawings for Croome Court by Robert Adam, Lancelot Brown and James Wyatt for the 6th Earl of Coventry in the possession of the Croome Estate Trust.

Robert Adam
Plan for altering the Gate at Croome s&d 1791
Plan and elevation of a Building (probably Severn Bank House)
Plan of a Bridge
Elevation of a Bridge
Plan of Foundations
Design of Architrave
Moulding d 1772
Design for Gallery Walls s&d 1763
Medallion for a Bridge s&d 1772
Design for a Tablet for a Bridge d.1772
Cornice frieze for a Bridge d.1772
Design for an Urn
Design of a Balustrade d 1772
Plan of Banqueting House and Menagerie
Elevation of Banqueting House and Menagerie
Design of East Window, Croome Church

Lancelot Brown
Design for Pirton Park, *c.*1760

James Wyatt
Plan of Bridge of Communication in Garden
Ruined Castle (Pirton) s&d 1801
Elevation of Lodge s&d 1794
Plan of Summer House (Panorama Tower) s&d 1801
Elevation of Summer House (Panorama Tower) s&d 1801
Elevation of Lodge and Gates s&d 1801
Plan and Elevation of Lodge and gate s&d 1801
Plan of Lodge s&d 1794
Plan of Apartment to be altered at Croome s&d 1799
Design for a Statue (Druid) s&d 1796
(Also Plan and Elevation of Saxon Tower (Broadway) s&d 1794 Plan of Tower s&d 1794)

Appendix IV

Drawings for Croome Court by Robert Adam for the 6th Earl of Coventry in Sir John Soane's Museum.

I am most grateful to Stephen Astley, Assistant Curator (Drawings), who is currently re-cataloguing Adam's drawings, for supplying me with this updated list.

It remains unclear whether certain items of furniture etc. were designed for Croome or Coventry House, now 106 Piccadilly. As furniture is likely to have been moved between houses at various times, the intended location of such items can be particularly difficult to establish. The list of drawings for Coventry House is more extensive and still awaits revision. It has been omitted here to avoid any confusion that might render it invalid prior to its revision.

21(111)	Front of the offices showing their appearance when lowered
50(9)	Gallery wall elevations
50(10)	Library wall elevations
50(11)	Lord Coventry's bedroom wall elevations
50(12)	Tapestry Room wall elevations
50(13)	Dairy plan and wall elevations
50(14)	Elevation. One internal wall with door
11(34)	Library Ceiling s & d September 1760
11(35)	Gallery Ceiling 'not executed' s & d September 1760
11(36)	Gallery Ceiling 'as executed' d March 1761
11(37)	Library Ceiling d January 1763
53(25)	Tapestry Room frieze
22(59)	Chimney-piece d 1762
22(60)	Eating Parlour Chimney-piece d 1762
22(61)	Eating Parlour Chimney-piece s & d 1762
22(62)	Best Bed Chamber Chimney-piece d 1763
22(63)	Mezzanine Room Chimney-piece d 1763 (possibly for London)
17(152)	Elevation of Bed
17(212)	Cloathes Press d October 1764 (possibly
17(213)	Cloathes press d October 1764 for London)
29(140)	Plan and elevation of Gateway d 15 Febuary 1799
1(5)	Sketch design for gateway 21(138)
21(138)	Gateway s & d 1791
51(83)	Gateway-a less finished version of 21(138)
52(155)	Gates d May 1781
51(84)	Plan and elevation of menagerie keeper's lodge
19(142)	Seat in Pleasure Grounds, plan & elev d.1766
19(143)	Seat in Pleasure Grounds, as 19(142) but less finished, s & d, 1766

19(145)   Pavilion between the Woods, plan, s & d 1766
19(146)   Pavilion between the Woods, elev, s & d 1766
44(104)   Pavilion between the Woods, elev
44(105)   Pavilion between the Woods, elev of alternative design
44(106)   Pavilion between the Woods, plan of alternative design
51(2)   Bridge, plan and elev d 9 March 1781
51(15)   Bridge, elev
51(16)   Bridge, similar to 51(2)
51(17)   Bridge, 3 arch bridge in sketch landscape
29(136)   Conservatory (Temple Greenhouse), elev, s & d 1760
29(137)   Conservatory, (Temple Greenhouse), plan, s & d 1760
29(138)   Greenhouse, elev & plan, d June 14 1759 (v. early drawing, not the Temple Greenhouse)
9(122)   Conservatory, (Temple Greenhouse) sketch for 29(136)
29(139)   Column with lamp & railings
17(121)   Grate & Fender (London or Croome)
17(73)   Sofa
6(177)   Tripod pedestal sketch
6(159)   Chair
6(161)   Chair

Croome Church

50(15)   Side wall elev and furniture sketch s & d 1761
50(16)   Wall elev
50(17)   Door and doorway. Feint sketches for garden buildings in landscapes on verso
50(18)   Wall elev and Ceiling design
50(19)   Ceiling design
50(20)   Plan and pulpit sketch
50(21)   Chair
52(167)   Gates for porch s & d 1763
52(168)   Gates for porch
25(209)   Pulpit, plan & elev

Appendix V

Drawings for Croome by Robert Adam at the V & A Museum (From Alastair Rowan's 1988 catalogue)

3324   Design for Park Gates, *c.*1781
3436.4   Elevation of an elaborate stained-glass window
3436.5   Designs (on 2 sheets) for Gothic traceried windows with stained glass

Select Bibliography

Beard, G., 'Decorators and Furniture Makers at Croome Court', *Furniture History Society Journal*, vol.xxix (1993), pp.88-113.

Beard, G., 'Robert Adam at Croome Court', *Trans Worcs. Archaeological Society*, vol. 36 (1958-60), pp.1-5.

Bolton, A.T., *The Architecture of Robert and James Adam* (London 1922; reissued 1984).

Clarendon, Earl of, *History of the Great Rebellion*, 4 vols. (Oxford 1704).

Coleridge, A., 'English Furniture supplied for Croome Court: Robert Adam and the 6th Earl of Coventry', *Apollo* (February 2000), pp.8-19.

Colvin, H., *A Biographical Dictionary of British Architects 1600-1840* (2nd edition, London 1978).

Colvin, H., 'Croome Church and its Architect', *Georgian Group Journal*, vol. viii (1998), p.29.

Country Life, vol 13 (1903), pp.536-42.

Country Life, vol.37 (1915), pp.482-9.

Cross, A.J.R., Severn Stoke Studies 1-5 (unpublished) especially Severn Stoke Parish Diary and Accounts (no.5).

Dean, W., *An Historical and Descriptive Account of Croome D'Abitot* ... (Worcester 1824).

Dickins, L. and Stanton, M. (eds.), *An Eighteenth Century Correspondence* (London 1910).

Frew, J., 'Some Observatons on James Wyatt's Gothic Style 1790-97', *Journal of the Society of Architectural Historians*, vol. xli, No.2, pp.144-9.

Gardening World, vol. 3 (26 February 1887), pp.409-10.

Gaut, R.C., 'Croome Park', *Trans. Worcs Naturalists Club*, vol ix (1932-41), pp.118-28.

Girouard, M., *Life in the English Country House* (New Haven and London, 1978).

Grice, F., 'The Park Ornaments of Croome D'Abitot', *Trans. Worcs. Archaeological Society*, 3rd series, vol. v (1976), pp.41-9.

Gwilliam, B., *Worcestershire's Hidden Past* (Bromsgrove, 1991).

Habington, T., *A Survey of Worcestershire* (1586-; Worcestershire Historical Society, Oxford 1895-9).

Halfpenny, W., *Improvements in Architecture and Carpentry* (1754).

Harris, E., *The Furniture of Robert Adam* (London 1963).

Harris, E., 'Robert Adam and the Gobelins', *Apollo*, vol. 76 (April 1962), pp.100-6.

Harris, J., *The Artist and the Country House*, (London 1985), p.271.

Harris, J., *The Artist and the Country House from the Fifteenth Century to the Present Day*, (Sothebys, 1995).

Unpublished draft on Lord Keeper Coventry (1996, History of Parliament Trust).

Hayward, H., 'Splendour at Croome Court', *Apollo*, vol. xcix, No. 147 (May 1974), pp.350-2.

Huddlestone, L., 'Viewing the Croome Landscape'. Newsletter of the Georgian Group in Gloucester and Avon, No. 3, 1986.

Jones, B., *Follies and Grottoes* (1953), pp.65-7.

Kelly, A., *Mrs Coade's Stone* (London 1990).

King, D., *The Complete Works of Robert and James Adam* (Oxford 1991).

Lane, J., 'The Furniture at Croome Court: The patronage of George William, 6th Earl of Coventry', *Apollo*, vol. 145, No. 419 (January 1997), pp.25-9.

Latham, R. and Matthews, W. (eds.), *The Diary of Samuel Pepys* (London 1983).

Lees-Milne, J., *The Age of Inigo Jones* (London 1953).

Lees-Milne, J., *The Age of Adam* (London 1947).

Lewis, W.S. (ed.), *The Yale edition of Horace Walpole's Correspondence*, vols. 1-48 (New Haven and London, 1937-83).

Lloyd, D., *A History of Worcestershire* (Chichester 1993).

Lockett, R., *A Survey of Historic Parks and Gardens in Worcestershire* (Hereford and Worcester Gardens Trust, 1997).

Nash, Dr. T.R., *Collections for the History of Worcestershire*, 2 vols. (Worcester, 1781-2).

Neale, J.P., *Views of the Seats*, 5 vols. (London 1818-23), vol. 5 (1822).

Parker, J.C., 'Croome Court Furniture', *Metropolitan Museum of Art Bulletin* (November 1959), pp.79-93.

Paton, A., 'The Botany of Croome Court', *Trans. Worcs. Archaeological Society*, vol. 6 (3rd series, 1978), pp.71-3.

Pevsner, N., *Worcestershire* (Buildings of England series; London 1968)

Reider, W. and others, *Period Rooms in the Metropolitan Museum of Art* (New York 1996).

Repton, H., *Observations on the Theory and Practice of Landscape Gardening* (London 1803).

Repton, H., *Fragments on the Theory and Practice of Landscape Gardening* (London 1816).

Rowan, A.J., *A Catalogue of Architectural Drawings in the Victoria & Albert Museum* (London 1988).

Shelby, J., *An Eighteenth Century Warwickshire Village—Snitterfield* (Warwickshire Local History Society. Occasional paper, No. 6, 1986).

Stroud, D., *Capability Brown* (London 1950; 2nd ed. 1975)

Sulivan, R., *Tour… in 1778*, vol. 1 (1785), pp.296-300.

Summerson, J., *Architecture in Britain 1530-1830* (London 1953, Pelican paperback edition 1970).

Tod, G., *Plans, Elevations and Sections of Hot-houses* (1812).

Tomes, C.S., *Life in Worcestershire at the end of the Seventeenth Century* (Evesham 1911).

Turner, R., *Capability Brown and the 18th Century Landscape* (1985; 2nd edition, Chichester 1999).

Victoria County Histories for Worcestershire, Gloucestershire and Oxfordshire.

Watkin, D., *The English Vision* (London 1982).

Willis, P., 'Capability Brown's Account with Drummond's Bank 1753-83', *Architectural History,* vol. 27 (1984), pp.382-91.

Woolf, J. and Gandon, J., *Vitruvius Britannicus*, vol. 5 (London 1771).

Young, A., *Annals of Agriculture* (1801).

Index

223